A LEWES I

1916–1944

Other books written and edited
by Diana Crook

Sussex books

The Ladies of Miller's, Dale House Press 1996

A Reader's Choice, Selections from books by Julian Fane, Dale House
Press 1996

A Peculiar Devotion: The friendship of Sir Philip Sassoon and Mrs Henry
Dudeney, Dale House Press 1999

A Box of Toys – An Anthology of Lewes Writings, Dale House Press 2004

Defying the Demon – Smallpox in Sussex, Dale House Press 2006

Ragged Lands – Viscountess Wolseley's College for Lady Gardeners
Glynde, Dale House Press 2008

Treasure Chest, A Seaford Anthology, Dale House Press 2012

Fiction

Open the Cage, Kindle e-Book, 2012

A LEWES DIARY
1916–1944

Mrs Henry Dudeney

Edited by
Diana Crook

Dale House Press

British Library Cataloguing-in-Publication Data.
A catalogue record for this book is available from the British Library.

First published by the Tartarus Press, 1998
ISBN 1 87262131 7
This edition published by Dale House Press, 2012
100 Marine Parade, Seaford, East Sussex BN25 2QR
ISBN 978-1-900841-07-8

Printed by 4Edge, 7A Eldon Way, Hockley, Essex SS5 4AD

PREFACE

In November 1945 Mrs Alice Dudeney died leaving precise instructions in her will. Firstly she required that a doctor open an artery to ensure she was dead, and secondly she bequeathed her diaries to the Sussex Archaeological Society with the proviso that they were to be kept sealed for 25 years. At the end of this period, the Society reviewed the diaries and, feeling that their contents might still upset local people, placed a further closure order on them until the year 2000. However, the application some years later of a researcher seeking information on the life of Ernest Dudeney, Mrs Dudeney's husband, led to the Society relaxing this ban and allowing access to the diaries from 1983 onwards. It was my good fortune that no one else had applied since this time to publish an edition of the diaries and I am very grateful to the Society for allowing me to do so.

Mrs Dudeney was born Alice Whiffin in Bloomsbury in 1866 and moved with her family to Brighton ten or so years later. She was educated in Hurstpierpoint and at 18 married Henry Dudeney (Ernest) a native of Mayfield. Ernest was a well-known mathematician famous for his puzzle columns and it is ironic that today his books, unlike those of his wife's, are still in print. After losing her first baby, Mrs Dudeney became visiting secretary to the head of Cassell's publishing firm. Her daughter Margery was born in 1890, by which time she had written several short stories. In 1897 the Dudeneys built a house at Littlewick Meadow, Horsell, Surrey and she published her first book *A Man with a Maid*. Two years later her third novel, *The Maternity of Hariott Wicken*, a melodramatic story of tainted blood, neurasthenia, suicide and murder, struck a chord with the public and attracted the attention of Henry James. Her next novel, *Folly Corner*, a Sussex love story, received over one hundred enthusiastic reviews, a quarter of them from abroad, and was later dramatised in the West End and America.

She was compared to Thomas Hardy by such distinguished magazines as *The Bookman*, and her novels were thought superior to those of her contemporary, Edith Wharton. Very aware of her highly-praised position in the literary world, Mrs Dudeney would be shocked to find that her many novels and stories have now fallen from favour, and it is sobering to realize how quickly her considerable fame has evaporated. Perhaps the rise of feminism has led to a lack of interest in Victorian tales where woman is usually a victim, trapped by marriage or made lonely by spinsterhood. Such neglect seems unjust, and anyone interested in reading her novels might try *A House in the High Street* or *Seed Pods*, both lively tales with unusually happy endings. I feel confident that Mrs Dudeney would have wished that her undoubted talent for writing, if not appreciated nowadays in novel form, should live on through her diaries.

It is to be hoped that the passage of time has removed the likelihood of offence being taken today by Mrs Dudeney's frank comments and revelations about her friends and acquaintances. She once said in an interview: 'It is not the affair of the novelist to whitewash humanity.' I similarly feel it is not the place of an editor to sanitise her diaries, especially since Mrs Dudeney's friends fall in and out of favour and her acid comments reveal more of her character than that of the persons so maligned. I have also left in remarks that would now be considered politically incorrect, hoping that readers will bear in mind the prevailing attitudes of women of her class at that time.

In editing these diaries, my main problem has been how to select from the mass of material available. The majority of the diaries were written in Boots Large Scribbling Diaries; no detail was considered too trivial to be recorded, even how many times the diarist washed her hair or wormed the dog. Every day, aided by an enviably efficient postal service, she wrote and received a quantity of social and business letters. She entertained large numbers of friends and in the mornings for two or three hours (domestic crises permitting) she worked at her typewriter turning out a novel a year, along with plays, articles and short stories. My quandary was how, in reducing the equivalent of seven or so full-length novels down to only one, I could avoid throwing out the baby with the bathwater and losing the sense of worried activity that constituted Mrs Dudeney's life. It has been necessary to keep in references to writings that are no longer remembered to illustrate her attempts to make enough money to run her household, and her compulsion for 'a life of the imagination'.

This edition does not include the first three diaries, written from 1910 to 1913 before Mrs Dudeney moved to Lewes. These cover her separation from her husband while they were living at Littlewick Meadow, and her subsequent move with her daughter Margery to The Pigeon House, Angmering, West Sussex. These deeply troubled diaries relate her dilemma over her affair with a married artist, Paul Hardy. Always known as David, he had met Alice at Cassell's when he illustrated her novel *Gossip's Green*. An accomplished illustrator and watercolourist, he was also an expert in medieval armour and sculpted for the Mond Nickel Company. A long-term resident of Storrington, West Sussex, he was responsible for the golden galleon weather vane on top of the parish church. His relationship with Alice had been broken off in 1905, then resumed in 1910. Ernest's jealous rages, blithely attributed by Mrs Dudeney to 'brain fever', led to her fleeing with her daughter to Angmering. 'I love David, my heart and my nature is his, yet Ernest has the tradition of my youth and he is Margery's father,' she writes in 1913. As no diaries were written for 1914 and 1915, the reason for the eventual ending of the affair and Mrs Dudeney's letter to Ernest asking him to join her in Lewes can only be guessed at. Her frequently expressed terror of loneliness no doubt played an important part in the latter decision, for her daughter Margery left for Canada to be married shortly before the outbreak of war. It seemed best to publish the diaries from 1916 when Mrs Dudeney was established with Ernest at 138 High Street, Lewes. Anyone regretting the absence of the earlier diaries can, of course, refer to the originals.

When I started my work, I had no idea that in 1916 Mrs Dudeney was written to by Sir Philip Sassoon and became his close, life-long friend. He was one of the richest and most glamorous men of his generation and at his mansions at Park Lane, Trent Park and Port Lympne entertained the leading figures of the day. To this glittering company Mrs Dudeney was regularly invited, and her cool and amused comments on that '18 carat crowd' are one of the delights of the diaries. This intriguing friendship, together with her tragi-comic relationships with her husband and lover, and the brilliant immediacy of the war-time entries, give the diaries a universal and not just a local appeal.

Addresses in the footnotes are in Lewes unless otherwise stated. I have given brief details of Mrs Dudeney's novels; any titles without footnotes indicate lesser works for which no records remain. I have retained Mrs Dudeney's characteristic spelling and idiosyncratic use of the capital letter. I have left untouched her invented words and odd sayings but have toned down her over-exuberant use of the exclamation mark and the dash. Italics have been substituted for her frequent underlining for purpose of emphasis. I have altered her punctuation where it distorted the sense and have in most cases expanded the initial or initials used to refer to her nearest but not always her dearest (eg E for Ernest). I have indicated where a word is illegible [?] or my interpretation doubtful [word?] and editorial comments within the text are inside square brackets. In all these matters I have been motivated by the wish to present a readable document while retaining anything personally significant. The diaries, closely packed with writing, often smudged with ink blots, cigarette burns or blobs of wax, are difficult to read. I hope readers will bear this in mind and not be severe on any mistakes of transcription.

Since publication of the first edition in 1998 Margery's children in America were traced through their unusual surname. They were delighted to learn more about their remarkable grandmother, whose diaries contribute so much to the town that she loved.

Diana Crook
Seaford, 2012

Acknowledgements to first edition

Firstly I must express sincere thanks to the Sussex Archaeological Society for permitting me to edit and publish these diaries and in particular to its Research Officer, Dr Richard Jones. I am grateful also for the help of the East Sussex Record Office with its patient search room staff, together with the County Archivist Roger Davey and Archivists Philip Bye and Christopher Whittick. Hove Museum and Art Gallery, Hove Reference Library and Mr Hugh Bailey assisted in the search for illustrations, books and documents. The Tate Gallery, The National Portrait Gallery, Country Life Picture Library, Edward Reeves Photographers, Lewes, and Alan Shelley of Bow Windows Bookshop, Lewes, kindly gave permission for the reproduction of illustrations and photographs. Professor Angela Newing generously gave me details from her unpublished biography of Ernest Dudeney. Rowena Bingham, Mr Peter Blake, The Marquess of Cholmondeley, Matthew Collinson, Pam Combes, Joanna Hallett, Don Harding, Mrs E Saxe, Mrs G B Shepherd, Mrs Edie Welfare, John Winter and Ivor Wycherley all supplied useful information. Colin Brent advised on local references, and Mr RA Elliston and Mr John Tillson shared with me their fund of fascinating knowledge regarding Lewes during WW2. Julian and Gilly Fane gave invaluable encouragement and advice regarding publication. Special thanks go to my husband John for his unfailing patience and good humour in extricating me from losing battles with the software. And finally perhaps I can acknowledge Mrs Dudeney for her foresight in keeping and leaving behind her splendid diaries.

SOURCES

Alice Dudeney's diaries from 1910–13, 1916–19 and 1921–45 can be viewed at the East Sussex Record Office (ESRO), The Maltings, Lewes, BN7 1YT, due to move to the Keep, Falmer, Brighton at the end of 2013.

Also under this reference is an album of her early press cuttings from 1897–1901, including interesting photographs. Local newspapers can be viewed at the ESRO either in storage or on microfilm. West Sussex local newspapers are on microfilm in Chichester Library. Volumes of the *Sussex County Magazine* are available on reference at the ESRO with some on loan from Lewes Library, the latter also holding a large selection of Mrs Dudeney's novels. The Sussex Archaeological Society Library, Barbican House, Lewes, contains the following two out-of-print books: *Bachelors of Art* by David Sox, SAS 2098 (a biography of Edward Warren) and *Lewes at War* by RA Elliston, SAS 942.25, both of which are also available at Lewes Library. *The Third Route* by Sir Philip Sassoon and *The Sassoon Dynasty* by Cecil Roth are out of print but available for purchase on Amazon, while *Sassoon: The Worlds of Philip and Sybil*, by Peter Stansky, published 2012 by Yale in paperback, and *The Sassoons* by Stanley Jackson, published 1968 by Heinemann, available at most libraries, give an absorbing description of the extraordinary lifestyle of Philip Sassoon. Other books providing essential information are *The Ladies of Miller's* by Diana Crook, *Historic Lewes and Its Buildings* by Colin Brent (the official town guide) and *Georgian Lewes*, also by Colin Brent. *Modern Puzzles and How to Solve Them*, and *Amusements in Mathematics* by Henry Dudeney have been reprinted by Dover Press and the Classic Reprint Series respectively.

A Select Bibliography of Works by Mrs Henry Dudeney

Novels

A Man with a Maid, Heinemann Pioneer Series, 1897
Hagar of Homerton, Pearson, 1898
Folly Corner, Heinemann, 1899
The Maternity of Harriott Wicken, Heinemann, 1899
The Third Floor, Methuen, 1901
Spindle and Plough, Heinemann, 1901
Robin Brilliant, Hodder & Stoughton, 1902
The Story of Susan, Heinemann, 1903
A Country Bunch, Hurst & Blackett, 1905
The Wise Woods, Heinemann, 1905
Gossips Green, Cassell, 1906 (Illustrated by Paul Hardy)
The Orchard Thief, Heinemann, 1907
The Shoulder-Knot, Cassell, 1909
Rachel Lorian, Heinemann, 1909
A Large Room, Heinemann, 1910
Married when Suited, Paul, 1911
Maids' Money, Heinemann, 1911
Set to Partners, Heinemann, 1913
The Runaway Ring, Heinemann, 1913
What a Woman Wants, Heinemann, 1914
The Secret Son, Methuen, 1915
This Way Out, Methuen, 1915
The Head of the Family, Methuen, 1917
Candlelight, Hurst & Blackett, 1918
Traveller's Samples, Mills & Boon, 1918
Spade Work, Hurst & Blackett, 1919
Manhood End, Hurst & Blackett, 1919
Made to Measure, Collins, 1921
Beanstalk, Collins, 1922
The Finger Post, Collins, 1923
The Next Move, Collins, 1924

Quince Alley, Collins, 1925
Seed Pods, Collins, 1927
Brighton Beach, Collins, 1928
Puff Paste, Collins, 1928
By Consent, Collins, 1929
Traveller's Rest, Collins, 1930
The House in the High Street, Collins, 1931
The Treasure Field, Collins, 1932
Trundle Square, Collins, 1933
Portrait of Ellen, Collins, 1934
Barbourbrook, Collins, 1935
Put Up the Shutters, Hutchinson, 1935

Books of short stories
Men of Marlowe's, Long, 1900
A Sense of Scarlet and other Stories, Heinemann, 1909
Thumb Nails, Mills & Boon, 1918
A Baker's Dozen, Heinemann, 1922
The Play Box, Heinemann, 1924
Fly Leaves, Collins, 1926

Mrs Dudeney (seated with bouquet) opening the Sussex Room
of Worthing Library, 1924.

Who's Who in A Lewes Diary

Alice Dudeney born 1866	Writer, using her married name of Mrs Henry Dudeney
Ernest (Henry Ernest) born 1857	Husband, mathematician, puzzle setter, author
Nelson, Emma, Spangles	Family Dalmatians
Esther King, Emily Gander Washer, (EGW), Susan Freeman, Lucy Wilson, Vina Gathercole, Winnie Sincock	Living-in servants
Mrs Breach, Margaret, Mrs Brown, Olive, Mrs Eliot, Welfare, Palmer	Part-time servants, cleaners, gardeners, CPH
Wycherley (Alfred, Charles, Ivor)	Estate agents, rent collectors
Emily Whiffin	Sister, looking after their mother in Brighton.
Kate Pocock, Emily Dudeney	Sisters-in-law
Tom Dudeney	Brother-in-law
Margery Fulleylove, born 1890	Daughter, an artist, living in Canada, then America
Christopher Fulleylove	Son-in-law
John, Barney (Julian), Jamie, Catherine, Elizabeth Ann	Grandchildren
Joan Fulleylove	Christopher's sister
Vere Baker (Sullivan)	Holiday companion, daughter of Surrey friend
Paul Hardy (David), born 1862	(Ex) lover

Ida Hardy	David's wife
Drs Loud, Vallance, Dunstan, Nicholl, Irvine	Doctors engaged by the Dudeneys
Pinker	London Agent
Skues	London Solicitor
Harold Blaker	Lewes Solicitor
Sir Philip Sassoon, born 1888	Bachelor friend with mansions at 25 Park Lane, Port Lympne and Trent Park
Mr & Mrs Hill, Mr and Mrs Amos	Tenants of The Old Poor House
Kitty Howard, Mr and Mrs Adams	Tenants of 'Lean-to' opposite OPH
Miss Parker	Ernest's secretary
Miss Hayward	AD's secretary
Dusart	High Street hairdresser
Mrs Hyeem, Lady Boyle, David Sassoon	Local relatives of Sir Philip
The Revs Belcher, Calvert, Rawlings	Rectors of St Michael's Church
Rev Ensell	Rector of St Anne's Church
Rev MacKay Clarke	Rector of All Saints' Church
Rev Matthews	Rector of St John's Church, Southover
Father Flannagan	Priest, St Pancras RC Church

Note: Castle Precincts House (CPH) is today known as Brack Mound House to distinguish it from the other Castle Precincts House close by on the west side of the Bowling Green. The SAS stands for The Sussex Archaeological Society.

Mrs Dudeney's Lewes

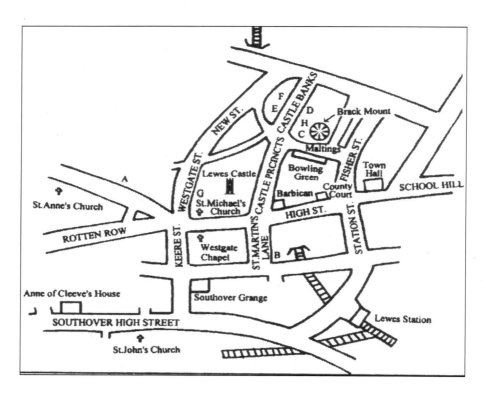

A 138 High Street
B Garden, St Martin's Lane
C Castle Precincts House (now Brack Mound House)
D Old Poor House
E Lean-to and garden
F Mount Cottages
G Westgate Street Cottages
H 9 Castle Banks

1916

What 10,000 pities I didn't keep a diary in 1914 and 1915 – such vital years: the war for one thing. And Margery getting married and going to Canada, and the Pigeon House[1] given up and my final goodbye to David, and Ernest and I are re-starting our married life.

1 January. At midday, horrid shock. Letter from Lock Hospital[2], saying Bessie G. [former servant] going to have a baby. I must 'remove' her. Poor Elizabeth (alias Bessie) the 150 soldiers at the Grammar School[3] were her undoing. And shall I ever forget that day when I took her to the Lock Hospital.

2 January. Very peaceful nice day and raining in torrents, which I rather like on Sundays. At Mass[4] the idea of Bessie G. was so insistent that I came home and wrote to the poor thing.

3 January. Nelson[5] stole 2 rashers of bacon. This jarred Esther, who 'jars' me. Then Ernest and I 'jarred' each other! Meanwhile Nelson – delightful spotted animal – was dignified and sad and a touch sulky, as usual. He resented being whacked. Bright, blowey, wind on the Downs enough to cut your head off. At night I worked at my nun's veiling[6] knickers of which I'm amazingly proud!

---

1 Angmering, West Sussex, AD's previous address. Left to Sussex Archaeological Society in 1940, sold back into private hands in 1970s.
2 The Contagious Diseases Acts of the 1870s forced any women with VD to stay in lock hospitals until they were cured.
3 Soldiers were billeted next door to 138 High St.
4 The Dudeneys worshipped at the Anglo-Catholic Church of St Michael, Lewes High Street.
5 Dalmatian with black eye patch.
6 Muslin.

4 January. The contrast between today and yesterday! Soft and dim and damp. Nelson and I to Offham, by the road right under the hill – wet through coming back. Wild gale at night and the wood fire and panelled room [7] – heavenly. Gave Nelson a bath, put frill on one knicker leg. Esther said of the war and the loss of the Persia [8] : "There does seem a lot of people losing their lives"!

6 January. Margery's dear little letter was nice but it unsettles me. Anything of the past, of youth, of fun, of slackening does. At lunch, I was so tired and when poor Ernest asked me to sew a button on his breeks I flew into a rage; then did it, then lay on my chintz sofa, then went and apologised; then went for a walk and bought him some chocolates.

7 January. Delicious wet soft morning, so warm that I haven't left off wearing nainsook [9] knickers. I've heard nothing from the Lock Hospital. I wrote and said they had wrung that promise (to remove her, if pregnant) by force and I said they must send her to her proper workhouse at East Preston. Wrote to her mother, in Devonshire (who had written to me asking what was the matter with 'Bessie'). I told her the truth as gently as I could: venereal disease and going to have a baby.

10 January. After lunch I walked a long walk alone, and met Mrs Moore [10] (which would have been nice) but 3 kids and all of them agitating Nelson! She is going – and trying not to go – to London to meet this man before he goes to Salonica [11]. Very often when these women talk of their lovers I find myself saying to myself "Is it true?" With her. Yes! She said of the children: "It is they who seem unreal and not me. He is mine, and real."

7 This panelled room still exists.
8 P & O liner torpedoed off Crete with loss of 400 lives.
9 Light, soft cotton.
10 The Frankfort Moores lived at Castlegate House, Castle Precincts. FM was a prolific author of historical and adventure novels, travel books, verse, plays and biography.
11 Salonika, northern Greece, where British troops landed to aid Serbia.

11 January. I found that Esther had rubbed the bedroom floors over with a turpentine rag and taken off all the polish. Then she was beastly rude. She's a sour beast and if she doesn't do as I tell her she can go. What pests they are. Went to tea with the Doyles, and one of those good Christian old maids [12] got up and literally danced on the hearthrug. "Aren't you glad the Kaiser's [13] going to kick the bucket? There's no mistake; it's cancer of the throat"!

14 January. Letter from Elizabeth, in East Preston Workhouse, thanking me for 'all my kindness' and promising to turn over a new leaf. Wrote again to her mother, suggesting that, when recovered, she should return to Devonshire and get a situation near home.

15 January. Esther had one of her mad fits and said that if Mrs Brown was coming to 'char' on her day out she wouldn't go: "For there's spies all over the place. You see 'em on the pavement across the road trying to look in at the windows." Gave in to her: worthwhile, for she's splendid.

18 January. Letter from Heinemann. Talk of breaking up my books, selling 'em off as 'nowt'. Broken up and full of terrors. Ernest no manner of good, no, not a bit. I came up here, and what a mistake to read old diaries, perhaps to keep a new one! I find that on every 18 Jan since 1910 I've been 'strained to death', 'too tired to live' and so on. Then turned to work, as I turn now: but that – yes even that – loses some of its passion and consolation. Things and people fail. Then, ever so weary, you turn to Jesus.

19 January. Very nice to have a sentry, with fixed bayonet walking up and down outside ...

22 January. Brief letter from Elizabeth's mother: 'Dear Madam, We don't want Bessie to come and scandal us'!

12 Edith and Agnes Doyle, 79 High St.
13 Kaiser Bill died in 1941.

25 January. Too tired to go to church. Have bought myself some Bynno [14]. Quite a nice day as it turned out; Ernest not 'nervous', Nelson unearthly good. What an up and down fool I am! At night, mending Ernest's gloves by the fire I thought what a nice thing he was: in many ways so much better than the other party – yet he had his points also! I'm getting most interestingly (to myself) cool and aloof!

27 January. Ernest had a letter from the *Strand* [15]. Terror took me lest the column was stopped and he left with nothing. Queer how the old horrors dog you and the old states return. Marriage does get its teeth into you and 31 years is a long time.

28 January. That beast of an Esther, with her economy run mad, has been rubbing all the brass over with 'an oily rag' to save Bluebell; remarking: "I should put food before polish". Been from ten till now (noon) cleaning my copper things. Damn her. If she wasn't half mad and so excellent I wouldn't stand her insolence.

30 January. Rowed at breakfast time. He flung off to his room, I remained staring into the backyard I've made so quaint: the blackish green tree in a tub, the whitewashed wall. The scene changes, the rows remain!

5 February. House all done, stair carpets down, Esther amiable, Ernest decent ... what an up and down affair life is. Mrs Moore to tea. The High Street is so quiet; the soldiers go by, Nelson and I sit at the small window in the panelled room and watch them.

7 February. Ernest in a most amiable mood – and then to thinking of last Monday! ... I miss Margery so much. I wish she hadn't gone. Men don't matter, over much! But being a mother does.

14 Restorative which in 1913 turned AD's face purple.
15 Popular illustrated monthly in which ED had a 'Curiosity Column'.

9 February. Been doing proofs. Some of the short stories . . . very good. Others *Harper's* [16] potboilers. Yet most are good. I can write, blessed be God. After tea . . . Margery's letter . . . She said: "I love you more than any mother was ever loved", oughtn't that to be enough for me? But oh to see you, dear, and hear you and touch you. Will that come?

12 February. I do wish I'd kept a diary in 1914-15 ... The soldiers at the Grammar School calling out of the window to Elizabeth in the yard on Christmas morning "Got the pudding in, Cookey?" And Elizabeth saying, when Scarborough [17] was bombarded: "Does that help us or does it help them Germans?" And, of Winston Churchill: "Isn't that him with the lots of hats?"

20 February. Sat behind Mr Verrall [18] at church. He beautifully groomed, a coat with a real waist. Looked like invisible blue, ought to be black. Some adroit female will certainly secure such an eligible widower. Two little pawmarks on the tail of his coat, where his dog had jumped up.

24 February. Useless for me to try to be anything but diabolical in such weather: snow and frost and glare. Everybody else seems to find it healthy and bracing. Ernest singing as he dressed!

28 February. Colder yet. Don't know how I can live through it. Stayed at home all day. Big fire in drawing room: my work table drawn to side of blue chair a great joy.

29 February. Warmer and thawing . . . Henry James dead. I didn't swear all day.

---

16 Monthly magazine published in New York to which AD contributed many short stories.
17 Shelled by German warships December 1914
18 Frank Verrall, one of the Lewes brewing family.

1 March. Posted 'Feather Bed' to *Harper*. Nelson disgraced himself by taking my eiderdown for a bird and gnawing a hole in it . . . Nelson and I walk on the hills; where they are breaking in mules to go to the front, poor beasts. Such a kicking up of heels and showing of rumps.

9 March. Margery's birthday. Of course I've been reading diaries like a fool. How badly from the worldly point of view David treated me! Losing me husband and home, imperilling everything. Yet I love him and shall, on the side where worldly things don't matter. And I know he loves me. What a glorious mad fantastic thing love is and how blind it makes you, how merciless!

14 March. On the verge of madness with 2 bad nights and Esther is in one of her lunatic moods. At lunch Ernest was very nice and I felt ashamed of being cross, but I can't help it and don't mean it! . . . After tea down High Street alone to buy green calico. Met Dr Renton, who said the Germans were quite expected to invade – Hastings!

19 March. Ernest said that during the 3 years I left him he never went to his club without looking for a letter from me and that it became: "a question of my emotion not my reason, for it was so hopeless". That he blessed the fact that letters for him went to the Pigeon House by mistake, for then he saw my handwriting, re-directing. It all made me feel tender and bewildered and so grateful that I did not leave him permanently outside.

30 March. Went to see Mother. She better and wearing a most lovely cashmere shawl belonging to a long dead cousin of hers, 'Mary Ann' (into whose coffin I as an infant dropped a cotton reel). Wish she'd leave it to me.

14 April. Little walk with Charlotte [19] after lunch: she a nice thing, but parchmenty! Ernest spoke so nicely about my work at night by the wood fire. I went to bed happy, feeling that he does begin to understand and not think I've got swelled head.

---

19 Charlotte Wicks, widowed friend of AD living in Basingstoke, then Lewes.

17 April. Went to church early, feeling very ill as I always do getting up early. A blackbird on a bare branch outside, the grey sky and the grey castle pulled me together.

23 April. Thinking it over, I conclude that I make this an ungracious diary, all my little ailments, little worries, hardly a word of the lovely things: the look of the hills last night, confession on Thursday and the joy that came of it, communion today.

27 April. Mortal hot. Rooks cawing like mad outside. How I adore this little turrety apple room! Outburst at lunch. After that, the usual black hopeless, squalid misery alone up here, hugging Nelson.

28 April. Then Charlotte to tea and we went for a walk. Her neat mind! Well! Mine isn't neat. Ernest played bowls, poor old soul, for the first time in a tweed suit, looking so nice. He is an old dear; but – ye gods – what a trial sometimes.

1 May. Esther been smearing paraffin not only over the floor but over the front of Ernest's piano. Shall have my little holiday and then, the next time she offends, fire her. In the afternoon to Depot [20]. Victor [21] girl there scraping lint. I couldn't be interested, the sense of mutilation was too awful.

8 May. Vere came.

9 May. We started for Alfriston, walking across the hills all the way. Hadn't got far before it started to rain, a fine drizzle. Sat under a thorn bush eating our lunch and getting steadily soaked. We were to lodge with Mrs Purless; a dear old woman who, many years ago, was a nursemaid in Mrs Hubert's [22] service. She opened the door; Nelson – dripping at every spot – made a bee line for a big kitchen fire he saw ahead! Mrs Purless was divine. She produced

20 Royal Sussex Artillery, Kingston Rd.
21 The Victors lived at 103 High St.
22 Old Lewes lady who taught AD to crochet.

a large towel. We wiped him down. He was admitted to the little parlour where there was another fire. And we changed and had tea – eggs and bacon, lots of jam. The one drawback, we later found, to dear Mrs Purless, was that about 9 o'clock, when we, in kimono and bedroom slippers, were digging in after a hard day, she'd appear with candlesticks. She wanted to lock up and, in her gentle old weary voice: "Was we ready?" I said to Vere how would she take it if I returned with spirit: "You can go to bed if you damned well like! But we are not ready!"

12 May. It snowed, but the south wind blew. Mrs Purless said: "This is the wind what blinds the conger eels. They come up for breath and the south wind blows their sight away." Every morning, snow or no snow, we start off the two of us for a day's tramp on the hills. First, we go to Miss Budle's [Bodle] shop to buy some lunch and have glasses of milk (Nelson too, out of a pudding basin).

13 May. Miss Budle [Bodle] was speaking with great pride of her brother at the front, and I said, thinking to compliment her: "Is he a Sergeant?" She returned with simplicity and perfect breeding. "No, Ma'am, he is a Brigadier General"! And took us into the parlour at the back of the shop and there he was, a very big coloured photograph and a 'bosom' covered with medals. He rose from the ranks in the Boer War. [23]

17 May. I gave Esther notice, because out of sheer venom knowing I will not wash my face in anything but rain water (hence my indisputably lovely skin!) she had emptied the tub saying the rain water "stunk"!

22 May. Esther went out. I swilled the yard. In the middle a caller – of course! A Miss Harvey Smith [24]. I conveyed her to the drawing room and explained. Promised her I'd go to tea on Thursday. 'Wetchedly depwessed' at night. A lunatic in the home is not exhilarating.

23 Brig. Gen. William Bodle, 1855–1924, is buried in Alfriston churchyard.
24 The Misses Harvey Smith lived at Hill House, The Avenue, and bought the patronage of All Saints' Church, now a youth/arts centre.

23 May. This morning she [Esther] was so insolent: "Higher trees than you have been topped" and: "Your conversation goes in one ear and out the other" that I told her next time she'd go . . .

26 May. I slipped on the attic floor; cut my face, blacked my eye and dislocated my wedding ring finger. Ernest came up. He was awfully concerned and sympathetic, got me on the sofa and went to Boots for stuff. ... Esther was a lunatic beast and said when she brought up tea: "It's quite nice to have you shut up here and the house quiet."

1 June. In the afternoon the Miss Harvey Smiths and Dr Parsons to tea. For a long time I wavered as to whether I wouldn't wear my shot taffetas. Finally decided that – no – it didn't go with a black eye that is waning to green. Dr Parsons a bumptious beast and not only that (perhaps because he's been a woman's specialist) curious to say the least! Started talking of hermaphrodites! Ernest, modest and embarrassed, trying to change the subject by flying round with a plate of cake. Miss Harvey Smith's eyes goggling in her head.

3 June. Bad news. Naval disaster [25]. Horrid depression everywhere.

8 June. No letters and I woke up in the mood for lots! Esther says: "Lady Miller comes for her character on Friday." Will say what I can. "Lady Miller's flat is as full-furnished as what this is plain."

10 June. Esther, now she's got her character, mad as mad: "You take care. Everything you say will be took down" – (pointing) – "you ain't the only one what goes upstairs and writes a diary"!

11 June. Whit Sunday. Made our communion together. I do try so hard not to hate Esther, and do fail so gloriously!

25 The Battle of Jutland where Britain lost 7 ships and 6907 men.

20 June. Worked at my play all the morning; after tea - and tea is so nice, with cakes on the dumb waiter and Ernest happy and amiable and Nelson on his cushion - went to get honeysuckle on the Downs, know just the place. Sat down midway in a little rough patch, all long grass and poppies and yellow stuff. Said my 6 o'clock Angelus, and other things. The beauty of the hills overwhelms me.

21 June. Mrs Montague Blaker [26] told me that when she was a girl – a Miss Beard at 16 Southover – she had every morning to go and turn the hams that were pickling in salt, and it was such a cold job! Letter from Pinker with Methuen's account which depressed me, as accounts always do.

24 June. I do get the hump, can't bear the idea of getting old. Ernest – having got through that stage and at no time holding on to life as I do – very wise and tender about it. In the middle, after a pause he said: "I see Miss Mercer's marked her strawberries down to 8d a punnet". We roared. It so pointed the elderly simplicity – the naiveté – of this Lewes life. Very good notice of *Travellers' Samples* [27] in *Daily Telegraph*. Didn't buck me any.

28 June. Ernest and I to Mr Verrall's to tea, to look over Anne of Cleves' house [28]. When I went and showed Verrall over the Anne of Cleves' house [little] did I think that it would be with Ernest I'd sit there to tea in less than 2 years! And Mrs Verrall dead, poor soul, and I pouring out. Life is always entrancing and full of surprise.

29 June. Thought of 10 years ago and David and I cycling in the wind to Fonthill! Wonder if he thought? Men are so odd.

26 The Blakers, a family of Lewes solicitors.
27 Published Methuen 1916.
28 Part of Henry VIII's divorce settlement. FV presented it to the SAS in 1923.

3 July. Now – 12 – just back from servant hunting. Heard of a young girl – Alice Simmonds – and sent to see her on School Hill. Dear little thing, but wears a spinal jacket. I couldn't set her to scrub. Went to Mrs Marchant, the station master's wife, for Emily W's character. Such a nice woman and speaks well of Emily Washer. Oh I'm sick of servants. If only we could do without.

6 July. Up the High Street two wounded soldiers surveyed Nelson with interest. "That chap looks as if he's had a bomb burst over him."

10 July. Riotous morning! ... advent of Emily Washer. What an increasing bore housekeeping becomes. Went to Wycherley [29] who thinks he's got a garden. Couldn't sleep for thinking of it.

12 July. The tradesmen are terribly rude. I went in to Pryor [30], the pork butcher, who had 3 pigs' tongues on a blue dish in the window. Pryor, sitting behind the counter reading a newspaper, asks after pause: "What's for you?" "Pigs' tongues, please." "You can't have 'em, they're going to be cooked for my tea."

19 July. Dear Nelson, his spotted pale face behind the wire blind when I went and when I returned. So touching! What a thing dogs' love is!

21 July. Mrs Hubert told me that when she came back from Australia – in the mid-seventies of the last century – that the last thing she did, before leaving the ship, was to put her crinoline through the porthole and the first thing she did on landing was to go to the first drapers she could find and buy a quilted swansdown petticoat.

29 Alfred Wycherley. His father started the estate agency at 15 Keere St (now demolished) in 1853, now at 56 High Street.
30 Pork butchers established over 100 years until recently in Lewes High St.

4 Aug Fri. Like a fool been reading up diaries since 1910. What volcanoes and vortexes! How I suffered and made others suffer. But now it is over. If Ernest suffers, if David suffers, their own fault. Heaven knows I've done my whack for both! And Margery is supremely happy. Been shopping. Three caravans on St Anne's Hill and a [bevvy?] of beguiling gipsies, all admiring Nelson. How strong and vivid they looked in their rags and their sun brown and their diamond combs and crescent shaped earrings, besides the little anaemic genteel shopping 'ladies' going by.

5 August. After lunch Ernest said would I like a walk on the hills so we started. A perfect day: rather flustered at the beginning by that old woman on School Hill who declared Nelson bit her collie and caused paralysis. Collie now dead. Composed myself – I trust – with kindliness and dignity, declining to accept any such mad cat story. Ernest and I to Falmer, tea there and home by train. I shall remember how nice he looked – in the homespun suit, his hat off and his grey hair – and how gentle he was. This is the sort of thing I want always to remember and nothing else.

7 August. For walk after tea. Divine! Firle and Caburn, then Windover in a round filmy ball beyond. A belt of poppies so red and thick and regular that they looked like a roof. The blue sea, children in white playing on the edge of the hill as it slopes to the town, fluttering like gulls. Lewes is the most divine spot in the world.

30 August. Determined – for Margery's sake and the little child's [31] – to make my Communion every Thursday until all is safely over.

10 September. After supper Ernest and I had a charming talk: not sure that it isn't more fascinating to have that type of man! Married 32 years, and still mysterious.

31 Margery is pregnant with her first child. The loss of AD's first baby started her on her writing career.

14 September. Pryor the pork butcher went to Switzerland for his holiday, climbed a big peak and there ate a pound of his own pork sausages: first meal he'd enjoyed since he left Lewes! How Sussex-y.

16 September. Remember what Mrs Hubert told me about smugglers: their tramping by in the night (riding) or when children were going to bed: the nurse: "There's the gentlemen". The way they stopped the doctor, then let him pass. The old man with rheumatism and his candid avowal: coming from Cuckmere, keg back and front on yoke, the snow fall [32].

21 September. This day I got my garden in St Martin's Lane [33]. From then till now – 26th – the whole thing is a joyful madness. Took Emily down with me, she carrying Nelson's basket. Had some straw sent to the garden to make his bed.

23 September. I was so dead tired by the delight and exertion of the whole thing that I sat in the lookout staring blissfully at Firle for hours. Ernest came in, read his paper and, clearly, liked the place. I've given him a key and the run of the place, on condition that he pays the water rate, 10/- a year.

7 Oct Sat. Heinemann's cheque £10. The young man at Walker's stores is a snuffling horrid creature and has never got anything you ask for, his invariable reply being that "the men at the front must come first".

16 October. Bad beginning. Ernest grousing about his bread and milk, probably with reason but I'm so worn out with peevishness and gloom. Flew out at him. What is this curious emotional disparity? The heaviness he brings, the sense of prison. He came home amiable, with chocolates – so he can be!

32 Rather confused recollections of Sussex's notorious smuggling past.
33 Rented garden in Lewes twitten. Bombed in WW2, now allotments owned by British Rail.

20 October. Mrs Diplock, delightful old dear, with Crown Imperials [lilies]. She was at school with John Dudeney [34]. Told me of her great grandfather, passionate old toper, who because the servant brought him a smeary tumbler, smashed a whole service of glass.

26 October. Crossed over the road to see how Dr Belcher was. Bulletin on door: "Died last night". I told Ernest, who looked mad at being interrupted, then crossed himself. I loathe these mechanical pieties and said so. He excused himself by saying: "You know I'm working against time to get off to Brighton by the cheap train." Made me realise how little death touches us, so long as we live.

11 November. Felt I must pull myself together over the housekeeping and get nice things to eat, whatever they cost in time and money. Went off down High Street alone. Got a rabbit and piece of boiled pork for tomorrow, kidney and bacon, apple turnover today. Most lovely misty day. The opalescent hills – mist threaded through with amber – and then, suddenly a misty pearly mass of sheep, just softly moving through a hollow. Their plaintive bells, the rigid black figure of shepherd and tall crook. Pryor the pork butcher, silly – very like a pig – on a high stool and surrounded by carcases and features of pigs, says savagely: "Miserable weather, bad for the meat."

22 November. Met Mr [Mackay] Clarke, took him to my garden. He told me of old Verrall who meant to sell his brewery business for not less than £70,000. Sold it for £120,000. His 2 sons, one a reprobate and kept on a small allowance – the eldest son – when he inherited he at once went on the booze, broke his neck in 3 days.

25 November. Can't remember much, except that it was wet and we quarrelled. Had I known that this devil-possessing dyspepsia still had hold of Ernest, nothing, no loneliness would have made me write to him, as I did.

34 The shepherd-mathematician who ran a school in Abinger House. A collateral ancestor.

28 November. Letter from Charlotte. She comes tomorrow to look for a house.

29 November. She arrived. With my usual genius for houses I find her one at Southover [35] by the simple expedient of asking the milkman. The young man at the Westgate Stores I had unkindly taken for a 'Conchie' came out, in the course of a brief affable conversation, that he had been torpedoed three times!

9 December. Letter from Sir Philip Sassoon [36], home from the front on leave, admires my work and will I go to lunch. Showed to Ernest who was chill and unsympathetic – as always! It is worse than being alone. Again, the old wild mad melancholy seizes me and I go down Rotten Row with Nelson for his little run, my eyes – my heart – asking questions of the hills! Will now write to Sir Philip and accept.

11 December. Charlotte gone. A very unsettled morning: her bobbing in and out. I get desperate with anything or anyone who gets in the way of my work. I am becoming nothing but a funnel for imagination.

12 December. I went to 25 Park Lane and met Philip (Sassoon) for the first time – I knock – the double doors fling back. A butler – pompous, discreetly pot-bellied: "Does Sir Philip expect you, Madam?" Perfectly calm – not having had a gypsy grandmother (and a royal Lee at that) for nothing – and I inform him that Sir Philip does! And sail past 2 rather flabby looking footmen in the background. His sister, Lady Rocksavage [37], there; also a nice middle-aged man, Sir Louis Mallet [38]. I enjoyed it so much . . . Oh I'd like to be rich for the mental leisure it gives. At the last, Sir Philip gave me a bunch of carnations: "Mrs Dudeney, I shall write to you" (and did).

35 16 Southover High St.
36 Connoisseur, politican, diplomatist. PS to General Sir Douglas Haig, C in C British Armies in France, 1915–1918.
37 Countess of Cholmondeley, wife of 5th Marquess, Joint Hereditary Lord Great Chamberlain of England.
38 Diplomat. Former Ambassador to Turkey.

15 December. In bed. Both these days dear Nelson hardly left me. Ernest always tolerant of mild flirtations and blandly amused, says: "If that young man, Philip Sassoon, were a tobacconist's assistant, you wouldn't bother about him". I said that at no period of my career was I likely to give a tobacconist's assistant a single thought. I think he's rather pleased with the affair. If a man admires his wife, it is a tribute to him and his power of selection.

25 December. Communion early. Sung Mass. Later I was most intensely wretched thinking of other years and other people, thinking of David and not daring to pray in case I cried. Then I looked sideways at Ernest. After all with his many faults he is mine: he has been wronged and I do suffice him. Came to the sensible conclusion that these acute unbearable miseries are half physical. At dinner Ernest produced dessert he'd bought, dear old soul. All the afternoon I dozed by the wood fire. After supper I read him the *Strand* serial.

27 December. Met Frankfort Moore with the three kids who've had scarlet fever. Greeted them at a respectful distance.

30 December. Ernest in bed. A most awful day. I say to myself am I heartless utterly and pure devil?! But illness, my own or anyone else's, anything that gets in the way of my work drives me mad. I loathe sickness and all the sick room paraphernalia. Then I'm short with Ernest and savage with Nelson and full of penitence all the time, yet swearing!

31 December. Always write a little speculative bit at the last! Will 1917 bring peace? That seems the one thing that matters to me! Will it mean a nice book about Beausire Fillery [39]? Already I'm in love with her. And will Christopher and Margery be in England next New Year's Eve? And what will my grandchild be like? And shall I get 750 dollars for the Film rights of *Trespass*? And will Dr Vallance cure Ernest's dyspepsia? Says he can, but I think he's bitten off more than he can chew! And will E.G.W be with me? XX. The answer to

---

39 The heroine of her book *The Head of the Family*.

all this I shall know on New Year's Eve 1917. If I'm alive?? And will I be here in my dear old High Street house with the panelled drawing room and the tubs in the back yard? And shall I have my darling garden in St Martin's Lane still? How fascinating, how always fresh life is, influenza – your own and other people's – notwithstanding.

XX This was partially answered by the fact that E.G.W came in 3 hours later, half seas over and hiccuping. "I've only been drinking the health of my sweetheart at the front." (You convinced she has too many sweethearts).

Anybody would think, to read this diary, that I was the most bitter, most unhappy and half-mad woman in the world. But not so! Ernest's temper is abominable, but he can't help it, doesn't even know it (that's my belief) and makes exquisite amends. After all, if you are married to a genius – and are by way of being one yourself – bound to be clashes ... and I've got such consolations, such joys that never fade, nor fail me. The look of the world, the delight of my work, the adoration of a spotted dog.

1917

3 January. I went up into the lovely panelled room, read the Psalms, thought how charming the faded red-wine of the rugs was, took Nelson down Rotten Row and looked at Caburn, hung up my coat in the attic and stood at the window staring at the sycamore – and now am here, starting on a clean copy of that thing for Harper.

5 January. Feel I must shove off for a bit. After all, life is more or less, through this present phase, an imprisonment! To Brighton by 11.30 . . . Got at Hanningtons a shawl for Margery's infant: 18/9. Just to buy it, just to realise, stirred me very much. Took shawl to show Mother. She approved. Home by the 4 train.

8 January. Went alone down the High Street. Tried for patterns of baby's bonnet in crochet, couldn't get one. EGW after supper came up blubbering: "Sister took bad and she must go home at once for a week." Told her quite impossible, but she could have a month's notice if she liked. Don't believe a word of it. Believe she is playing an Elizabethan game. Men here whitewashing kitchen, EGW fulsome in her meekness. Letter from *The Gentlewoman* asking for my opinion on peace. Gave it.

10 January. Seems as if never shall I settle down to work at 11 again! Housekeeping such a niggling fret of an occupation. If I were happy and the house gay, shouldn't mind, might even enjoy it - but as things are! 'All is gloom like the tomb', and I say to myself, why the dickens, why the devil, why and what for am I ordering these endless, these cheerless meals?

11 January. EGW's day out, and she must go home for a week to "help Mother with the soldiers[1]". I said it was preposterous, she could only go with a month's notice. She went off in such a mood that I hardly expected to see her back.

---

1 Soldiers were billeted with Lewes families.

14 January. In the afternoon went by invitation to tea with Miss Harvey Smith.
Mr Warren[2] there. Charming, but uncertain – perhaps a little silly. The first
magic of him sitting on my sofa his eyes lolling at the panelled wall and "Well
now, isn't it lovely to have a room like this?" gone. Feel I won't bother about
him. S'pose I'm getting old.

22 January. Another day of ghastly cold and trying to snow. By lighting the
gas fire early I was able to work. Nelson insisted on coming up, not being
very well after his bath. I whacked him, but made him comfy and put up
with him. Actually succeeded in working, but this is the coldest house I ever
knew. For my old age I shall have a little tiny snug house, looking full south:
old or new – as long as it's warm.

24 January. Went to view Dr Belcher's things. Nothing there I wanted. The
squalor and heartlessness of sales. His hat box on the bed and 'lotted'. I
remembered Sunday mornings he, scrupulous in tall hat, and our little walks
up the street after church. Meanwhile, it's the coldest winter for 22 years so
they say. I can't sleep or eat or think. Brain and soul set solid in ice. At night
Ernest played chess at Dr Vallance's.

31 January. In the afternoon went for a little walk. Came up against Charlotte
and we walked together. I was glad, because it had been snowing and was
slippery, but oh that intelligent, pigeon-holed little mind! Yet I'm fond of her,
tired as she makes me and (egoistic as always) I'm glad she's at Southover,
ready if I want her! That is what they are for, what they give you in return for
the originality and colour and life you give them. It thawed. When I went to
bed I opened the window and listened to the ravishing glug-glug of the pipes!

1 February. When I wake in the night – as last night – warm, while the world
is so bitter cold, and pray for the homeless, desolate, sick and endangered, is
it because I'm so afraid of these things for myself? And so petition for myself?

2 Edward Warren, American art-collector and aesthete, lived at Lewes House, School
Hill. In 1900 he commissioned Rodin to make him a version of *The Kiss*. In 1914 he
gave it to the town, where it stood in the Town Hall but was returned for fear of
exciting convalescent soldiers. Funded a Military Hospital next door during the war.

4 February. Just the usual quiet day, seemingly: but the excitement of the war keeps you in a topnotch mood.

6 February. Letter from Sir Philip. The perverse postman put his red wicker parcel carts outside the window at breakfast time, so I thought it was a parcel, but he took 'em down Antioch Street. Man just been with fresh asbestos for the gas fire.

9 February. After lunch paid bills as usual on Fridays. Great shock at Walkers! They could only let me have a quarter of sugar! Also no golden syrup. The factories closed down. Also Pannett wasn't sure if he'd ever have any more wood and if he did it would be £2 a ton. Came home horribly depressed.

10 February. Letter from Sir Philip, asking for loan of *Secret Son* [3] to be forwarded by his Secretary by 'King's Messenger' to France. Sounds splendid. He's a splendid and captivating sort of young man. What a queer affair it all is!

8 March. It, the weather, is trying to snow. I have a gas fire, an oil stove, bedsocks, mocassins, two woolly coats, and I perish.

21 March. Oh the loneliness, plus disharmony, of this life! For the usual sweet little Rotten Row walk with Nelson: all my tenderness nowadays on a spotted 'wow'! I come up here – why write about it? The hideous nothing worth while-ism, the constant chill and repression. Oh my God, what is it, this disparity? Then like a fool cried, making myself uglier than ever. You can't afford it at 50! After tea had a really truly real talk with Ernest, confided all my worry and work worries. It cleared the air between us. Met Mrs Moore in the afternoon. She in the deepest hump. So's everybody. War, I suppose.

22 March. Ghastly cold. Feel I never want to work again, until it is warmer, until the world is at peace. Went to the Bank and down the High Street, paying bills, spending money like water. Don't care if I am ruined (3 bob for cakes for tomorrow's tea fight, defying the Food Controller.)

3 Published 1915 by Methuen.

30 March. Again peace after dinner. That's the trick, evidently: keep away from each other. To the Blakers to tea. Such nice people and we didn't squabble going or returning. Ernest, dear old soul, said he had enjoyed it more than any party in Lewes. Mr Blaker said there was a church St Martin's in St Martin's Lane, Remains still in the walls to be seen. Thought of the archway in my garden.

2 April. I say to myself that now, at last, I turn over a new leaf. A curious beautiful sense of the consolation, the reality of Jesus came to me when I made up my mind to this. . . . went to my garden and actually found hinge marks on the arch. So my garden is perhaps consecrated ground. This delights and awes me.

15 April. Went down Rotten Row before church for young nettles: 'Southover Spinach' – delicious. EGW wouldn't touch 'em.

18 April. ... Ernest in tantrums at tea time, just like a naughty child. I told him afterwards that if he couldn't behave he must have tea in his own room, that I simply wouldn't have my friends alienated.

19 April. Ernest asked me when I came in from nettle cutting in Rotten Row to "get me a bunch of primroses and pin them in my coat". I said – in a hurry to get up here and provoked, as always, by his morning easy chair habit: "Plenty in the drawing room, get them". I got them, of course, but coldly, wearily. And once I should have done it gaily, made a play of it! But now. Oh he has worn me out, driven me off, shooed me away at last. I came up here feeling very, very sorry and so hopelessly tragic.

20 April. Ernest and I came to a certain understanding. Dear old soul! If we could worry through. At night couldn't sleep in case there should be an order to destroy dogs.[4]

4 It appears that this was an unsubstantiated rumour.

25 April. Two [letters] from Margery: 'John' born 24 March. No cable. Ernest cabled ... At 4.30 to tea with Miss Harvey Smith. Charlotte there. We came away together. I brought her in and showed her 'John's' photo - at 2½ days old, the darling.

29 April. Remember the nice row the Mamma and infant rooks make in the big sycamore.

1 May. Went to Brighton. Took 'John's' photo to show mother.

2 May. Letter from Heinemann: I am 'the nicest author he has ever known.' Wrote him. Wonder if he'll pay what Methuen pays?

3 May. I met a lovely tramp with lovely windmills 1½d each. Bought one for 'John'. I'm sure he wasn't human, nor his windmills. Just sent for me: because I was good and got up to go to church.

5 May. Letter from Heinemann: quite insulting in its way, and declining. Must spar off a German and a Jew [5]. That seems clear!

7 May. Wrote Heinemann as diplomatically as I could.

11 May. Wrote Pinker. Put on thin combinations. Exquisite day.

12 May. Sunday, at Mass, a darling wren 'as bold as brass' singing in the churchyard, *when the choir sang*! Made me so happy: mixed up with prayer and became one with it.

13 May. Who dares say that wrens – and dogs – don't have souls?

15 May. Went off down Rotten Row with Nelson (remember pale green sycamore blossom thick on road and, always, the splotches of wounded blue soldiers against the lavender background of hills).

5 Heinemann and Methuen.

19 May. Letter from Pinker. Methuen offers £100 advance. Wrote Heinemann. I feel relieved. I could live on the £100 (given a little luck with *Harper*) but not save.

31 May Thurs. Began *The Journey* . . .

7 June. Ernest took the Mass [6]. After lunch decided I must have something thin. Bus to Brighton: Linen coat and skirt at Medham's: £2. Sir Philip sent me an evening coat; rose coloured brocade, lined with ermine, or something that looks like it: anyhow, there are tails!

16 June. Lewes Communal Kitchen [7]. I give it 3 weeks. And the elderly man and those women: their indignation, their spotless blouses and conscientious home- trimmed hats.

19 June. EGW suddenly demands a week's holiday. Scene. Shan't stand another. Has so shaken me that I can't settle my thought to work. Must. How I loathe servants. But for me one is indispensable.

22 June. To London. Bitter cold. Perished in frock! Travelled up with Mrs Hubert. Lunched with Skues: borrowed £2 off him and went to Selfridges. Taffeta coat, steel grey, £2.12.6. Very nice. To Sir Philip's: he, Lady Rocksavage and the Countess of Essex.

3 July. Ernest went off after breakfast with a Gladstone and a great fuss. He looked very white and thin, but I simply mustn't let everything wring me.

4 July. Posted gold cross for John. It got there ... Letter from Ernest. Distinctly cold and on his dignity.

7 July. Air raid in London. Wired Ernest, was he safe? Very distressed. Tea party.

6 ED, an accomplished musician, played the organ.
7 Non-profit-making restaurant in the Corn Exchange. It lasted until 1919.

8 July. Bad night ... wire from Ernest and letter – quite genial . . .

13 July. Ernest returned. Very penitent, loving, gentle, with a love offering of a Liberty bag.

15 July. Made my communion. Said, returning, that never would I lock my bedroom door again. He came in, dear old thing, to kiss me good night when I was in bed. This made things human and sweet between us once more. Nelson very much perturbed and outraged.

28 July. Ernest got a disquieting letter from *Strand* man, made me feel the column might go. Oh the old terror! ... everything is so flat, so unprofitable, so moneyless; the war squashing us all flat. Ernest was so tender. He took me in his arms and wiped my eyes and said: "In my heart, I am always tender". My dear! I will remember that. I came upstairs, opened Thomas à Kempis [8] at random and there saw "That a Man should not be fretful in Business" – took it down to Ernest. . . . If Margery, if David could see the lovely town, the panelled room, my garden – oh – if! But as fast as you pick up one love you drop another!

1 August. Poured. Most awful day, cold as well. In despair, went to the pictures. Vulgar, asinine affair. Methuen sent proofs of *The Head of the Family* [9]. The whole weight of the war, the accumulated sadness of the war seems to be killing the world, not only in battle.

3 August. ... Oh if I only had a £150 a year without lifting a finger. My world would be changed . . .

8 August. Went off for the day, Ernest having gone to London ... Got home just before a thunderstorm. Ernest returned. *Strand* column not only secure but booming. I was so relieved. What a faithless devil I am. 'Journey' back from *Harper*. Will I alter the end? Will. Anything nowadays!

8 *The Imitation of Christ.*
9 Published 1917 with dedication 'To P.S.'

22 August. Hell of a rage! "What the devil do I pay for?" No dinner or tea prepared yesterday. Knew there would be. However, EGW is back now [from holiday] so I shall be able to keep away from him. At tea he brought home scones and was urbane – to the dog – I'm not so easily mollified that way.

29 August. Very nice tea party... Mrs Young a most beguiling old thing. She says this house is haunted by an old man called Langridge, the usual miser, who lived here alone. This would account for Nelson's nerves sometimes in the drawing room [at] nights . . . EGW late again. Gave her notice.

30 August. Letter from Sir Philip [10]. Wycherley in garden at 11. Gave him a trug of apples.

4 September. Got called "a bitch" after supper! I walked down to post in the lovely moonshine, stark with misery, red with rage. Then I looked at the belfry of St Michael's, at a little star, at the pretty street and grew calm, devout, cynical – a little of each.

8 September. Six years since Margery and I departed from Littlewick. What courage and desperation, and how unexpectedly it has panned out. Ernest's book [11] out.

2 October. Mrs Moore says Frankfort Moore is in the depths, Hutchinson won't take any more books . . . She said to him: "Why don't you do other writing?"! Poor devil! They never understand. As Ernest, who came up for a chat and was affable, said: "Doing the pork-butcher's books?"!

3 October. The whole town full of poor deplorable Cockneys who have fled from the air raids in London.

10 'When is *my* book coming out? I am sorry that you did not put 'To Philip Sassoon' on the flyleaf, as I'd have felt so *proud* – no one will know who P.S. is and I should like *everyone* to know.'
11 *Amusements in Mathematics*, published Nelson. ED's first book, *The Canterbury Puzzles*, published in 1907.

6 October. The new people [next door] are cutting down the sycamore. Cried and cried. Ernest was very nice, though he couldn't understand. Mopped up and made for a story 'The Tree'. Very good notices of *Head of the Family*. This bucked me.

10 October. Sausages, divinely cooked, for dinner. While I was doing them in a splutter and flare of fat, wire from Lady Rocksavage. Would I lunch there Saturday? Declined. Struck me as very droll: sausage-frying and an invitation from a Countess!

21 October. Letter from Sir Philip [12] by King's Messenger – very splendid! My birthday. Ernest gave me cigs and O'Henry's stories. Couldn't be better.

29 October. Ernest now "got a temperature", "shaking all over" and stumbling about: "Can't guide myself, can't see". Pure hysteria! Makes me savage and sorrowful.

30 October. Still alive and active, but a thundering headache. Ernest – for I gave him no encouragement to stay in bed – down: but walking and floundering about bent double . . . it made me laugh. Gave him hot tea, cut him thin bread and butter, plonked him down close to the fire and told him not to be so silly. Dr Vallance came. He's got pleurisy. This makes me seem a monster, but I'm not simply boy and the wolf. We got his bed down into his study. Two nurses came in and gave him fermentations. Charlotte who, by mercy was here, went off and got a pleurisy jacket and malted milk and heaps of other sick things. I didn't feel remorseful, because how can I, after all my long experience of him, sort out the real from the false. Poor old dear! He was very gentle and grateful when we got him comfortable.

1 November. Three years since he came to Lewes. No good asking oneself mad helpless useless questions. He is in a vile temper. I've just got called (in Emily's hearing) a blasted fool. I come up here, control myself and send

12 This letter and the previous one dated 25.8.17, both written from the front, are kept in this diary.

Methuen the 2 amazingly good notices (in Sussex papers) of *The Head of the Family* ... at night when I gave him his last dose of milky stuff, he was ineffably sorry, said he was delirious. We will let it go at that! He bent his head, so grey, so ill-looking, and kissed my hands. It broke me up inside, but I had the sense to keep calm.

2 November. Hope, by mercy, to keep quiet and work till one: that the doctors won't want to see me, that the nurses won't want any more rags, towels and so on; that I shan't be packed off kerslap to Carvills for the commode. Worked very well. But it left me so fearfully tired.

12 November. Ernest up again, but weak . . . EGW drunk-ish and insolent at night.

18 December. Philip sent me a blue silk hand-bag in a tortoiseshell frame and with my initials AD in tortoiseshell.

21 December. Just snivelled – idiot – by the fire after breakfast, getting warm ... everything wrong, of course. Lavatory water stopped, gas fire giving no heat, oil stove gone mysteriously wrong, utterly empty and unhappy. Life with Ernest is always prison, and for over 30 years I've been beating at the bars.

24 December. Awful day. No warmth in gas fire while I dressed ... went off down the town for a final Xmas shop. Mince pies 3d each, I ran to earth a 3 lb pot of marmalade . . . so far the most frozen, unhappy Xmas Eve I've ever spent.

25 December. Ernest was able to get to church at midday . . . Charlotte and I for a walk at 3, then Evensong and Carols, then she came here to tea. Best tea things and all the rest. Very nice. Big log fire. Ernest went off to his room directly after, which chilled me. However, he came up later, very gentle, gaunt and penitent: "hadn't realised it was Xmas". So I went and sat with him and a peaceful evening was our end.

26 December. After lunch a row. My fault very likely. I was frozen and diabolical. I came up here into this little room, hopeless, wretched, rebellious at the whole thing. It is a constant, subtle, incurable torture. It is a net – I can't get out. The blue sky, the old red chimney, the tracery of the great sycamore made me glad: but they are cutting down the sycamore . . . At tea time he was perfectly sweet and said I must have a real fire in my writing room: "I'll pay for the coal." This relieved and sweetened me. He has been so mean, or given the impression of meanness.

28 December. I hear from Pinker. He has fixed up with Hurst & Blackett for 3 books. Just to know I am going to have a foil and that I am safe for 3 years transforms my world.

29 December. At midday a great whack and the sycamore fell! I was heart-rent - cried and cried ... made a sort of top muslin blind to the little landing window to hide the cruel patch of branchless sky, then arranged a jug of holly on the window ledge to spray across the lower panes and give the illusion of branches.

31 December. Got all my papers into the bureau and got a fire. For the first time since I came into the house I find myself with a proper writing room!

1918

2 January. 12.30 – Just back from futile shopping, no margarine, butter tea or cheese. Ernest bland as usual trying to soothe. Mad with him. Told him he'd have to take his share of the bother.

8 January. Tea party ... Ernest behaved nicely and we were all quite gay round the wood fire. I thought of David.

29 January. Start Communal Kitchen meals [1]. Went to Australian concert with Mrs Moore – delightful. Heavenly day. Walked on the hills. Finished first part – 22,000 words – of the Blanchflower [*Candlelight*] book.

7 February. Ernest sent Emily out with a note and between them they let Nelson steal half the dinner. I came down after working and before then getting drenched through shopping in rain down the Cliffe. When I fly into a very natural rage get told – in a shout – to go to hell. Came up here, finished John's ball and posted it.

4 March. Hideous east wind . . . Prowled down the High Street looking for grub à la scavenger dog.

7 March. Went to Dr Vallance and insisted on a certificate for the Food Controller so that Ernest may have more butter.

10 April. EGW's day out and also Ernest's birthday. He was weighed: lost 1½ lbs. I was wretched. Cake for tea, the only bit of rich that even Brighton could provide. Gave him Patience cards.

17 April. No good attempting to keep a diary. War news awful, the whole of life grim.

---

1 As voluntary helper.

8 May. EGW really thinks she will get married and gave me a month's notice.

2 June. Tea at Mrs Moore's. Wore my new hat. Got twice roared out and called a fool. Up here now – 8.30 – sternly determined to make notes for book. Anything so that I don't break down. He downstairs playing the piano most ravishingly! Odd pair!

12 June. Emily left, to my great regret and to hers.

15 June. After dinner Wycherley came. The Castle Precincts house [2] is to be sold. Wildly excited. Told Charlotte. Had to tell Ernest. To my amazement he was quite approving, complimentary even, and consented to trundle round and look at it.

19 June. Bear [3] burnt down. Got Margery's letter; with information that another infant is expected in September . . . Letter from Wycherley saying he will make an offer for house.

23 June Sun. Queer stomachic upset. Perhaps fish rissoles – tinned – from Communal Kitchen.

1 July. Met Mrs Moore. Mrs Burbidge [4] is after Castle Precincts house. My heart beat like mad. I told Mrs Moore, had to. Said that if I got 'em Mrs Burbidge should be tenant. Arranged for them to come round after supper.

19 July. All three act plays back from Pinker who says that at present there is no chance of placing them. . . . got a servant - Susan Freeman by name, with a very indifferent character. She comes August 12th.

2. Built 1813 as a watch-tower by the London-Lewes Carrier John Shelley. It stands against the second motte (mound) of Lewes Castle.
3 The Bear Hotel was beside the Cliffe bridge over the River Ouse at the bottom of the town.
4 Doctor's widow, friend of Mrs Moore.

3 August. Told Wycherley I'd give Edge £450 for house.

21 August. Went over it [Castle Precincts House] with Mrs Moore and Mrs Burbidge, who wants it for 3 years: "I must have it". Forsee difficulties in that quarter!

26 August. Got the Castle Precincts House!

27 August. Went to Bank and told them to sell out my War Loan. Wrote to Mrs Burbidge [5]. (About the most unfortunate act of my life. The woman is a tigress. 24/8/20)

30 August. Title of house from Skues. Told Mrs Burbidge she could have it for 3 years. Sent £5 5s to Wycherley, his fee. Feel delighted of course, equally of course exhausted. Very tired but sort of glowing inside because I've got my home.

2 September. Went all over house by myself with Nelson, deciding what I'd do with it. Meanwhile Ernest goes to Public Library, Brighton, plays chess, plays bowls, never suggests going to look at it! So, chilled – as he always chills me, mournful – as he always makes me, I took the key back to the house agent. Such *incredible* stupidity on his part, if he really loves me. But of course he doesn't. He loves himself and always has and will and loves nobody else.

5 September. At night told Ernest what I felt. He was instantly tender, penitent and all the rest. We went over the house. Returning letter from Margery: John died on August 11th [6]. Oh what are houses now.

6 September. No sleep, wept myself blind. Wrote her, wrote Christopher. Sent them my Thomas à Kempis. Went to Brighton and told my mother.

5 AD, fearing Mrs B would buy CPH, wrote offering her a tenancy. Letter was 'stamped', making it legally enforceable.
6 The reason for the death of AD's first grandchild at 17 months is never given.

16 September. Just before dinner a cable. Margery has a son [7]. Cabled Margery. Ernest didn't "see any necessity" and refused to pay half.

19 September. Susan went to the Circus : "Oh it was a sell! Only a few 'orses and the ladies dressed up in their silks what done the cakewalk. An' I went to see wild beasts: elephants an' camels and lions and tigers and" – her eyes getting round and her voice and her bust rising – "jackals!"

28 September. Lawyer's letter from Mrs Burbidge.

1 October. Getting this room into order. Blacksmith came. Am going to put pot hook up drawing room chimney to save gas ... Cut Mrs Burbidge dead. She, unfortunately for her, was coming out of a wine shop with a bottle.

8 October. Another bout: at breakfast time was called a fool, a swine, a bitch. I come up here, broken, furious, degraded. Chimney pot broken. Drawing room fire impossible ... my nerves on end, cross to my nice Susan, to the blacksmith who is putting a bar up for the pot hook, to Nelson – everything and everybody ...

13 October. Letter from darling Margery, from a Maternity Hospital.

3 November. Oh! Had a scrap with Ernest because he will kneel with head practically on the floor at Mass. So neurotic, eccentric. Makes me want to chuck a chair at him. He thought my attitude "monstrous".

6 November. Wretched. Bad notices of Candlelight [8]. Why am I so faithless? Why do I get so afraid?

10 November. Terrific excitement. Waiting for the Germans to sign Armistice.

---

7 Barney. Later called Julian.
8 Published Hurst & Blackett, 1918. Later dramatised as The Old House by Richard Pryce with Gertrude Elliott (Lady Robertson) playing the main part.

11 November. *Armistice signed*. I was typing in the middle bedroom when Ernest called up from the yard: "Alice, it is over". He wouldn't come out again but I tied on Nelson's red, white and blue bow and off we went into the High Street. Everything and everyone delirious. All the dogs out, all with bows and all twisting round your legs in the crowd. A lot of soldiers outside the Town Hall collared Mackay Clarke, the Rector of All Saints, bundled him up on to an impromptu platform, roared at him to make a speech. So there he was, with his ginger moustache and his sweating carrot red face, waving his arms about, moving his lips, and nobody heard one blessed word for the shouting and laughing and roaring. And lots of people were crying and one old woman outside Stone's shop said: "But think of them poor boys what 'ull never come back."

13 November. Lovely weather. This, and the Victory, makes us all as light as air.

23 November. Sir Philip sent me official photographs of the war. Wrote him . . .

24 November. Yesterday after tea I went to Mrs Burbidge and asked her, finally, if she would let me have my Castle Precincts house at the end of a year. She refuses but admitted "I know I've behaved badly".

9 December. Mrs Burbidge moved into my dear home! Pulled myself together and paid 2/- for a pot of flowers which I left at the cottage for her.

27 December. Sir Philip sent me a lovely rose brocade wrap, lined with fur.

What's the good of speculating over next year or prosing over this. Yet! How do things stand? I've got the Castle Precincts House, the war is over, Christopher and Margery may be coming home. Little Barney is born but John – oh little baby, I did not see you but I grieve for you. And just now packing up the new ball I thought of the red, white and blue one I made for your first birthday last March. *Little* John Gabriel! No good writing and maundering any more; for it seems so silly when you read it over a year or two later. I shall read this, if I live, and smile and shrug and sigh, and turn away, become absorbed by the year that is then.

1919

Something rather invigorating and nice about a New Year and a nice new big diary. Glad to put away that wretched little 1918 one, full of war miseries and grousing.

5 January. Very nice day. Ernest read *Les Misérables* [1] at night: I am enjoying it so.

7 January. Woke up feeling delighted. Tonight I am not going out. Kimono, swinging pot over the logs for my bath: sitting in candlelight looking at the silky oak panelling, all the delight of a home winter evening.

9 January. At night took all my note books into the drawing room and, by the fire, picked out two ideas for short stories the man wants: 1500 words, ridiculous length.

16 January. Been shopping in torrential rain. Came in, flew at Ernest who (not to put too fine a point upon it) is beastly selfish. That habit of sitting by a big fire half the morning reading the paper enrages me: I who am always working, hand over hand, at a dozen things. However! What's the good? And I am sorry. Just taken him a bit of holly as a peace offering . . . At night a row, thought it would be a marvel if we got through *Les Misérables* without one. He explained to me, in that smug way I detest, what a cicatrice was: "thought you might not know". Instead of being blandly ironical and meekly asking what a cockatrice was, and a cockchafer and a cockroach, I flared out. What an ass I am!

17 January. Made my communion. Tried not to feel ruffled any more. Came home and kissed his face of thunder!

1 By Victor Hugo.

18 January. A little hard not to feel bitter and very sad: not grudging and envious a bit, but lonely. Just now down Rotten Row with Nelson, heard such light happy laughing and there was Mrs Victor hugged up and walking in the sun with a third daughter home from Salonica. Oh I do want Margery. If I could have had lots of children and a lover-husband and bright, bustling family life. But after all, I've had and have got lots of things and I wouldn't be Mrs Victor for a King's Ransom. I'll plunge into Missing: and that's the sort of pure, unspoiled joy *she* hasn't got. An hour later! What a fool I was to whimper like that. I've been in the 7th heaven working at Missing.

22 January. There has been a town meeting over some memorial to Lewes soldiers who have fallen. One illuminated idiot suggested an obelisk with an urinal and cloakrooms underneath. [2]

31 January. Finally decided that this intense irritation which Dr Renton months back diagnosed as 'war nettlerash' and which becomes unbearable must be seen to. Went to Wyborn the chemist for a lotion, showed him my arm. Itch[3]! Came home – howled. Degraded beyond measure. Mopped up my face and flew to doctor. Itch!!

3 February. Got to have baths, baths, baths and rubbings in of sulphur ointment.

4 February. Shall I ever forget it. The house gaunt, no fire in the breakfast room. Frost intense. No fire in drawing room. Fire in the middle room and baths; baths and anointings. And no servant. Only a morning woman.

8 February. Am getting better.

9 February. Went to church. Feel better still. Burned, on doctor's advice, a sulphur candle to fumigate my outdoor clothes. Filled the house with stinking fumes.

2 Lewes War Memorial erected, without urinal, 1922.
3 Scabies, a parasitic skin infection, considered a disease of the working classes.

10 February. No irritation but my skin blazes. Got a letter from Richard Pryce [4] . May he dramatise *Candlelight*, which he admires immensely? Wrote consenting.

11 February. They [Christopher & Margery] are not coming home after all. So I must get broken to that also. Went to doctor. He says I am now absolutely well, that I might have caught it in a railway carriage; from paper money – anyhow or anywhere. The sulphur ointment is making my skin burn, but it will pass.

17 February. Flew into a silly wicked rage at supper time, but I do get so sick of Susan being away. Also there is the sense of this revolting ailment. I feel as if I can never recover my self respect, never feel sure.

25 February. Charming letter from Sir Philip. Wrote him and then the morning was gone. Ernest got his *Blighty* [5] column.

18 March. I was desperate, done for. Remained in bed, sent Ernest for Dr Loud, who arrived and gave his verdict. Yes, it is back. He says I must have a bath up to my neck and suggested going into a nursing home. I thought of Charlotte's bath. Sent Ernest to her, she nobly consented. Then it was arranged I should go there at 7.30 and a nurse would be there. Nurse never turned up till 8.30, was without ointment and was instantly fetched away altogether by a distracted person who said a little boy in Leicester Road was "took bad". Add to this that the beastly geyser never heated the bath; that I lay in "loo [luke] warm" water and walked home at quarter to ten in the rain. That was my day.

19 March. Again no sleep. Dr Loud came. The nursing home can't take me _ only one bath. Susan is splendid. Impossible to part with Susan. Don't suppose she gave it me???

4 Theatre director.
5 Patriotic magazine during WW1, revived in WW2.

20 March. Slept like a top. Am normal again, human. Dr Loud came; he suggests that I hire a bath. Went all over the town in vain. Punker down Cliffe thinks he *might* and will let me know tomorrow . . . now – 6 – I'm happy although I tickle like mad. Lovely fire, pot on, Nelson, bewitching scatter of spots asleep, got up and rolled him over, he was irresistible.

21 March. Ernest very good and peaceful. He's on the upgrade. £150 in the bank, lots of work coming in, man coming to interview him on Monday. Had my bath in the drawing room. Ladling boiling water out of the pot.

22 March. *English Review*, with my Taking the Waters. Same old damned skin irritation. Of one thing I'm sure, no more sulphur ointment. It has burned me up. The whole thing is a minor sort of misery. I tickle all the time. The one blessed interval is when I get into my boiling hot bath at night.

4 April. After dinner tore my legs to rags. What am I to do? A minor misery very likely, but it spoils life. And doctors seem such helpless fools. What's the use of spending money on 'em?

5 April. The most heavenly day. I dined at the Communal Kitchen and afterwards walked over the hills with Nelson to Glynde where we had tea, then walked back. He was overjoyed, looking so enchanting with his mouth open, laughing. Then he threw back his head and barked and barked and barked.

7 April. This last chapter [*Spade Work*] [6] possesses me. I want to do it all the time: and all the time I'm thinking of words, then losing 'em. Ought to take a day off.

8 April. Money came in [from] *Harper*, Heinemann. I've got £80. So I've bought the Castle Precincts house and mended the stable [7] roof without borrowing a penny.

6 Published Hurst & Blackett 1921. Set in Angmering, West Sussex.
7 John Shelley's original waggon house.

10 April. Ernest's birthday. Gave him – by request – a prayer book. Nelson gave him a box of matches and some spills! Saw in the butcher's half an ox hanging up, with the printed notice of a Fancy Dress dance pinned on!

18 April, Good Friday. No Three Hours for me. Nelson can't be left. Went to the Reproches, afterwards took him on the hills which did me good. Got tea ready and Ernest came in. We had ducks' eggs and a jolly good row.

22 April. Past my darling house, saw Mrs Burbidge and asked if Sands had done the chimney nicely. She asked me up to see. Oh I do hate her and the other tenants for keeping me out. Will 2½ years ever go? Shall I be alive when they are gone?

16 May. Joan Fulleylove came. I liked her instantly and immensely.

19 June. Ernest got a rise on the *Strand*. He is now making £300 a year! 2.30. These charming warm sunny days and loafing afternoons! Just up from my sprigged sofa; Nelson stretching on his cushion, languid after a beef bone, Margaret scrubbing the flagstones in the hall, which always gives cool sound.

20 June. I'm afraid my diaries would make squalid reading, but beautified here and there. Let's hope they'll be cremated with me! When?? All the morning I turned out china, pots, pans and so on preparing for the grinding slavery of a new servant. If only one could live and, more, work without these wretches.

23 June. At night I went into finance and found that at present I am paying out £130 for the house and Ernest is only paying £75. As for a long time his share was only £50, I must be a good £150 to the bad in 5 years – and this, *honourably*, he owes me. But I shall never get it. He is now earning £300 and has about £800 capital. His appalling meanness over money alienates me more and more as I grow older and so tired.

24 June. I made a list of my expenditure and enclosed it with a letter to him. Dared not talk it. I was so dreadfully afraid of a row, shrink from them, they destroy me. All the same, I won't go on losing money like this. He was out,

playing bowls, when I came in I went up in the drawing room and sat in the little window, doing crochet to calm. I trembled when he came in and when although Nelson ran down barking, he didn't speak to him as usual. However at supper he said very gently: "I got your note, dear. I'll talk it over another time, when I'm not so tired with work". All the same, I'm afraid it means eventually some terrible scene.

28 June. Peace signed ... bells started ringing, guns thudding at Newhaven, squibs went off in the High Street. Nelson much alarmed, bolted into his bedroom. After tea I took him down the High Street to buy a flag (my Armistice one got loose and flew out of the window) and a bit of ribbon for his Victory bow. More squibs. He, in stark horror, fled down Fisher Street, going like a streak and out of sight. For nearly an hour I lost him and was desperate. He was clearly afraid to come home. On my way with Mabel Smythe [8] to the Police Station to report his loss met the poor dear sneaking up Castle Banks, his eyes starting out of his head.

2 July. Invitation to go to Alice Clemmison's [9] wedding. Her 3rd marriage: this time to Sir William Bryne. Some women do go it!

11 July. I've hung the crucifix where John's photograph used to be. Sometimes I get a gust of misery about his death and then I think of darling precious Margery and what it means to her: such infinitely greater sorrow.

19 July. Peace Day. To the wedding. Met Vere looking quite charming: violet silk, little black silk coat, black hat. Had a cup of coffee and a sandwich, then to Grays Inn. Chapel shut up. Went to porter's lodge. Wedding postponed. Furious of course. Decided to get out of London at once. Tube to Victoria, two changes. Buried alive in a veritable hell, packed with swaying, sweating humanity. A sprinkling of full blooded niggers in immaculate grey suits ... At night torchlight procession. Mrs Young sent a note would we view it from

8 Mabel Smythe and her sister Bertie lived at The Corner House, High St. Bertie was known for wearing a trilby hat.
9 Cousin of ED.

her attic windows. I went, Ernest wouldn't. Later I went alone on the hills and saw the bonfire on Firle [Beacon]. Got in at a quarter to one.

21 July. Letter from bride with the belated news that wedding is postponed.

30 July. It comes to me with anguish and rebellion that he isn't a bit like any other husband. He isn't asked to keep me, I can do that. But he never does anything for me, nor gives me anything. He is flush now and could give me either a typewriter or a wrist watch, both of which I want so badly. Simply never occurs to him. This looks like whining – *Damn!* Bought a Smith Pressive typewriter £6.5s!

2 August. Letter from Sir Philip. Will I go to Hythe [10] for a night? S'pose I must: but it means all sorts of fuss. He's too rich.

6 August. To Brighton with Ernest. Perfect day. He was so good and gentle and generous. One of the days to hoard up, one of the days that atone. He bought me a wrist watch.

25 August. These two days I was busy getting ready to go to Sir Philip's. I've got a new evening frock – thick satin the colour of an elephant's skin: with a net overdress embroidered in gold.

26 August. Bought a blouse, also a ridiculous nightgown. I shall be very cold in it. I wasn't. The house most lovely and luxurious. I seem to be staying with a fairy prince. While I was in my bath before dressing for dinner, he – Philip – who was out when I arrived – came knocking at the door: "Mrs Dudeney, are you in your bath? Get dressed and come down quick. I am *dying* to see you". All very boyish and gay and much emphasised.

27 August. There is a wide and wonderful herbaceous border with a vista of the sea at the bottom. We walked up and down at sunset time and he quoted

10 Port Lympne. Mansion on Kent/Sussex border built in 1911 for PS. Now part of Howlett's Zoo.

something lovely about the colour of phloxes. I said: "Where did you get that phrase?" He laughed: "From your *Secret Son*." A Mr and Mrs Gubbay in the house, his cousins, very Indian and Jewish-ey looking [11]. Also Sir Louis Mallet. I like him. He has a villa in the South of France and said: "Now you have stayed with Philip you must come and stay with me". I can see Ernest's bland look of stupefaction if I announced that I was going!

28 August. Returned. Enjoyed myself very much; but so nice to get home. Also a Lady Edward Grosvenor [12] there. And people from all over the earth seemed to come and go all the time! Gubbay said: "To stay at Lympne is like being at Piccadilly Circus". So awfully sleepy with all the excitement that I loafed all the morning and slept most of the afternoon.

13 October. Blazing, God-given sun, the Virginia creeper making a heavenly vallance to the window ...

21 October. My birthday. Ernest is giving me silk stockings. I am happy today ... And yet, because he will gobble his food then blunder up and fling open doors, we had a jolly good row, and so my 50 odd birthday ended. But it is too barbarous. One day he started smoking before I was half through and another day he actually changed his shoes while I was dishing up the pudding!

31 October. In the afternoon dipped my Mitchell frock into water with a bottle of red ink in. As that only turned it pink, poured in a bottle of violet ink and it looks quite promising.

2 November. Ernest morbid: miracle if he could keep rational for long. Elbows on table at dinner time, face black and wild. "I am very ill." Simply got a bit of a cold coming.

---

11 The Sassoons were an Anglo-Indian Jewish family of Spanish origin that settled in Baghdad in the 16th century. David Gubbay was an expert financier who managed PS's investments.
12 Daughter-in-law of Duke of Westminster.

4 November. Letter from Sir Philip saying he had been to Paris and had brought me back a sweater . . . Ernest in bed. I took his breakfast up, seeing with meticulous care that everything was on the tray, including marmalade and a filthy-smelling red herring (he adores them!) But he wouldn't touch a darned bit!

11 November. Armistice Day . . . Went to Requiem Mass for the fallen. Very impressive, the pause, with sirens going and a bugler playing the Last Post outside. Inside, the full and motionless church.

12 November. Been reading the prophet Amos and St Peter. Everything in the whole world blazes with content and beauty (just remembered that there is no mustard in the house, sausages for dinner, pig's tongue for breakfast).

28 November. Wrangling all day. My fault probably but I do get so over-wrought. And after swimming down the High Street in hail and rain and up it with a loaded basket to see him sitting there in that sleek, self indulgent way I have always detested, before an immense fire: and to remember that he calls me a skulking lazy beast! I want to murder him. And then I come up here and have my little temper and read the Bible and pray, and get out the typewriter! ... Oh, I bought a sweet white velvet dog for Barney and ordered a book of poems for Christopher.

25 December, Christmas Day. Ernest gave me silk stockings. I gave him gloves. Margaret delectably cooked a delectable chicken and everything passed off beautifully. I purposely crocheted hard all the evening because I didn't intend to get sentimental and mawkish!

29 December. Bought Xmas number of *Lloyds Magazine*. My Another Opinion not in, although he said it would be. Very annoyed, for it's a bob wasted! Before supper played the old game of biscuits with darling Nelson, turning up the rugs and putting chairs out of the way.

30 December. 1919, which I started rather joyously, has been a beast of a year. My fault perhaps. Glad to see it go, anywhere.

1921

[Mrs Dudeney burns her diary for 1920. Her reason and regret for so doing is recorded on 23rd March 1927]

15 January. Met Mrs Burbidge in High Street ... we had a heart to heart talk, I saying that as she had given her word of honour to leave my home before Michaelmas if she could find 'a roof to go under' I could not understand why she refused all my offers of homes . . . She said she'd heard of a house in Southover and would take it if she could get it.

21 January. Went up and spoke to the hideous woman with the even more unfortunate would-be Dalmatian dog that Nelson used to go for until she shouted that she'd 'summons' me! Asked how he was. Dead, poor beast: she very moved and asked after Nelson. I said that was nice of her, as she'd no reason to love him. She told me that her poor, altogether wrong, Dalmation was the dog of her daughter who died seven years ago. And that he used to sneak off to the churchyard and sit on her grave.

25 January. Miss Doyle very funny over Pryor crying in the shop when his second wife died but pointing to photograph of first wife hung up in shop amidst the pork: "But it was her I loved. She was the one".

1 February. Worked like a horse on fire at the *Harper* (to be, let us hope) short story 'The Festival'. My books *Harriott*, *The Orchard Thief* and *Candlelight* back from film man. No letter, so conclude he makes nothing of them. Unfortunate. But I clearly wasn't born to make money.

1 March. Queer how the sublime and the ridiculous blend. I dreamed in agony that Nelson was shot, woke with joy to find it was only a dream. Went in to kiss him and found he'd been sick on the floor.

7 March. Letter from Margery with the first snapshot of Jamie [1] . . . As I came off the Kingston hills, Firle on one side and the burial ground on the other, gave me a funny feeling. Here am I counting the hours for six months to get itself over and Firle has been there for centuries, and will be. I, soon, shall lie under some little stone.

16 March. Sir Philip at 1.30 [Park Lane]. Mrs Lowndes [2] there, Mrs Cornish, a nice man called Baring [3], Lord and Lady Lovat [4]. . . Later I went to Richard Pryce and found him in. Then to Nigel Playfair [5]. Came home by the 6.40, very tired but quite triumphant.

25 March, Good Friday. To the Three Hours. Later on maddened by traffic in the High Street. Went to bed with such a horrible headache.

6 May. To tea with Mrs Moore. Very nice man there, a widower, Gale by name, who is 3rd on the list for this house [6]. Asked him if he'd like to look over it. Frankfort Moore appeared and was pleasant. Talked to him – deferentially – about his garden and he bounded and boomed as usual.

12 May. Finished – at last – and after gargantuan difficulties my book. And how am I going to get through this airless, noisy summer?!

14 May. Appalling day: exquisite weather which make it worse. Traffic made me want to scream and as to work, entirely out of the question. Ernest with lumbago. Got a flannel body belt which I insisted on him wearing. Also got some ribbon and put new bows and bands on 2 of his hats. He was so rapturously grateful that it was lovely to do it for him.

1 Born some time in 1920.
2 Mrs Belloc Lowndes, author of *The Lodger*, sister of Hilaire Belloc.
3 Maurice Baring, diplomat, man of letters.
4 The 14th Baron Lovat, founder of the Lovat Scouts. He became Parliamentary Under-Secretary of State for Dominion Affairs from 1926–8.
5 Actor and Theatre Director.
6 To rent 138 High St after the Dudeneys move.

23 May. Fearful artistic blow: The *Post* gave £50 for the American rights of *The Legacy* and I sold the World Rights to the *Strand* for £25. *Entirely* broken-hearted and sitting here crying like a baby. Ernest doesn't understand: says coldly, "It is business". Very likely.

25 May. Ernest to Edenbridge to see his sister . . . it feels like thunder and I've got the hump and hate Ernest to be away. Feel quite in love with him.

27 May. At night I wrote 8 commandments [7] on a card and hung them up in my wardrobe ... It became bitterly cold and I rolled up on the sofa with Sir Philip's coat (God bless that gilded youth) and the eiderdown.

18 June. After tea went to cottage to paint. Mother Burbidge has taken down her dog kennel! I instantly went mad with joy – for she must be going. How much it means to me, my darling home. I went about from one empty room to the other – singing, croaking like a late cuckoo. Coming home saw a row of Canterbury bells in a garden. If I can have my home and an herbaceous border, and a play acted, can be happy for 1,000 years [8]. At supper time, I put on my pearl earrings.

20 June. Letter from Nigel Playfair saying he will write to Sybil Thorndike about *Eating Cake* : "One of the best one act plays I ever read". This bucked me very much. 2nd post enthusiastic letter from Sybil Thorndike about *Eating Cake*: "I would love to play it". But Joseph Levy [9] "chooses". At noon to station with Ernest to see his sisters. Funny affair. In a way I enjoyed it! Emily [10] unchanged, with her expression of dignified, troubled sweetness. Kate, as ever, absolutely deadly. Those intent eyes of hers, that rigid mouth.

7 It is interesting to speculate which two she omitted.
8 She achieves all three.
9 Sybil Thorndike's manager.
10 Dudeney. Not to be confused with Emily Whiffin, AD's sister.

23 June Thurs. Emily and Kate over for the day. Passed off very well. I showed them snapshots of Margery and her children. Emily overflowed with love. Kate unmoved – Kate. Went to my cottage with them, as Ernest wished it: then back to tea – the best china and he took them down to the bus. Rum world! Never thought to see them again! Better that it should be botched up, however – for Ernest's sake. His sisters, after all. And I like Emily, for her own.

4 July. *Eating Cake* back from Sybil Thorndike. A blow but I become philosophic.

5 July. After supper Ernest, very seedy, went to bed. Mr Gale came in. A nice creature. So dreamily verbose.

17 July. Have written to *Daily Telegraph* man saying I will do an article as he asks, on the 'New Woman'. At tea time Mrs Moore came in and later Mr Gale. Ernest getting restive about Mr Gale, which is absurd: an elderly, very lonely widower.

23 July. Curious day. Intensely warm, violent south west gale, very dull but no rain. Worked away at *Daily Telegraph* article, it is as much trouble as a short story. Wonder what I shall get for it! Will leave space! [£6 6s].

29 July. Very delighted. Got a proof of my 'New Woman' *Daily Telegraph* article. Ernest was so perfectly sweet about it, although he can't agree with a word … at night we talked of where we would put the furniture and how arrange it.

24 August. After supper Mr Gale came in with acute hump. Thought he was going to cry. Talked about his flat and his furniture. Then, very lugubriously: "I've got two turkeys in the sitting room". I – dropping my crochet – what?! But he meant carpets.

1 September. Lympne. At lunch a Baron Henri de – something [11]. Cousin of Philip's. After lunch I slept and it pulled me together. After tea I poked about the gardens while they played tennis. Philip said: "I'll send a gardener with you", which was exactly what I didn't want and wouldn't have. Early to bed and slept like a top.

2 September. At 10.30 in a car, of course – though it isn't 10 minutes' walk – to Sir Louis Mallet. He's got some lovely things and we had such an interesting talk. He said: "You must come and stay with me, not always with Philip". Returning, on my legs, had a delightful talk with Philip on the terrace. After lunch to the races and he put some money on a horse for me and said I'd won and that 'my winnings' would be sent on to me. [£3 5s]. At 3.30 the car fetched me and I left them there. Got home to a heavenly welcome.

3 September. Very tired. Very gratified that it is over: yet I loved it, in a way. Not very well, all those horrid rich things and I had to eat something.

7 September. Wrote Philip Sassoon who is a delightful creature. If I were young I would be head over ears in love with him . . . for some absurd reason I had a bad attack of Burbitis [Mrs Burbidge] all day . . .

14 September. Note from Gander saying he could move me 28, 29, 30th. Wrote him 28th.

17 September. I for an enchanting half day alone with dear Nelson on the Downs, the best way to go – and he thinks so too. Ringmer way with a gale blowing: it blew the devils and dreads out of me. I came home at 2, loafed gloriously on the chintz sofa till tea time. Later to cottage, then to Evensong. Got back and Ernest was at home. The whole day so happy and sweet 'making melody to God in my heart'.

11 Rothschild. PS's mother was the daughter of Baron Gustave de Rothschild.

25 September. Our last Sunday! Packed hard, doing also various squalid jobs.

28 September. Day of madness. At 9.30 sweep arrived at Castle Precincts house and that viper – the Burbidge – had not given up key. Returned to High Street, no Gander to move us. Tore to his home to know why. He out. Later he came to say I'd fixed 29th but I showed him his card, fixing 28th. Compromised by one van today and one tomorrow. We arrived and slept here. The first wonderful night. I was of course abominably uncomfortable but deliriously happy. And all day long the bricklayer was knocking holes through and the place buzzed with every species of working man. And the blacksmith came to put up rods. And the gas man came with the cooker.

29 September. I sat in the sun and saw the van unpacked, saying that 'this' was to go 'there' and so on. In the afternoon hypocritical note from Mrs Moore which I didn't answer and don't mean to.

30 September. The last load of junk came. The cottage was full of bricks and mortar. What a waste of time to polish those floors as we did. Vina, most awfully good all through, did almost mutiny when she saw all her kitchen china on the floor as they hadn't brought the kitchen table. It came with the trees in tubs at 3. It did thrill me after 3 years waiting to see those trees in the courtyard. Such a darling letter from Margery and I went to bed so dreadfully, tearfully happy.

1 October. The house already looks entirely different. People stop and stare. Meanwhile, inside the confusion is lunatic. And as fast as we clean up, so do the nice cheerful apologetic plasterers, carpenters, painters, plumbers and the rest come clumping over the place with more mortar on their feet.

4 October. Ernest came home and it was wonderful. He was so tender, so charming, so plainly thrilled and proud with the whole thing. We were happy, happy. Has God answered prayer? And shall we live more peacefully, prettily in this heart's desire of a home?

7 October. Mrs Gander put up the hangings on my four post bed, so I really do begin to feel at home. Slept in my own lovely big room for the first time

and to wake in the morning and look at hills and autumn tints (after 7 years of waking up to look at a chimney pot) was almost too exquisite a joy.

13 October. To my mother, took her birthday chocolate: also for a drive along the front. Made her very happy; but it cost me ten bob which I can't afford! However, that is not the way to look at things, Alice Dudeney.

19 October. Letter from Skues. The Burbidge affair in full blast. Shall I ever get quit of that pestilential creature? Delightful letter from Philip and one, equally delightful, from Vere. Altogether, just now I am about as happy as I ever was in my life.

3 November. To London in streaming rain . . . To Vandyk [photographer] at 12 . . . to Joan [Fulleylove] . . . she says it is on the cards that Margery and the babies will come home for 6 months next summer. This moved me enormously.

4 November. Ernest in bed with a slight attack of lumbago and as usual a pig. Got roared out, called a Fool and told to "get out". So we are beginning again! Got off Hammond a curly-wurly, hideous but most comfortable mid-Victorian armchair. Shall cover it. Wrote to William Morris for some Corncockle. The new window at the end of the upper corridor is knocked through. Always a great thrill with a nice window as to what you'll see! It is divine: Caburn, little old roofs and trees.

5 November. Ernest had breakfast in bed. Carrying up trays gives me a veritable brain storm. Funny, but I can't help it and mustn't do it ... I was a beast to grouse about Ernest. He is sorry.

18 November. Such an entrancing day. Perennials from Philip. Woke to the sound of a spade: and there was the gardener down below. Tore off to Mrs Fawssett [12] for perennials, got them. Returned to find 2 'shooge' boxes of plants from Lympne. The rest of the day was sheer abstract joy. I got grass

12 The Fawssetts lived at 83 High Street. Daughters Winifred and Evelyn.

seed and the gardener sowed 'the lawn' It is a horseshoe shape and a darling. Then I got half dozen Madonna lily bulbs. Don't think I ever was happier.

19 November. Such a change! Ernest in an infernal temper and, as usual, abusive. Photos from Vandyk in which I appear as an affable gorilla. Shall burn 'em. Bad first notices of *Made to Measure* [13] . . . Had no dinner; never wished to eat again...

22 November. Charlotte here at 10.30. Dear little soul and amiably oblivious of the fact that too much talk spoils my morning!

6 December. Quite the most blissful day I've had for a long time. Turned out all papers in the basement and then started in the garden an immense smother fire, my first for 7 years. The smell of it made me cry with joy (did cry – with smoke!). I rushed in to dinner, then back, rushed in to tea, then out again, in sweetest dark and fine rain, to tuck my bonfire up for the night. I smelt it last thing and first thing when I woke. The scent seems to have got into my hair.

9 December. Making a real shot at last at a novel. But it's hard going although, for a wonder, I've got 2 ideas and both obsess me.

15 December. At 5.30 Calvert came to bless the house. Quite a beautiful service. Every room sprinkled with holy water. Nelson came round on the lead, very devout, bless him. So now I cast out for ever all Burbidge devils.

18 December. Most horribly sleepy and therefore disgustingly cross! Yet may as well put in on record that, just about now, I'm as happy as I ever was in my life and a darned sight happier than I deserve to be!

13 Published Collins. 4 impressions. War novel included by French in their war literature.

1922

Mrs Stewart-Jones was wandering about with the Sunday dinner she always takes to a woman at the alms house[1], who was ill and couldn't eat it. Mrs Stewart-Jones very upset and meeting Mrs Ingram coming out of church said: "Oh do you know anybody who wants a Sunday dinner?"

Mrs Breach's husband was lying à la tramp under a seat on the Pells upon which sat a lover and his lass. Breach, seized by a cough which he couldn't suppress, gave voice and was seized by irate swain and chucked into the water, from which he emerged muddy and sober.

10 January. I started my book.

19 January. I wrote to the Lincoln person giving her conditional permission to dramatise *Secret Son*. Now – 9 pm – been drawing the final cheques for Constable and Fuller. So my darling house is paid for. Entirely happy day.

28 January. Savage notice of *Made To Measure* in *The Times*. I seem to get nothing but whacks!

1 February. Wonderful notice of *Made To Measure* in *Sussex Daily News*. I at once went up like thistledown and hated myself for being such a faithless, terror-stricken cur!

8 March. Letter from Kate: has seen Tom, who confesses to 3 sons: Renée, Kenneth and Douglas. Because I looked sceptical Ernest flew into one of his coarse furies and remained there all day.

---

1 A refuge for poor widows in Keere St, now St Michael's Court.

22 March. Mr Gale . . . everlasting coming and going, talking of his absurd love affair. At 65!

2 April. Mr Gale came to tea. E. Harvey Smith has refused him: I was quite done for – probably as a result of his everlasting confidences, so went to bed at 8 and slept 11½ hours.

9 April. Mr Gale came and the dear creature actually gave me those jet beads because I'd been "so sympathetic".

4th May. Margery sailed . . .

7 May. Another heavenly day. At Mass Calvert prayed at my request for a "family travelling by sea".

9 May. Another lovely day . . . I bought deck chairs and actually sat out in my own garden – after 7 years.

17 May. At night, about 6.30, a wire from Canadian Pacific people: '*Scandinavian* lands passengers Friday morning at 8'. Another horrid delay.

19 May. Margery came and the children. Wonderful day! Indelible moment when the cab came, when I saw the little weary – precious – group in the hall. Jim [Jamie], the baby in Margery's arms, Barney a lovely child, holding his mother's hand. We hugged and cried, Margery and I and then she said: "Mother, we are so ill." They arrived absolutely ill with flu. I caught it and we had a horrid time.

30 May. Dr Vallance sent me to bed, temperature 103 degrees. He says I've missed pneumonia by a narrow squeak. Vina went home with it. Awful time, no servant. I unable to do a thing.

10 June. About midday I felt suddenly better. Barney got into trouble for smacking his baby brother. He said, through sobs, "But to smack Jamie, cheers up me"!! He is an angel – and so naughty.

18 June. To church. After tea took the babies on the Downs. Delightful.

30 June. Margery took Barney to Brighton to see his great-grandmother.

6 July. Suddenly I get horrid hump and try to persuade myself it is my gouty feet! But – no, it is the old terror – of old age and poverty: and the knowledge that – financially – I'm a failure. Then comes a letter from *Review of Reviews*. Will I send photograph for inclusion in Article on 100 Eminent English Women. Me one! And what *does* it matter?

8 July. Ernest to Brighton, thank God. His gloom is poison gas.

11 July. Jamie is plain and grave, but he breaks into a sudden ravishing smile. "His grandmother's smile" says Charlotte.

21 August. Lympne. I was so enchanted to take Margery to Lympne to show her off to Philip and to show her Philip's wonderful house. We were met at Ashford by the Rolls-Royce which I'm always so thankful to get out of, for it makes me feel sick. There was nobody staying but Sir Louis Mallet, the Dowager Lady Gosford and the Gubbays of course. Mr Gubbay a dear little man, but so palpably Oriental – the palms of his hands looking as if they were sprinkled with soot. Mrs Gubbay handsome: in the short-necked Jewess way but, as I have felt from the first (and Margery agreed), take off her fine clothes and her ropes of pearls, put her behind a banana stall in the East End on a Saturday night – and there you are! Dozens of her anywhere. Lady Cholmondeley is quite different – and yet there is a certain likeness. At dinner I wore emerald green chiffon with a brocaded sash: green and silver. Philip, quite adoring, picks up the hem: "You must always wear green". Oh, and a floating lovely scarf borrowed from Margery. How he – or anybody else – could look at me or look at anybody while Margery was in the room I can't think. She is the sort of person who can look almost plain if unhappy; but bewilderingly beautiful when she is feeling the other way round. Her figure is always lovely – the slim long lines which we all, she, I, my mother, get from the Royal Gipsy Lee. She had some sort of diaphanous pink and primrose frock which she'd run up for the occasion and which looked like

ten pounds at the least! Her dark, demurely parted hair: her pale skin and dark eyes! Oh my darling, my only one! Why are we parted?

After dinner the usual repair to the small library: Mrs Gubbay doing her quilting; she is a great needlewoman. Next morning Margery came into my room for breakfast; and we just caught sight of one of last night's stately footmen, slipping up the back stairs with a tray which he handed to Agnes, the head housemaid who waits on us. In his shirt sleeves, his hair rumpled! It came out at night that Sir Louis Mallet had been on the point of buying Knockwood at Tenterden where Christopher's uncle, George Elgood lives – but Uncle George got in first. So Philip said, in that gay boyish way of his (Philip can be irresistible when he chooses!) "We'll all go off tomorrow and see Uncle George". So off we went in the accursed Rolls Royce, Philip, Sir Louis, Hannah Gubbay, Lady Gosford, Margery and me. After a few miles I felt awfully sick. I controlled myself by saying: "Alice Dudeney, are you going to bring irreparable disgrace on yourself and your beloved daughter by being sick in this multi-millionaire's car?" And it worked – for the time being, only. And then I asked in a faint voice: 'How far is it to Tenterden?" "Oh, no distance – seven or eight miles?" My God! How am I going to hold out? "Alice Dudeney, are you going to bring disgrace . . ?" And just as my "tummy" gave that upward twist which says "I'm *going* to be sick, millionaire or no millionaire," we stopped at the gate of Knockwood!!

27 August. Jamie is a wicked baby! Yet wicked as he is how adorable! He loves kippers and haddocks; Margery says they don't get them in Canada. "What is there for breakfast, Jamie?" "Pippers?" "No, not this morning". "Aggocks", says Jamie with his heavenly smile. And when he wants more to drink he says: 'More Yilk" – and waves the cup round his head. And when he doesn't want any more porridge he picks up the plate "Elkel" – which means give it to Nelson, and unless you catch the plate it smashes. They love Nelson but at first sight of him they screamed; this big dog with spots. And when Jamie (which is often) gets sent by his grandmother out of the room at meal times for being a little fiend, he goes whacking at the kitchen door for Vina. He can't say Vina but she's told him her other name is Gathercole

"Gaggergool, Gaggergool" roars the exiled Jamie. Ernest is very, very good and patient . . . He's so proud when he is playing on the Bowling Green and the children on their way home call to him through the railings: "Hallo Grand-daddy", pipes Barney. "Gang-gaggy" says Jamie, with his usual solemnity.

12 October. The journey down to Southampton was awful, Margery and I not daring to look at each other for fear of breaking down. All the way down to Southampton Barney was standing on the sea and pretending to be the Guard. I was afraid when we stopped at the stations that he'd pitch forward and said that the Guard always sat down just before the train stopped. "Yes, but you see, Grandmummy, this Guard doesn't." He is always pretending to be something: the other night when I went to kiss him in the bed, he turned away: "I'm an engine driver." "Yes, darling, but doesn't the engine driver kiss his Grandmummy good night?" "Yes", arms flung round my neck and wet little mouth on my cheek, "he *always* does". Getting them to bed is an elaborate affair. Jamie will never lie down. He howls, smiles, climbs over the cot; until at last, quite worn out, he falls on his back saying "Kitch". So you kiss him and we come down here to what dear Margery calls "elegance". I'm afraid she doesn't get much of that in Canada.

12 October. In the train to Southampton docks, Jamie was yelling, the carriage was filled with sailors. One asked Margery: "What's his name?" "James." "Oh, you'll never have no luck, old chap, with a name like that."! We got into Margery's cabin. There was nothing to say; never is at these riven moments of parting. So Margery and I took our last embrace, crying – crying. The babies were on the floor playing. Barney looked up gravely: "Grand-mummy, I would like to kiss you again." And so they went!

13 October. Breakfast in bed, and stayed there till tea time. I was nearly dead with crying, and with trying not to cry.

27 October. Went for a walk on hills: the way I used to go with the children. The heap of flint stones, the 'castle' they built, still there. Touched me enormously.

15 December. Antony Guest is coming for Christmas. I'm so glad. The feud[2] between him and Ernest is ended. My fault: no – not my fault. Just fate! The inevitable break up of Littlewick, when Margery and I ran away. Antony realising that to live with Ernest's mad temper was impossible. And – so – taking my part, realising that the fact of David being in love with me was merely incidental. And 1911 is a long time ago. And David is off the map for ever. And Ernest and I are pulling together – somehow.

25 December, Christmas Day. It was too beautiful: and I shall always remember; if I have twenty more Christmases – unlikely! The three of us, two old men, one old woman, close friends since I was eighteen and they were twenty eight, with just that emotional break of 1911. And of that nothing was said. It was lovely to sit in my chair, of so many memories, the chair that has known my life for thirty years, and just listen to them talking; of dead and gone times and for the most part dead and gone friends. And Nelson was in his basket at my feet and surveyed his master and his new Uncle Antony with grave approving glances. After early dinner on Christmas day, the three of them went out for a walk and I sat in my chair by the fire and watched the sunset come. And it was the most wonderful sunset. Lovely sunset, lovely occasion, I felt that all storms were over. I didn't dread the future any more. Not old age, not poverty, not Ernest's temper.

2 Antony took AD's side when she left Ernest. Her early diaries show that her affair with David was the main reason for the separation, not 'incidental' as she preferred to believe.

1923

9 January. So happy in my work. Ideas flow in like mad. If only I can succeed (and I am succeeding) in getting away from terror, grudging and striving, then I am at rest and in delight.

20 January. Mr Gale came in after supper. He would like to go for a walk with me "but for the conventions"! I'll jolly well see that he doesn't.

28 January. After church Ernest and I got at cross purposes. Is it just reaction? After tea we had a tender and enlightening talk, admitting the tragic difference of temperament but firm on the affections. So all was well and I returned to my lovely fire, leaving him by his, and both of us happy.

1 February. Most cheering letter from Pinker. Thinks he can not only get a further contract from Collins, but perhaps better terms. I go up like a ball! And then I could cry, because I'm such a faithless beast and always in terror. And then my common sense tells me that this is only one side of imagination.

9 February. Agreement from Collins for 3 more novels after this one. Wonderful! I am safe for four years! The most perfect day, like June. And I was never happier. Worked all the morning in the garden, spreading the bonfire – now beautiful pink ash – upon the grass . . . Ernest says that Philip and Sir Louis Mallet are at Tut – Someone Amen's tomb[1]; now becoming quite a fashionable resort.

14 February. While I was making my bed I looked out of the high window and down at Castle Banks: 3 huge black bullocks standing - steaming - in the brownish air, the greyish rain. An old, gentle uncertain sort of drover and his

---

1 Tutankhamun's tomb was discovered in November 1922.

caressing way of urging them on (how much better this sort of simple, traditional sight than all the 'foreign' travel people jaw about: rushing everywhere, seeing everything, retaining nothing) . . . Ernest to Brighton. More everlasting chess. However, I am glad for it keeps him interested and amiable.

2 March. To my mother. She in bed and a very pathetic figure. Gone all to bits and looking 100 without her teeth and no cap.

3 March. Ordered a copy of *Vogue*, wrote to Harrod, Liberty and Barker for patterns . . . got a bit of lace for cap . . . made a cap for Mother. Great success. I've got the hang of it.

4 March. Assize service [2] at 11. Horrid nuisance and bother the Judge.

8 March. Finished the last cap of four, made it narrower and, so, without elastic it's a first rate nightcap into which I bundle my hair loose. Can't think how I've managed all these years without one.

23 March. Going to communion met a working man, very conversational and pleased with himself. Told me he was the soldier, mentioned in the papers at the time, who was deaf and dumb but recovered his speech suddenly at a picture palace, three years ago.

17 April. Miss Smythe said of Mrs Grant: "It's certainly a happy marriage – but then she had new teeth put in."

24 April. Muddle about sort of morning. This is the way I get into when I'm not working and it is what the British Matron calls being 'so busy'. Bless her kind heart and thick head.

2 Held at the commencement of the Lewes Assizes at St Michael's Church.

25 April. At night I read Freud's Psycho-analysis book. Very clever and fascinating, but stuffy and one-sided, seems to me. Anyhow I read myself blind. Very stupid.

26 April. Possibly with a desire to air myself after too much Freud (for really this merciless analysis leaves you naked and ashamed!) felt I must have a morning out, bus to Brighton, a walk out to Black Rock, bus back in time for dinner. The sea was heavenly, greyish, greenish – everything -ish.

4 May. Went to the police and said they must stop children tobogganning down Castle Banks.

5 May. Perfect weather and I live in the Gazebou, which is piled up with goosedown feathers. Opened garden gate about tea time and outside 3 charming mites, 5, 4 and 3 as I learnt on enquiry. Looked awfully frightened and the biggest said – pointing to a few blades of grass they'd scattered on the path "Please M'm, will the policeman be after us for spilling this". I *did* feel an ogress. Went in the garden and picked them some flowers, the darlings.

9 May. Weather changed, of course as I am off to London . . . To Philip at 3. The great bare room, with one lighted picture and great jars full of crimson rhododendrons and white lilies calmed me. He'd brought me from Egypt a pink coral necklace. We motored to Ranelagh, where he played polo and I watched. Back to tea and caught the 6.40 home. He told me in the car – with occult constraint – that the pictures had gone back to Canada. I was very upset[3], but showed nothing. And we slid on to other topics.

11 May. Wrote to Philip saying no thank you very much I would *not* come up, dine, sleep and a theatre.

17 May. This morning for the first time I saw the man (a baker) who goes by every morning ringing a bell at 8 to the minute, a signal that I *must* get up! So he is flesh. Liked him better as a symbol.

3 The reason is unclear. Possibly PS commissioned Margery, an artist, to paint some pictures and did not honour the agreement.

31 May. Frankfort Moore sent off a cartload of garden statuary. Miss Falconer[4] said it was *most* embarrassing to have those naked females outside her house all the morning as she had two nuns staying with her.

6 July. So hot that I furtively undid my stays but not the suspenders. Strange lady arrived from Mrs Fisher. Did I know of lodgings in the Isle of Wight? Heard I'd just returned. Did what I could and then proceeded to let her out the garden door. Sartorial *contretemps*. Found my little stays hanging down behind!! Sat down on the steps with an "afraid I'm coming to bits" smile and she departed.

8 July. After tea Ernest and I strolled round the Bowling Green[5], quite happily, until we fell out about the Pavilion! . . . washed his gloves, hair brush etc, getting him ready for London.

9 July. He went off dear old thing looking very nice in a new Panama hat and not so nervously gloomy and irate as usual, when off on a journey . . . The Lewes ladies are going about in their typical summer rig: large patterned foulards, worn either with hefty boots or shoes and always black wool stockings – or very airy voiles with same shoes and stockings.

10 July. Timed chime of St Michael's bell between the thunder. Drunken man cursing and shouting on Castle Banks, until Batup[6] rather superfluously shouted from his window that he'd heave a bucket of water over him. Found out that it was a bargee who had absently missed his way, fallen into the river and swum across it!

11 July. Letter from Margery enclosing a draft of hers to Philip. He deserves it, but it means that his and my friendship is ended. Pity. Pinker wrote that *Eve* will pay £20 guineas for a short story.

4 Miss Falconer lived opposite Castlegate House at Castle Lodge, once inhabited by Charles Dawson who 'discovered' Piltdown Man.
5 Medieval castle tilting ground. Bowling with distinctive old flat-sided woods continues today.
6 Disreputable dealer, neighbour and one-time tenant of AD's stables.

12 July. Met Miss Falconer in a new hat: Tuscan straw with a rigid black bow, like a pork pie in mourning. All the time it is beautiful, boiling, burning hot: stupid people and stupid papers are talking about a heat wave. Mr Gale must have come to tea once or twice – certainly more than once or twice.

25 July. Astonishing letter from Joan. Margery's letter to Philip has done the trick! She – Joan has seen him. The pictures are to be sold and [burned?]. Why doesn't that cable come? Can think of nothing else and can't write another word till I get a new note.

27 July. When I returned, there was the cable. Just 'Catherine' [7]...

2 August. Went into the garden where it was boiling beautiful hot and sat in a deck chair in the full sun supremely blissful and staring at my border. The scarlet penstemon, blue campanula and double poppy of a blackish purple, with a grey green spray of Michaelmas daisy behind made the loveliest patch and the hollyhocks were wonderful.

1 September. Vina gave me notice. Going to get married. Very glad for her sake, but feel curiously lost and topped!

3 September. Vina says she'll go to the Registry office [8] and give me a thoroughly good character!

14 September. Answered Methuen's letter about the Doll's House library [9].

3 October. Brighton in torrential rain . . . to my mother, found her very tearful poor old darling (her 84th birthday) and being fussed over by a sympathetic half char: half nurse sort of party. She – mother – gave me a wonderful silk shawl which she bought of a mysterious foreign pedlar when she was 17.

---

7 AD's first grand-daughter.
8 Agency for the hiring of servants.
9 AD's short story 'Feather Bed' was included in the miniature library in Queen Mary's Doll's House at Windsor Castle.

And which has been lying by ever since. Never knew she had it. The other lovely cashmere shawl – her grandmother's – had been given to Emily – *who had it cut up and made into a dressy blouse!* She brought it with pride from the wardrobe. I could have wept at this incredible vandalism, and said so.

5 October. Lucy Wilson seems to be shaping well and she really is a better cook than Vina.

20 October. My portrait and an account of my distinguished self in *The Sussex County Herald*, tomorrow being my birthday.

3 November. Mrs Godfrey 4.15. We went. The home [10], of course, is wonderful. Henry VIII rafters, beams and so on. But, too *museum*-like. For instance, great open hearths with dogs and all the rest merely forbidding caverns. No fires: central heating, also electric light. I wanted a wood fire and candles. He very interesting, full of vitality. She pleasant. Her papa, also pleasant, but *not* off the top shelf.

5 November. I write so many books – or have written – that I become quite dizzy. And, anyhow, life is a rum performance – and to think that the little strut round *this* world ends it! Incredible . . . Wrote to Philip saying I wouldn't [visit] and explaining why.

11 November. Mrs Sampson and Phyllis to tea. She – the girl – will make a china figure of Nelson for £2 2s. So glad.

30 November. After lunch Mrs Hart turned up. Fur coat – Australian black rabbit – which only cost £7 7s! Feel increasingly that a fur coat I must and will have.

10 The 16th century Bull House, High St., once the home of Thomas Paine. Walter Godfrey was an eminent architect and local historian.

3 December. To Brighton . . . after lots of tryings on and indecisions, during which the sales lady became restive – got a *real* beauty for £12 12s! Came home. Told Ernest who was amazed at my downfall! Went out in it and met Mrs Hart in hers. So funny.

8 December. We went outside the County Hall to hear the poll declared [11]. Campion in, but with a much reduced majority. Lord Gage[12] made the announcement, nervous, insignificant young man . . . Wore my fur coat.

16 December. After lunch knock at the door and who should arrive but Philip. Long, agitated explanations – and reconciliation! Ernest was introduced. They seemed to like each other.

17 December. *Such* a morning. Cabled Margery then wrote her. Also wrote her yesterday, also wrote Philip after he left. By second post letter from him and enclosing one to her. Wrote him again. This disposed of the morning.

19 December. What a delightful gamble life is! Went off by 'bus with Nelson and Mrs Miller [13] to a sale at Alfriston for the outing only, wanting nothing and determined to buy nothing. Bought – by borrowing £1 from her – for £2 2s 6d a goose down feather bed [mattress] – 5 ft – for my bed. It looked like new. The man whose sister's sale it was (a delightful gentleman farmer) spoke to us afterwards: said his mother made it. This gave it just the right personal touch I needed. Altogether a delightful day . . . Mrs Miller came back to tea. At night snow and in the night I was so cold – I cheered myself up by thinking of my goose down bed at Alfriston!

11 Hung Parliament. Labour and Liberals threw the Tories out. Ramsay MacDonald became first Labour PM.
12 Viscount Gage of Firle Place, near Lewes. Lord in Waiting to George V and Edward VIII. PPS to Secretary of State for India 1924–29.
13 Mrs Miller had a flat at Dusart's, 84–5 Hight St., later moving with them to 8 Prince Edward's Rd. She became AD's close friend, later referred to as Auntie M.

22 December. Off to Alfriston by 'bus. Stormed at the Carrier's wife. Said the bed I must and *would* have. She had assumed I wasn't in "no hurry". Then tore off – 3 miles in 40 minutes – to Berwick station and just caught the train. Found that Lucy had broken two plates and also the pudding wasn't cooked. Just as we were sitting down to tea THE BED CAME!

23 December. Fired off a few greeting cards . . . After this a furious damnable row– only because he couldn't find a clean nightshirt. There all the time.

24 December. Broken hearted. Awoke feeling I'd give a year's income to get out of Christmas and the farcical – ghastly – gaiety of the whole thing. In the middle of the morning he came up and apologised, but I cannot react all at once. At tea time Antony arrived. Slept on the feather bed. It comforted and petted me.

25 December, Christmas Day . . . Ernest practically never spoke all day. Sour gloom. Most embarrassing for poor Antony. I went to bed early and – after trying to keep gay and Christmassy all day in such an atmosphere – broke down. Again the feather bed caressed me. Mr Gale sent a great big box of chocolates. Miss Doyle to tea.

27 December. Very flat day, the usual detestable Boxing Day feeling – no letters, papers nor shops . . . At tea time Ernest and I overjoyed to be alone. We can grub on quite nicely if not interrupted.

28 December. Communion at 8.30 and I was specially sorry I had felt so bitter towards him all Xmas time.

1924

1 January. Letter through Post Office returned one I wrote to Philip at Southampton. Sent it him. Letter from dear Christopher [Fulleylove]. How much more valuable family love is than intermittent friendship with an attractive millionaire.

25 January. Worked away at Chapter III, am all behind but it is coming along nicely . . . Ernest and I had a little tussle at night about the lovely tradition of putting a tuft of sheep wool in a shepherd's coffin, so that he explained to his Maker why he didn't go to church on Sundays! Ernest laughed in the end and said I never made a proper defence. Ought – when he said it was "pagan" (and I flared up) to have retorted that they bury a chalice and [?] with a Bishop – equally "Pagan".

28 January. Phyllis Sampson turned up and Nelson sat for an hour [for his china figure].

11 March. Finished off Chap IX with a regular flourish! Heavenly day. At tea time a devil of a row because I said he could go for a walk if he liked. 40 years pretty well of this hopeless business of trying to make him lead a healthy life. I GIVE IT UP FINALLY.

17 March. When I told Ernest that Cathy had 2 teeth and weighed 22 lbs he looked up abstractedly from his newspaper: "What! Two teeth – 22 lbs?"!

19 March. Summoned to serve on the Grand Jury!

24 March. Letter from the Curator of the Worthing Art Library, will I open a 'Sussex Room' on April 12. Accepted.

4 April. Wrote Miss Frost saying I'd come by 12.57 at Worthing. She meets me in a car. I lunch with an Alderman, tea with a Mayor – and open a room. Begin to feel horribly nervous.

8 April. Grand Jury 10.30. It was an eyeopener! The foreman without an 'h' to bless himself with: my next door neighbour – a nice enough creature in the same plight – and with filthy hands. Six other women jurors – the St Michael's Miss Etherington one. I froze on to her! Answered to my name "Alice Dudney" with a feminine pipe of "Here" (should have been "ere' to match the company).[1]

12 April. I open the Sussex Public Library Room. Oh – Lord! Went off. Did open it. Made a speech. John Oxenham, who was there, said the best woman's speech he'd ever heard! Didn't feel frightened a bit once I was on my legs. Got photographed. Was given a bouquet. Came home, reported to Ernest – who was delighted.

15 April. Got after all to go to Brighton. Meeting Emily 'secretly' at Fulgens – and by Jove she spoke her mind. I respected her for it. She says Mother must have an attendant. I flatly refused to bear the whole of the cost – as they seem to think me rich. Said I'd pay half and she is to pay half – spending her savings. But then so am I spending what would otherwise be mine. At her request went and interviewed the doctor, decent sort. He says Mother may die next week or live till 90. Saw her afterwards – poor desolate, tearful old thing. Then home . . . told Ernest, who was very kind. Also there was a notice in today's *Sussex Daily [News]* [2] and the Librarian wrote a charming letter. So I cheered up, but couldn't go to sleep.

1 May. Sent my sister a cheque. This new development added to the brandy money [for mother's tipple] means about £20 – hard earned – yearly out of my pocket and I should be a humbug if I pretended not to grudge it..

1 No more is recorded of AD's jury service.
2 Records AD's 'delightfully spontaneous speech' and that messages of goodwill were received from Conan Doyle, Hilaire Belloc and Margery Allingham.

4 May. Mr Gale to tea smelling abominably of mothball.

17 May. Just about now I'm so happy. Weather perfect. I potter down the High Street; dream and idle in the garden. Nelson sits with his nose on his paws, his paws crushing daisies and butterflies (not buttercups!) round his head. After lunch, actually fled from this idyllic picture and called on the Galsworthys. Wore my nice blue, embroidered frock which I bought at Pallants. Mrs Galsworthy a snob, a sentimentalist, a spiritualist. "You're a novelist, aren't you? Now tell me about your books." I was – as usual – frigid: and turned the subject. She then talked without ceasing of a defunct Pomeranian bitch. They, or rather he, is a cousin of John Galsworthy (reason I called!). But she has never even seen him.

24 May. Another perfect beast of a day. The sweep again put his cart outside the dining room window. I said if he did it again I'd complain to the police as I would not put up with it: "Yes" – sticking his suet-coloured soot-strewn countenance close to mine: "You complain to the p'lice. There's a lot of things you won't put up with, ain't there?" Exit Mr James from my life [3]. His income less by 4/6d a year. And if he does do it again I write to the fat Superintendent of Police.

31 May. Kate came. I had been dreading and loathing this visit. To my amazement and heavenly relief we – after the first inevitable frigidity (on my part) settled in. And, later, as a complete bond found that we suffered from precisely the same form of foot trouble. (2 months later. Queer! The way I was taken in by her tigerish softness! Found later she'd been making mischief as usual ...)

3 June. Ernest sent on [AD is on holiday with Vere] a splendid notice of *The Play Box* [4] from the *Daily Telegraph*: 'This is a masterpiece, or rather a series of masterpieces'. Went up like a kite! Also a letter from the Queen!! About the Doll's House.

3 When Mr James was ill in later years, AD supplied him with meals and visited him in hospital.
4 Short stories published by Heinemann.

11 June. Horrible notice of *The Play Box* in *The Times*: 'machine-made' stories. Came down like a sack of coke.

14 June. I felt so disgusted, and yet so infinitely pitiful with all that. Vere told me of her various — and too literal – love affairs. Yet not disgusted with her or alienated in the very least. I blame her mother for everything. The *atrocious* upbringing. Actually allowing Sullivan to be in the home as a paying guest!

19 June. Beautiful service at St Michael's. Outside some street musician playing on a sort of musical box. The most liquid, innocent, joyful sound. Seemed to fit in . . . had a chat, as usual, with the nice vagabond scavenger who always has a flower, a feather or – at a pinch – a playing card stuck in the band of his hat.

20 June. Ernest funereal in black having decided to go to Canon McAuliffe's[5] Requiem, demanded his black hat (said hat bought in 1912 and discarded long ago). I rooted it out, minus ribbon and lining. Got a ribbon from an old panama, cleaned the whole affair with petrol, was told to go to hell, said that was a nice prelude to his giving somebody else a send off to Heaven! Quite breathless! But not angry. I can now – but it's taken a lot of learning – see the humour of these scenes. Added that if he wasn't a born fool, he'd call in at Hugh Rae's [6] (Hurr-ay!) the hatter and get a new lining put in for a bob. Agonised grunt from behind the *Daily Mail*.

25 June. Ernest departed in his usual sullen flurry, poor old dear. Probably born of an excess of love. Doesn't want me to miss him too much, so – of design – shows himself at his beastliest. Rum idea! . . . Welfare came and cut the grass, tidied up the pinks. He doesn't think we shall have any lavender. Let this be a lesson to all who follow after me. Never cut back lavender as the experts advise. Didn't at Littlewick and always had heaps.

5 Former Priest of St Pancras RC Church.
6 Gentlemen's Outfitter, established 1923, still at 74–5 High St.

4 July. To lunch with Mrs Bates [7] . . . Mrs Bates beautifully turned out, a black frock, a string of pearls 'nood' [nude?] stockings, black suede slippers. Her hair, an ashey blonde, shingled. How do these other grandmothers do it? She confessed to being "close on 60". The house lovely, exquisite taste and (as Rosario [8] said of this) "plenty of money, nozzing but money".

9 July. A charming day. Ernest looked so nice and was such a dear. What a wonderful marriage we might have had! And should I have written all those novels – or any novels at all? Went and voted, by the way. Beamish [9], our Conservative man, got in. Thank Heaven! No Socialism for Lewes.

15 July. Most exciting day. Went off to Miss Hillman's sale to bid for the really charming mahogany bed I saw there yesterday . . . I got the whole caboodle – mahogany bedstead, hair mattress, bolster and feather bed – for £2 7 6. Told Ernest, he simply took my hand and said: "You've bought me a bed. You are a dear". Made me so happy. Yet what a rum cuss! All along he's been saying: "I don't want a mahogany bed. Why can't you leave things as they are?"! Great excitement in the town over the Crumbles murder [10]. Crowds and crowds in the High Street all day long. Saw the Judge, trumpeters and the rest. Love the pageant of it. But oh that wretch, the murderer.

17 July. Somehow one can't get away from the morbid drama of a murder. I won't stand in the High Street: too much of of a hypocrite perhaps, but they bring the murderer in a closed car from the prison past this house about 9. So

7 The Bates lived at St Anne's House, built 1719, opposite 138 High St.
8 Italian owner of doss house at Old Poor House, close to CPH and later bought by AD.
9 Tufton Beamish won the Bye-Election. George Bernard Shaw appeared in support of Labour Candidate.
10 The Bungalow Murder. This sensational trial concerned the murder of Emily Kaye by her lover Patrick Mahon in The Officer's House at The Crumbles, Eastbourne. Mahon cut her body into pieces, burnt the head and left the rest in trunks in a bedroom. That summer crowd arriving at The Officer's House were charged 1/- for admission, with drinks sold at the gate. After an outcry, the property was closed. Two weeks later it re-opened with an increased admission fee of 1/2d.

why do I sit about over my breakfast, near the dining room window? Great excitement, Ernest's bed came and was put up.

19 July. Horrible excitement in the town about the Mahon trial. The most ghoulish touch was the crowd in Castle Ditch, a spot always deserted. I came home that way as a short cut, being late for lunch. The gates leading to the Assize Court well back, a covered grey motor lurking there, guarded by bobbies, waiting to take the prisoner back. At that time we didn't know the verdict. But a man in Roberts' shop said he knew it was 'Guilty' and so it was.

22 July. Dreamed I had heaps of letters. Ernest said, rather funnily, that he dreamed someone threw a plaster at me and it stuck on my mouth so that I couldn't talk at breakfast time. No letters ... Mr Gale turned up ... very dandified in a tweed gold suit, greenish, and a white waistcoat. He looked like duck and green peas. I believe he's after Mrs Stenhouse!

29 July. Sent a cheque for brandy [for mother] ... Ernest gone to London, first displaying the hideous temper he always shows when he's off there. Roaring like a postman! And Lucy listening, no doubt. She always listens. Felt so degraded ... I started off on another story altogether. *Ancient Lights*. Emily wrote. More brandy! Mother has had more fits. Sad.

5 August. Delightful tea party in the garden ... Later it was Nelson's Private View and he behaved beautifully. We went into the drawing room and they [guests] 'viewed' his china effigy.

12 August. Letter from a Mr De Burgh – will I contribute to a book he is compiling on England's Foremost Women Writers? Consented. Letter from the Hove Poetry Society. Will I make my speech Jan 7th or Feb 7th? Said Feb 7th. Begin to feel rather afraid.

15 August. Mr Gale came in after tea extra jaunty and foolish: which means, I truly do believe, that he means to propose to Mrs Stenhouse.

16 August. Letter from Philip. Had I got the fan he sent from Paris and when was I coming to Lympne? Wired him . . .

18 August. Philip wrote: 'Another fan will be awaiting you at Lympne'. What a nice, easy way millionaires have of doing things! Charlotte arrived in her best dear little soul mood. So glad to see her.

3 September. Lympne . . . very nice welcome from Philip and his cousin. Assembled there Mrs Arthur James [11] (presumably of baccarat fame) old, pleasant, vivacious – also Lady Edward Grosvenor, a young woman with a sweet, non-committal smile which drifted to you at intervals across space. In the hall later cannoned up against Miss Boyce, the secretary. Edith Wharton also was there. I thought her detestable. Before dinner – Philip having gone to Folkestone and the women playing ping-pong – I went for a walk. Returning, found a tall, bald man with very thin legs there. We talked and later I was introduced, Lord Hugh Cecil [12], no less. A pleasant simple evening. The men and Mrs James playing bridge. The rest of us doing our crochet or knitting and chatting.

4 September. Never slept till 5, but, oddly, wasn't tired. We, that is Philip, Mrs James, Lord Hugh and I, motored to Canterbury. At the Cathedral Lord Hugh was fastened on, with great joy, by a pleasing, voluble, sacristan person, and we did the tour in great style with a "Lord Hugh" here and a "Lord Hugh" there. Bunches of open-eyed sightseers surveying us. Amused me very much. Very gay tea party that afternoon: a 'New Thought' woman, a Mrs Philipson came, with a Lady Cheetham [13] – a divorcee – so Mrs James wouldn't meet her. Slept like a top in my favourite green room , to which Philip had thoughtfully changed me.

11 One of King Edward VII's Marlborough House set.
12 Politician and famous speaker, 5th son of 3rd Marquess of Salisbury.
13 Daughter of Russian Ambassador to Rome, divorced from Sir Milne Cheetham, a diplomat.

5 September. In the morning he and I had a long talk on the tennis court. Also
– his suggestion – I went round with the head gardener and chose perennials
which will be sent to me at the proper time. Came home. Dear Ernest gave me
such a sweet welcome and Nelson was nothing but an ecstatic shower of
spots.

11 September. Finished and posted, thank Heaven, *The Next Move* [14] proofs . . .
I read Edith Wharton's *Ethan Frome* right through. Wonderful! But what a
pity she's such a hateful person.

22 September. I do like Winnie. I do hope she will stop [15]. After tea a divine
walk Kingston way, as far as where the 6-sailed mill used to be. My feet didn't
hurt a bit. Altogether it has been a happy day.

24 September. Letter from Pinker saying *Eve* will take a short story. My
suggestion. What are these agents for?

5 October. It was a relief to be in bed [with cold] and about 6 my brains
suddenly returned to me and I thought out the first part of 'Safety First' or it
may be called 'Quince Alley'. Winnie was very good. Dear Ernest also. He
came up with a boiled egg in his pocket.

9 October. Labour Government fell, thank God. Poor Ernest in bed all day
and not feeling very bad – as long as he's in bed: but that's the treachery of
these infernal colds.

10 October. Ernest in bed for breakfast. His success is wonderful. Practically
got a column on *The Daily News* now. He must have a Secretary. As for me!
This cold doesn't seem to get a bit better. I'm an absolute wretch. Met Mr
Gale. Felt I couldn't stand him. Waved him off. Nelson got his ear bitten by a
beast of a sheep dog.

14 Published Collins 1925. The theme a strong endorsement of marriage.
15 Winnie, the new servant, stopped for 21 years.

17 October. To Brighton at 2. Found Mother alone and so peaceful and pretty and happy – no fits now for 4 months. I went on to Brighton. Great crush. The Duke and Duchess of York there. Tea at Pavilion Creamery . . . Reference in *East Sussex [Gazette]* on 'Mrs Henry Dudeney' and her views as expressed in *The Bookman* on the chances young authors have.

22 October. Ernest met Mrs Byron who so hoped we'd come to tea and meet Mrs Sotheran [16]: "such a clever woman". Considering that old dear has twice in ten years heavily snubbed me (a course of treatment I don't respond to) the tea party is not likely to come off.

25 October. Met Mrs Byron and the whole silly social Sotheran tangle is unravelled: after 10 years. Mrs Sotheran has read my books, always wanted to know me – but thought I came first to the town and has been semi-sulking because I didn't call!

27 October. . . . so excited about the election.

28 October. Great blow. 'Ancient Lights' back from Harper. This – combined with the letter I had weeks back saying the management had changed – makes me feel that the position, as far as I am concerned, is changed. I tried very hard not to be frightfully down in the mouth and – more or less – succeeded.

29 October. Went and voted, of course. Bought Conservative colours for me and Nelson. Nice man in the shop – Morrish's – buying 6 yards "for a cat". . . Bought myself a 1925 diary – Venture of Faith!

30 October. Poll declared. Conservative majority of over 8,000 [17]. We – the crowd – enchanted.

16 The Sotherans lived at The Old House, Southover High St.
17 Massive Tory victory. Baldwin returned as PM.

1 November. Letter from Frankfort Moore [18]. Will I go to lunch in about two weeks time? Hastings Literary Society as 'Leader of Sussex movement in novel writing'. . . wrote accepting. This means a speech, but I feel now, once having broken the ice that I could speak in the Albert Hall. Sent an SOS to Charlotte. Must have advice as to what to wear .

13 November. My lunch at Hastings. In the train finally rehearsed speech. Jolly affair. Rider Haggard [19] in the chair. The Frankfort Moores met me at the station. Made my speech without turning a hair and got clapped and complimented . . . home, dirty, weary and triumphant at 7.

20 November. Leaflets arrived, advertising Mrs Henry Dudeney to lecture in the Hove Town Hall. Rather frightens me . . .

25 November. Horrid news in the *Evening Standard* of all papers. Wonder how it got there? Poor old Huggett [20] has hanged himself. Quite haunted me. I could see his lean and little old body packed up so tightly in a frock coat and his sad protuberant eyes. Ernest had a very good offer – £500 a year from the *Daily News*.

26 November. At lunch no Ernest. I waited till half past one, worried myself into a fit of acute indigestion, kept looking out the window for an ambulance: actually (how mad it seems!) went to the outside lavatory to see if he had hanged himself. Then remembered that he'd said he was going to Brighton.

27 November. Went to Huggett's shop and told young Mrs Huggett how very sorry I was.

3 December. Ernest to London. Important interview with the *Daily News* . . . a minimum fee of £500 one year certain. I feel so proud and glad. My star being, financially anyhow, on the wane hardly matters.

18 The Moores had moved from Lewes to St Leonards-on-Sea.
19 Writer of adventure stories, remembered especially for *King Solomon's Mines* and *She*.
20 Lewes shoemaker.

5 December. Wire from Margery. Will we send baptismal and birth certificates at once. Ernest entirely callous, pushing the wire away and reading a mathematical postcard! I felt I was going mad at such callousness when he knows the whole facts and that it may mean her getting – or not getting – into America with Christopher. Didn't rave, haven't the stamina in these days. I just said – and meant it – "I could kill you as you sit there. You've never cared a bit for your child". And came away. And sent her wire to Skues, asking him to get the certificates, and sent a note to Margery. He came up penitently at 11 just as I was settling to work, but by that time the mischief was done. However, it blew over as things do by mercy nowadays.

20 December. Welfare came and planted the Ceanothus. I went up in the attic and found a poor young blackbird frightened to death. Brought him down. See him fly out of my bedroom window like an arrow. Philip sent me a chest of china tea.

24 December. Wild Xmas shopping . . . Ernest came home. A most successful day, dear old thing. I do so rejoice and riot in his success. He stamped his *Daily News* agreement and saw the *Daily News* [21] people. They are enchanted with the work he has done.

25 December, Christmas Day. Last night I sat by the fire trying to make out which was the happiest Xmas of my life. Now I know, take it all round – this! Communion at 8 for us, Winnie went at 7. Nelson gave his Master a chocolate dog for a Xmas present. At 11 Church again. Home to a lovely chicken, and the usual Christmas fare. After supper Ernest came up and I read, from *Eve* first, Michael Arlen's [22] extraordinary story and then my 'Parrot Food' [23]. He enthusiastic of 'Parrot Food'. Says it's absurd Pinker not placing my short stories and offered to see him for me.

31 December. Ernest came up after supper and by warm mutual agreement we tabooed seeing the old year out!

21 In 1925 the *Daily News* published *The World's Best Word Puzzles*, a compilation of ED's columns.
22 Chiefly remembered for *The Green Hat* published 1924.
23 Short story, published in *Sussex County Magazine*, Vol. 1, March 1927.

1925

10 January. Decided to take a day off. Hard brilliant frost . . . after dinner for a nice walk on the hills but it is disquieting to find that dear Nelson gets so easily tired.

14 January. Letter from Margery . . . she enclosed delicious photographs, one each of herself and the children. Delighted and upset me!

17 January. Thought I was going to have such a gay, money-spending morning, buying shoes at bargain price from Huggett. But Mrs Huggett said quite unconcernedly: "Nothing to suit you, Mrs Dudeney"! Mistake to sympathise when old Huggett hanged himself. These people are simply not fine enough to bear kindness.

23 January. Poor dear Antony seriously ill, bladder trouble and carted off to a Nursing Home . . . Dear faithful Mrs Brown came and cleaned the dining room carpet.

27 January. Ernest and I talked it over and it was decided that I, not Ernest, should go up tomorrow. Ernest is frightfully busy, but at the same time I don't think he quite grasps how serious Antony's state is . . .

28 January. Got to King's College Hospital where Antony is in a paying ward £4.14.6 weekly. Ruin! He was looking so awful that I, armed with votive daffodils didn't know him . . . He said, hardly above a whisper : "Alice, let me hold your hand". And when I left: "Give me a kiss, dear". So very unlike Antony, handsome and a little aloof. However, I complied on both counts! And I asked him if, when he was a tiny bit better, he'd like to see a clergyman. To my surprise and joy he would and he'd be grateful if I'd arrange it. On leaving him I found there is a resident Chaplain, finds he believes in confession – is not, thank goodness, a 'Church of England clergyman'. Reserved sacrament in the chapel and a Daily Mass. So I was happy for Antony on that side of things.

30 January. Dear Antony died in his sleep last night . . .

3 February. Ernest just gone off to the funeral, looking lugubrious in black but nice and carrying a vast cardboard box with the wreath . . . He returned with an account of the affair: unreal, leaving him untouched as these ghastly funerals do.

9 February. Awoke more dead than alive. Got up and dressed, took Ernest his breakfast. Said I'd got a bad cold and had him to thank for it: "You're a Fool. I didn't give it you. You're" – voice rising as usual – "A FOOL." What is one to do with such a savage? What I did was to go off to Brighton with dear darling Nelson, my one true friend, by 'bus and walk like mad along the sea front in a gale and with lots of gulls (beautiful). Came home and went to bed. Ernest penitent, but that doesn't quite heal the place.

10 February. Mrs Miller, who really is a brick and you can't expect to find everything in one person, came and took Nelson for a walk. He, the dear beast, is a most devoted nurse and never left me. Winnie was splendid. Ernest frightened me to death by coming in and saying he'd been spitting up blood. Sent for Dr Vallance who says it is nothing: some little vein at the back of his throat, caused by coughing.

13 February. *Black Friday*. Dr Vallance came and asked to see me before he went in to Ernest . . . The analysis is bad: his lung certainly touched again [1], as it was before in 1910. All the terror of that time came back, but then I had Margery, a tower of strength – now I must bear it alone. Dr Vallance said he was bound to tell the nearest relative but we both thought it best not to tell Ernest who is so highly nervous.

14 February. Have put Ernest on cream with his porridge, also got some Cow & Gate milk. I did howl all alone, just once but wouldn't, first because I don't mean to be a fool and also because I don't want to look a hag at the Pavilion

1 Tuberculosis. Before the discovery of streptomycin in 1944 there was no effective treatment.

on Tuesday . . . Called to ask how Mr Gale was. His housekeeper says nerves and "too sorry for himself".

17 February. Off to Brighton in my best togs. Lunch with Slingsby-Roberts and his mother, a delightful woman of 88, a piece of puckered ivory who spoke of the Duke of Wellington's funeral[2] as if it were last week. To the Pavilion where I spoke my little speech[3]. Every one *most kind* and *complimentary*.

26 March. Mrs Stenhouse came after tea. She says that Mr Gale (wily old codger!) asked her to tea and said he did not ask "consolation" from her, although he was so wretched without a wife – only friendship! And could he be of any use in helping her with her affairs?! And he tried to find out what her income was.

27 March. Bitter, blasting, beastly day. Couldn't allow Ernest to go out. Went to station and made all arrangements for his journey on Monday . . . Quite wild about the idea of 2 bathrooms. I simply must.

6 April. Of course through all this time there was the thrill of the new bathrooms but by now glamour is gone and I am merely wondering how much it will cost and will the *Play Box* money (£38) cover it? If only *Harper* would take 'Dirty Weather'. But nowadays *Harper* takes nothing.

7 April. While we [Vere is staying] were at tea who should be announced but "Mr Sullivan"[4]. I was intensely annoyed, disapproving, ended disgusted at the whole affair. Couldn't be rude, so he came to tea, made himself charming (although physically I find him slightly repulsive). I – who'd have believed it – ended by dining with him and Vere at the White Hart[5]. Wore my grey crepe de chine and best hat. His verdict on me was that my eyes were

2 In 1852.
3 The location and date of AD's speech were changed.
4 Vere's 'unsuitable' lover.
5 The White Hart Hotel, Lewes High St., established since early 18th century.

"unexpected". Might be anything, a squint even. Vere was very grateful to me for being civil – as indeed I had to be. But I said I would really be seriously annoyed if he turned up again: although I rather like him (shouldn't have dined with him else). There's a curious appeal about him. Perhaps it is the horn-rimmed glasses.

17 April. Mrs Brown came and scrubbed the basement kitchen. She is quite good at a hefty straightforward job which doesn't include eating . . . I bought a tortoise and named him Edgar.

22 April. I'm extremely happy all day long ... Gas man came and said the geyser is "foolproof" and showed me how to light it . . . Tea in the summer house watching Edgar take a really brisk constitutional on the grass!

12 May. A perfect day – our first . . . All the afternoon in the garden where lying on the fat cushions in my lovely summer house or cracking snails or doing a bit of weeding. Edgar very active, in the long border opening his cruel, crooked mouth for insects. Nelson doesn't know what to make of him and gets out of his way when he waddles over the grass.

13th May. . . . changed into thin underclothes.

21 May. Edgar was very tiresome and would go on the border and eat delphinium leaves. He came here with a false character as an insect-eater. Finally settled him in a bush of balm.

23 May. Queerest letter from Pinker. He is just back from America and all the publishers think my work 'very good' but haven't 'the courage' to publish it. The impression being that I am 'finished in The States'. Very crushing, but I have been crushed lately . . . He said would I publish under another name in America? Wrote him saying it struck me as a very amusing notion, and why not! But I wasn't amused at all and all day long I had an uncomfortable sensation of being dead and buried.

26 May. The chief event of the day has been that Edgar the tortoise having been caught 3 times eating 1: pansies; 2: ranunculus; 3: pinks, got translated to the Brack Mount. I stood on a kitchen chair and put him over the wall and watched him go – rather sad! But he just could not be borne with any longer. 27 May. Letter from Margery. They are building a home and buying a car.

30 May. Was telling Charlotte about Edgar when she said calmly: "But I can see a tortoise on the Brack Mount now," and there was poor Edgar halfway across the stony bit on his way back to us. So touched that I got the steps, climbed on to the Brack Mount and brought him home. He instantly made for some young asters! Got a wooden box, and knocked the bottom out and put some wire on top to make him a little cage.

2 June. Another gorgeous day: a salmon sunset going on now (9.30 – as I write by the window). Ernest and I at teatime watched with great interest Edgar get out of his cage – he's a clever reptile. Kemp came and repainted 'tradesmen' on the door.

12 June. Mrs Hart came about 3. Asked her if she'd like a tortoise and to my surprise she jumped at it: "Frank loved them". After tea Nelson suddenly made a savage onslaught on poor Edgar. Just as well he is going.

28 June. Very nice tea party at Mrs Byron's and the Sotherans very nice people. Pity we've managed to lose 10 years of each other's society...

1 July. Mr and Mrs Rawlings, Sir Alan [6] and Lady Moore at 4. Mrs Rawlings, as Grant aptly puts it, belongs to the "Order of Fluff" but a nice little soul. Ernest enjoyed himself and likes both Rawlings and Sir Alan . . . I suppose these parsons so often marry pretty little youthful barmaid-ey persons in a mood of violent reaction. So seldom do they hitch up with the really truly good churchworker who would jump at the chance of 'helping in the parish'.

6 Surgeon. His wife, née Burrows, daughter of late Bishop of Chichester.

10 July. Trent Park[7]. Nearing Trent whole strings of cars, the road lined with people and on every tree and at every corner placards: 'To Trent'. Arrived. Philip and Lady Cholmondeley received us, Mrs Gubbay came up – I must be presented to the Duchess: And I was and hope I managed my curtsey properly! Great fun, altogether .

13 July. To Mrs Sotheran's. She looked delightful and was. The whole setting: house, garden and graceful old woman, enchanted me – probably because it is becoming rare to find a truly well-bred person in a suitable atmosphere of house and dress. Nothing rough nor jarring.

14 July. One heavenly day comes after the other. I live in the garden and just pass through the drawing room on my way to bed. . . . I went to bed in daylight, falling asleep with my eyes on the hills and blessings on my lips.

16 July. Mr Sotheran called at 12.30: quite a Cranfordy[8] hour – felt I ought to produce cake and wine! Most fascinating man . . . Quite an exquisite. Never before have I seen such a white, white hankey! Found we loved the same things: our own land, – always; the very hot weather – and wandering alone on the vast hills. He very much admired the old piano: "Quite a John Leech[9] look". I was glad to know (and that he would see) how very well my jet necklace and long jet earrings kept up this early Victorian illusion.

22 July. Mrs Gubbay: 44 Hertford Street, London. I went up in boiling heat. Nice little time. The home lovely. A Mrs Dudley Ward[10] came in: "You've of course heard of her?' asked Mrs Gubbay and seemed surprised I hadn't: "A great friend of the Prince of Wales" (whatever that may mean). Philip came in after lunch to see me, and remarked on my going to Lympne as usual! Said

7 PS inherited from his father this ugly Victorian mansion in New Barnet with a park landscaped by Humphrey Repton. He refaced the front, transforming it into a handsome country house. Now part of University of Middlesex.
8 Mrs Gaskell's novel *Cranford*.
9 Artist and *Punch* cartoonist 1817–64.
10 Prince of Wales' mistress before advent of Mrs Simpson.

I would (although I hate spending more money on clothes). He then took me in his car to the House of Commons, got out there and I was carried on to Victoria and just caught the 3.15.

27 July. Isle of Wight ... Rain, wind raging . . . The steamer crowded, lots of scouts going into camp and some of 'em were sea-sick. Not me, in the least.

28 July. Rain again, but the whole of the visit I intensely enjoyed . . . In the afternoon we [11] motored to Ventnor to have tea with the De Vere Stacpooles: he [12] a big Irishman rather inarticulate: shy and jerky at the tea table, but all right later in the garden where he and I got alone and talked shop.

29 July. Good 'voyage', the sea and sky leaden but beautiful. At Lewes, Ernest, dear thing, met me and insisted on carrying the bag. He looked, I thought, wan, and I felt a beast for having been so angry with him but he can be so devastating . . . Darling Nelson went mad with joy.

2 August. Miss Doyle and Mrs Miller – back from her holiday and brisk as ever – to tea. She is going to have her head shingled [13] on Tuesday. Rather a daring experiment! But these quite plain women can dare things which the moderately goodlooking can't.

7 August. Letter from Pinker, he has sold 'Ancient Lights' to *The Windsor* for £18.18s. Presented dear Mrs Brown with the red feather out of my last winter's velours hat – she always used to stare at it in fascinated admiration! I said: "I believe you've always liked it, Mrs Brown." Her shrill ecstatic pipe came: "I always *did*, M'm" and she blushed with joy. Queer creatures women – even charwomen!

11 AD stayed with Governor of Parkhurst, Frank Wintle, and his wife Irene, son-in-law and daughter of Mary Carr, an old friend.
12 Novelist remembered for his best-selling romance *The Blue Lagoon*, published 1908.
13 Hair cut short in latest fashion, tapering from back of head to nape of neck.

17 August. Such a dazzlingly lovely morning felt I must do something, so paid £1 3s for a trouser press for Ernest. It came. I was automatically thanked and he never even unpacked it! Went off first to Bowls and after supper to Chess. In a *fury*, not with him but with my own fool self (for not knowing better), put it in his bedroom.

18 August. After lunch in the garden on a peerless day, the storm broke! The usual "What's the matter with you, darling?" When I told him he was vile as usual, wound up by calling me a liar and a fool . . . I came indoors, took the trouser press back to the shop with some rigmarole about "Mr Dudeney" not wanting one and would they put the £1 3s to our credit . . . came home and just howled and howled sitting on the floor and holding dear Nelson's paw. He very distressed trying to lick my face. So for his sake I left off. Grotesque for an old woman to cry like that, anyhow.

20 August. Same old silence, broken, by him, at tea time, attempting a row and – finally – threatening to alter his will. Interesting, if it wasn't agonising. The way the old mastery over money breaks out at these times . . . Afterwards I went into the study and said very calmly: "Won't you come upstairs before you go to the Chess Club and settle this unhappy affair?" He came and a sort of peace was botched together.

26 August. Lympne. Off I went. Really rather a diverting annual event! Found 4 Americans there: 2 men, two women, one pair enormously rich – both pairs delightful. Philip said later "You got off with them splendidly, you do with every one and you know it. Even with Lord Hugh who is quite unimpressionable."

27 August. The Americans went. We had a quiet day. I like Mrs Gubbay more and more. After tea Philip and I went off for a long drive to see the most wonderful little Saxon church in a tiny village.

28 August. People to lunch, a delightful Dr Gomez, for one. After lunch, Lady Edward Grosvenor came with her cool, inscrutable smile. Rather a fascinating person. At 6 I left provided with a packet of fruit cake and sandwiches, which Ernest and I shared when I got home.

4 September. Packed the portmanteau, never sure what to take and what to leave behind. Mrs Miller came to tea and we had a general pow-wow about things she is to do and isn't while we're gone. *Awfully* good of her to look after Nelson: "He shall be my dog". You overlook quite a lot in a friend for a thing like that.

5 September. The portmanteau went off, so we really are going! Can't believe I am going to leave Nelson for the first time in 11 years (nearly) for a whole week. Made a little cushion for Nelson's chair in the dining room window where he sits at meal times, bless him. Locked up my drawers, diaries, best china, tea tray, lacquer box, candle-lamp, sewing machine and so on.

7 September. We go to The Bugle [14]. I'd arranged that we – to spare darling Nelson's feelings – should not leave the house together. Met Ernest at the station. We had a charming journey, I always love the crossing.

9 September. We lunched with Irene and Frank at Camp Hill . . . we went round the prison. Irene showed me the snaps she took of me and De Vere Stacpoole. She has sent them to *The Bookman* and they'll appear in the October number.

14 September. At 9.30 we sorrowfully departed from dear Yarmouth and the Bugle, lunched at Ryde, arrived home for tea. Darling Nelson, moved to loud sobs and barkings. Found no letters, but Philip has sent me a big photograph of himself.

15 September. Busy unpacking and arranging myself . . . Nelson and I had such a happy day, not parted for a second – he so afraid of losing me again!

16 September. Dear Nelson quite ill. Hasn't barked all day, nor – it is 4 now – got out of his basket . . . seemed so dull and listless that I went down to the vet alone after tea and he came up about 8. Thinks nothing really serious with Nelson but that he is old and must take things quietly . . . But the whole thing

14 Hotel at Yarmouth, Isle of Wight.

is so sudden: he was radiant when we came home on Monday and – yesterday – so delighted to go out with me again and after lunch he sat watching for cats in the garden while I replanted pinks.

17 September. Nelson didn't wish to get out of his basket, had great difficulty in walking downstairs and wouldn't go out on Castle Banks . . . Settled him in his basket in the kitchen . . . the vet came at 10 and pointed out to me a curious little swelling behind, said it was dropsical . . . [later] he seemed so much worse that I was frightened to death and began to *dread*.

18 September. The vet arrived at 10 . . . then said Nelson would be a chronic invalid. I went upstairs, asked Winnie to send Ernest to me and there, upon the chintz sofa, we howled in each other's arms. I sent Winnie to Miss Falconer's for the address of their vet, as I was determined to have another opinion . . . I felt I would go mad in the silent house and with that dear, my spotted love, lying in his basket so ill . . . I sat here in the drawing room on the floor by his basket, holding his paw and talking to him. But he seemed dazed, only just once or twice did he look at me in the old bright adoring way. At 6.30 the vet arrived: a curiously sympathetic man and you relied on him at once. When he knocked at the door Nelson aroused and barked as usual – his last bark. He let the new doctor handle him . . . the swelling has increased enormously, there was absolutely no hope. He must be put to sleep at once. I wanted to stay until the last but was told he would be quite unconscious and that it would add to my distress. Mrs Miller stayed. I went upstairs and stood looking numbly out of the little east window. All so sudden, I couldn't grasp it. Before that, I had fetched Ernest from the Bowling Green and together, left alone, we bade him goodbye. Mrs Miller came up when all was over. I looked at him lying in his basket, the chloroformed wool on his mouth. Then she and I carried him downstairs and put him in the servants' bathroom.

19 September. No sleep all night. I stayed in bed till lunch. Mrs Miller went down the town and shopped and told the tradespeople and any friends she met what had happened; so that they shouldn't sympathise, which I couldn't bear. In the afternoon Welfare came and dug a grave at the bottom of the garden. She and I carried him down in his basket and he was buried in his

blanket. Then I gave Welfare his armchair out of my bedroom and gave Mrs Miller his basket, a new one, and had his cushions burnt and made a parcel of his collar and lead and put them away.

23 September. It was so *awful* to go down the High Street alone, to have no welcome when I returned, to see no graceful spotted body and lovely eager head at the ante-room window. I spent the morning writing letters and, also, crying!

24 September. Quite forlorn – and with £7 10s in my pocket, determined to spend every penny on clothes, if that would comfort me! . . . Two most tender letters, one from Vere, one from her mother. Whatever else is – or isn't – you simply cannot afford to surrender friends like that.

26 September. Welfare came and edged the grave with London pride then planted red and white roses, also a bush of lavender and one of rosemary.

28 September. Mrs Sotheran arrived – 4.30 – in a hired brougham, very lame, poor dear and very stately – in those hereditary sables and family rings which some old ladies affect . . . I went to bed early in a state of gusty misery remembering the lots of games we used to play when I put him to bed.

1 October. Must pull myself together and not cry so much. Ernest is so tender and so percipient. He said at breakfast: "A dog's love is so wonderful, so unspoiled in memory and so pure". That's it: nothing mars it, a sinless, perfect love. And nothing, ever, can fill the blank in my life.

8 October. Just about now old men are sweeping up leaves on Castle Banks. Amongst them the paralysed or aguish man who walks with a dance. He jigs about with a broom and a sack, the leaves fly – they comically evade each other . . . I've got a fire and will and must settle down to work and normal life.

24 October. Bought a paper *The Dog's World* where to my rapt tearful joy I saw Dalmatians advertised . . . I feel faithless to Nelson and yet it is a sign of devotion to him that I simply cannot live my life without a Dalmation dog.

28 October. To Mrs Stenhouse's. Found Gale there alone with her and grinning over a gas fire. He *may* pull it off!

31 October. Very thrilling day. Off to the Dalmatian Kennels at Mayfield. Mr Kemp met me and they gave me lunch. Very nice people, elderly, of the retired tradesmen-cum-farmer sort. The 'lovely spotted dog' he advertised for £8 was a misprint for 'liver spotted'. He only had two dog puppies and lots of little ladies. One – only 6 weeks old – quite adorable. Both he and she assured me that lady dogs were not so tiresome to keep. And anyway, 'Emma' [15] was irresistible. So got her – £3.13.6d – and brought her home, the funny mite. Then had tea, then off to Tickners and other shops for a basket, collar and lead – such a touchingly small collar! – and a blanket which I couldn't get. Ernest arrived and was introduced and pretended to be quite indifferent.

1 November. No dog can ever be so dear as Nelson and simply to have a tiny bunch of spots about the place makes the hurt worse and yet makes it so infinitely better. For one thing she's a baby and keeps you on the hop: if she isn't making streams of water in one place, she's chewing up carpet in the other . . . And it seems too fateful that she should be 6 weeks old, born when Nelson died.

2 November. I took Emma for 2 tiny walks, morning and afternoon. She already is very attached and follows me about all over the place. The whole aspect of the house is changed. Nelson is Nelson and I look at the china image and kiss it and talk to him, but little helpless Emma brings tenderness into the house, and endless very practical jobs.

5 November. We went to Mr Gale's Guy Fawkes party. Lots there – people, not guys! Mr Ensell said – of dogs and of my loss of Nelson – that he believed we should have our dogs later on: "Heaven 'ud be a dull place without them." And he quoted a passage from St Paul.

15 Named after Lady Hamilton, mistress of Horatio Nelson.

10 November. Fate doesn't leave you long without a thump! Ernest has started to haemorrhage again, slight but *there*. Dr Vallance says he must stay indoors.

2 December. Snow in the night. Got a blinding headache. Horrible. Darling Emma – her first snow – quite enchanted and playing ball in the garden.

4 December. Freezing cold. I bought handkerchiefs for Margery and the 2 boys, a doll and doll's bedstead for Cathy, socks for Christopher.

6 December. Packed the Christmas presents for America: Emma grows in grace. Sir Alan and Lady Moore came in to see her after church. Wish she hadn't made a small pool on the floor!

21 December. Awful day, wet, foggy, dark. Emma can't go out, so have been playing blankets, rags, bones with her along the passages. She is a little love.

23 December. So lovely to have Joan [Fulleylove] here. We went out and shopped, but I . . . simply could *not* grapple any more with food. We got a nice turkey: 10/8d. I felt such a miserable kill-joy, a very nice Christmassey feeling about and I only longing for one thing – get to bed, get warm and forget there was such a thing as food . . . At 8 arrived a wooden box marvellously packed from Philip. By this time I was really feeling too ill to care. Ernest and Joan unpacked it and drew forth a quite lovely old glass bottle of a heavenly pinkish colour, with silver mount and stopper. Probably a pot-pourri jar. Also Joan gave me a shawl, Winnie gave me some flowers, I have Ernest's hassocks and Mrs Bates sent the most adorable tea cosey I've ever seen in my life.

25 December, Christmas Day. Had a cup of tea in bed. No church of course. Joan took Emma out. I much better, so long as I keep warm . . . ate a little dinner which Winnie cooked beautifully. Joan and I worked at my frock. Seemed to me the rummest Christmas, but so kind and loving.

27 December. I went to church at mid-day. Coming out Winifred Fawssett said would I stand by Jackson's shop and look up at her mother's window to see if she waved. They've rigged up a glass so that she can see all that goes on in the High Street. She did wave and I went up. She was looking so pretty: such a comfort to know that, when our time comes, we all look nice in bed. The heart affair is angina and she must keep quiet.

29 December. *Harper* rejected *Yeast*: 'Full of life and power but too tragic'. Sick of *Harper*.

31 December. Am getting on so nicely with the Marcelline Book [*Seed Pods*] ... Now – 8.30 – Ernest just gone down, Emma asleep: her eyes very tightly screwed up. Winnie out at a New Year's kick-up . . . So the year has gone. And Antony is dead . . . And I've lost my sweet Nelson and am putting myself together with Emma. Goodbye 1925. You leave me feeling quite happy and so very grateful to God.

1926

1926 begins quite well. No money worries, no servant worries. Am filling up the big hole in my heart, which Nelson dug, with Emma.

2 January. *Quince Alley* [1] came. I sent a copy to Philip . . . I spent the morning reading *Quince Alley* and thinking what a fine piece of work it was!

5 January. Quite an exciting afternoon. Took Emma by bus to the prison and then on to the Downs and let her off the lead. She was bewildered at first by such great space, then started skipping about but keeping very close to 'mother'. Afraid it was a little too much for her. She nearly fell asleep over her tea and has been in a dead sleep ever since . . .

7 January. Wanted some sort of 'citement and I'm hanged if I didn't get it! Letter sent on to me from Heinemann – *from Ida* [2]!!! Very affable, regretful, will I write? Will I meet her at Worthing? Wrote . . . Really, rather a wonderful resurrection, this of Ida. Wonder it doesn't stir me more.

26 January. Started training her [Emma] to go to heel. She quite grasped it until we met Miss Falconer and Miss Densham. Then she went mad with excitement. She really is a darling and every day at coffee, while she sits on my lap, Ernest hums to her and she is entranced, moving her head from side to side.

3 February. Philip at 1.30. [Park Lane] Such a nice visit. We were alone. After lunch we went up to the ballroom which he has lent for an exhibition of old books – the most beautiful bindings, some dating from the 12th century. Then he showed me his bedroom and, in a locked cupboard, was a Venetian glass flamingo which he said I must have to go with my Bristol candlesticks. But

---

1 Published Collins. Set near Steyning, West Sussex. AD's favourite novel.
2 Her former lover David's wife, who knew of the affair.

the key couldn't be found. Miss Boyce tried dozens. So there my mysterious bird remains and I am to fetch it later on and get taken to the Sargent[3] pictures at the same time. He motored me to the station, bought me some flowers, saw me into the train and 'so home'.

5 February. How *delicious* work is . . . after tea Ernest came up with the *Church Times* and a very good notice of *Quince Alley*. Didn't expect them to approve of it. Nice letter from Collins, very nice, saying 'it's a pleasure to publish for me'. Altogether I feel that it's a particularly nice world just now!

8 February. Sent Philip the vests he wanted.

3 March. Philip. Chauffeur met me at Victoria and I *really* did enjoy the day. Not tired a bit. Philip and I went to see the Sargent . . . Back to lunch. The Spanish painter[4] there - who decorated the ballroom at Park Lane and also the drawing room at Lympne. As he and I could only speak each our own language we got no farther than friendly smiles. Another man there – Honourable Evan Charteris[5] – who is writing a life of Sargent and after lunch we all went to his place in Mount Street where he has some lovely pictures. Left him and the Spaniard there and the car took us to Mrs Gubbay. Philip went off to the House: chat with Mrs Gubbay – she says the Duchess of York, who was coming to tea, is having a baby[6] in May. Philip sent the car back for me at 4. I took back my flamingo and a great bunch of carnations. Slept like a top.

12 March. At night armed with a hat pin and a bottle of brine went down the garden in the dark with my electric torch and caught two (*only* two) slugs glutting themselves with Crown Imperials. I shall go down every night.

3 John Singer Sargent, society portraitist and intimate friend of the Sassoon family. Painted portraits of PS, his mother and sister. PS lent 2 dozen canvases to the exhibition at Burlington House.
4 José-Maria Sert (Misia), a Catalan artist. His exuberant murals at Lympne were destroyed in the war.
5 Chairman of Tate Gallery. His biography *John Sargent* published 1927.
6 The present Queen, born on 21st April.

19 March. After dinner for a walk . . . dear Mrs Fawssett waved from her window with a towel tied on to a stick. Hasn't waved for weeks. She must be better.

21 March. Great talk over the proposed sea trip for Ernest and Gale. Not the Canaries but a coasting trip round Ireland starting from London. Mr Gale so nice I quite loved him. He is to do all the arranging...

8 April. Sent the film man *Quince Alley* registered. Started on the second part of *The Mayor's Parlour*[7]. So glad to get away from the squalid first part, clearly 'squalor' is not my line.

28 April. Mr Gale looked in. They are both looking forward like boys to their trip. Men are often tiresome, but always rather appealing, the great mistake is ever to regard them as grown up.

30 April. Sent Ernest off - saw the train go out: hope they'll have a nice time. Vere arrived. A tiny coldness at first, clearly owing to my attitude over Sullivan. But we talked it out and got warmer. ... Went to bed and never slept a wink.

5 May. We [Vere] took the bus to Brighton – the last one as it proved, all the men on strike[8]. Went round by Newhaven (and *what* a hell Peacehaven is! Hadn't seen it before). At Brighton big crowd. Strikers turning back the buses to the Garage. By luck we got one (the last, a Maidstone and Chatham) driven by non-union men – home.

8 May. Sullivan came to fetch Vere. I had to call a truce and ask him to tea. A violent Revolutionary and, as he describes himself, "an Irish peasant".

7 Published as *Seed Pods* by Collins in 1926. A woman with a colourful past marries the Mayor of Lewes (a brewer) and fears disclosure. AD hoped this would annoy the real Lewes Mayoress whom she considered self-important.
8 The General Strike, first in British history. The TUC backed the miners' strike with a strike of all essential services. Ended 12th May, but miners continued to strike until November.

14 May. Took Emma after for a walk down by the Meads, Southover. And it was, of course, quite lovely in its way. Vividly green water meadows, sleek cattle, lots of buttercups, the steely, sullen hills, cut by the pallid quarry, standing round, seeming to close up. Railway strike ended.

15 May. Welfare came and I pointed out to him that one of my life ideals was to get rid of the manure heap, not add to it.

21 May. The home looks very lovely, but what's the good? That face of his would turn Paradise. Letter from Collins – quite delightful. *Quince Alley* has sold nearly 4,000 copies and still selling. Like the fool I always am took the letter in to show him. No comment! Went to bed with a thundering headache.

25 May. His face at breakfast was horrible and his barking voice was worse. So now, 9.30, here I sit, my heart thumping like mad . . . Tea with Mrs Miller and her crippled sister. How vulgar they are and how kind . . . Went on the way home in to the Bowling Green and spoke to poor, unhappy-looking Ernest. This seemed to touch and melt him and *"all* of a sudding" there is peace and sanity.

31 May. Letter from America. Margery had a girl, Elizabeth Ann[9], on the 15th.

5th June Sat. Off to Trent. Met at Victoria and motored there. Park of 1,000 acres. Home – once early Victorian and transformed (or in process) by Philip – at a cost, his cousin told me, of £150,000, into a genuine William and Mary house. Lord Hugh Cecil there, also Lady Edward Grosvenor: know and like them both, also the architect Freeman Smith came to lunch and Lady Cholmondeley came to tea. At night as I was beginning to undress, and happily, in the new rose and black kimono, slippers to match, also cap – a knock at my door and there was Philip, bearing a delightful paper weight, a white china hound on a grey granite base: "It was my mother's and I'd like you to have it."[10] Then a funny little talk, half laughing, half serious. "I would

9 AD's 5th grandchild. She had seen only 2, Barney and Jamie, in 1922.
10 PS was devoted to his mother, whose early death may have contributed to his underlying melancholia.

like to have you always with me. I said so to Hannah just now. I've been faithful for nearly 10 years and all I get is a few illiterate letters, not warm at all." We laughed and I said then, quite seriously: "Well. Keep faithful, because your friendship means a lot to me." And he went off.

1 June. To church with Lord Hugh. Heaps and heaps more people there when we got back: Sir Hugh Seely, Lord and Lady Londonderry [11], Sir Samuel Hoare [12], Lord Lanesborough, Lord and Lady Ednam, and one or two others. Lunch out of doors.

7 June. Motored up to London with Philip, Lord Hugh, Mrs Gubbay. Dropped Lord Hugh at Arlington Street, Mrs Gubbay at Hertford Street, Philip and I went on to Christie's where I got introduced to Ramsay MacDonald [13], then to Curry and Paxtons; where I was measured for hornrim specs (a present from him) then to Park Lane, lunching alone. Then off to Victoria dropping him at the Air Ministry. At Gorringes I bought myself a blouse and arrived here for tea, having enjoyed myself enormously.

8 June. Arranged all the flowers – a big dress box full – which Philip had put with my luggage. Wrote him, also wrote Margery, also bought a bonnet for Elizabeth Ann and sent it off.

9 June. Returned Mrs [Lady] Sassoon's hound. Wrote to Philip.

15 June. She [Emma] at last has suddenly grown up enough to be a real house dog and barks at every knock and ring. Rather a squeaky bark for the present. But Ernest says feminine!

11 Lord Londonderry, Air Minister, later leader of House of Lords; Lady Londonderry a formidable political hostess.
12 Secretary of State for Air 1922–29, later first Lord of Admiralty, Secretary of State Home Affairs.
13 Former Prime Minister, then leader of opposition.

28 June. Postcard from Ida about tomorrow. I want to meet her – naturally – for although I don't see David he is in the background. But why on earth does she want – and eagerly – to meet me; must be the middle-aged woman's positive ache for drama of *any* sort.

29 June. Worthing. Put on all my best clothes: foulard frock, short satin coat and the rest of it. Ida arrived, ill dressed – but she always was. Touching queer affair. At 3.20 I watched her go off on the top of the bus to David. Went to Brighton and on the way home bought myself two summer frocks to "cheer up me"!

24 July. Very exciting day. Wire from Philip, will I go to Trent: "We all long for you". Wired back I couldn't, also wrote. Very gratifying, however.

26 July. What a climate! And what's the good of talking about it. Here I sit in 2 coats, 2 pairs of stockings and have raked out a pair of silk knickers and yet am cold! At this point I went and got a blanket to wrap round my legs! Borrowed Horsfield's *History of Lewes*[14] from Mabel Smythe. On page 164: 'The south wall of Mr Shelley's Warehouse on Castle Banks is part of the old fortification refaced.' Thrilled me exceedingly, unreasonably, to feel that I – yes, Me! – had got a bit of medieval wall for my very own.

27 July. Got into the garage and find that the south wall is certainly only brick but that the *north*[15] wall is undeniably ancient, yet not refaced.

1 August. Great shock. Winnie tells me that our dear Madonna Brown, so linked up in my mind with the very early and strangely anguished days at Lewes, was buried yesterday. Doesn't seem credible that never any more shall I hear her shrill voice and see her patient, calmly brooding face, nor give her any old stockings, nor see her polishing the floors on a Friday. Winnie will miss her too. After church I called to say how sorry I was and found the whole family in very solemn black.

14 *The History and Antiquities of Lewes* by the Rev T.W.H. Horsfield, published in 1824, with introductory essay by Dr Gideon Mantell.
15 Composed, as is Brack Mount, of medieval blocks of chalk.

2 August. David's birthday - 64!

24 August. Philip: Lympne. Arrived and found I was in the yellow room where 2 years ago I never slept one wink one night. Got transferred to the green one and slept like a top. Perfect weather. No one staying in the house but Lord Edward Grosvenor[16] is at the Aerodrome. He and some of the officers came to dinner.

25 August. Philip came to my room about 9.30 when, by mercy, I'd had my bath, my breakfast and had a cap on my unbrushed head. Very charming, abrupt, affectionate, inscrutable in fact. He then went off flying which he does in state with an escort of two other machines, he being a Cabinet Minister. Again Lord Edward and some air men to dinner. Before dinner Philip and I for a walk to see a very early Tudor cottage he's doing up and proposes to lend to his friends. He will lend it to me. Wonder if Ernest would come. In the morning Mrs Gubbay played golf and I motored to Hythe[17].

26 August. In the afternoon Folkestone with Philip and Mrs Gubbay to a gymkhana. After tea I went up in a flying machine with one of the air officers. Not afraid a bit, nor sick, nor anything. Sent a note to Ernest that I wasn't coming home till Saturday.

27 August. In the afternoon Philip and I to Folkestone, he played polo and I watched. After that we motored to the Fish Market and saw the boats come in and the fish auctioneer; they all crowded round him – not the fish, the men! Very Conservative. He dined with Lord Edward, Mrs Belloc Lowndes arrived, enormously fat and very friendly, also a gardening man, Lionel Johnson.

28 August. The Rolls Royce was going to Tunbridge Wells to fetch Sir Austen Chamberlain[18], so actually got motored from door to door. Also got presented

16 At school with PS. Under Secretary of State for Air 1924–9, 1931–7.
17 PS was MP for Hythe from 1912 until his death.
18 Foreign Secretary 1924–29, half brother of Neville.

with a heavenly cake, a regular wedding cake. Philip came into my room after lunch when I was getting ready to go and again fidgetted about, saying nothing much. In the morning I had a long talk with Mrs Belloc Lowndes about work, which may prove useful. Though I doubt if I am a money maker. Winnie and Emma so pleased to see me – also Ernest when he came back from Brighton.

3 September. Letter from *Morning Post* [19]. Will I write in form of a letter 3000 words on 'Women as Creative Artists'? Did and got it off by 12. This exhausted me.

10 September. Before I got to Mother's I was feeling: 'Oh I can't'. But when I saw her face light up and when I saw Emily looking really sweet in one of the cotton frocks I gave her, I felt a *Devil*!

16 September. Very ingratiating letter from one called 'Michael Joseph' on the staff of Curtis Brown. Could I see him? Wrote and fixed 12 next Wed . . . Finished chapter XVII. Shall be so glad when this book is done.

22 September. Michael Joseph [20] quite a nice young man who I do think may be a real help. Pinker is none . . . Came home . . . everybody was happy, though I am bound to add that I am most "wetchedly depwessed" because the *Daily Mail* – curse it – has an article on the best novelists – and doesn't mention me! So petty of me – but I can't help it.

30 September.. Very nice letter in the *Daily Mail* from Allan Fea saying what a gifted creature Mrs Henry Dudeney is. So I'm quite reinstated. And how stupid to care at all one way or the other.

5 October. Letter from Pinker. Will I do a short story 850 words for the *Daily Chronicle*? Wrote him and did (it) in the rough, against difficulties for there was a domestic row before I began . . . Coming up Keere Hill [Street] I saw a sight quite Greek in its tragedy. Little squeaky-voiced comic Pinyoun the baker

19 Amalgamated with the *Daily Telegraph* in 1937.
20 Founder of publishing firm in 1937. Now a subsidiary of Penguin Books.

has lost his wife. And there he stood in the middle of his open shop, with the one black shutter – *oblivious* – his head dropped, his face grey as the dried dough on his bare arms.

18 October. Took Emma for a walk – Southover. We met Mr Bates with 'Zeb' [Dalmatian] who to me is a touching puppy, quite immense, already bigger than Emma although he is only 5 months old. And very shy. Lives out in a loose box. I hate that, as an idea.

29 October. In the afternoon got out the machine and turned up the hem of the red dress and also put tucks in my petticoats. The fashion now is to be short, almost to the knee. Very comfortable and if one has decent legs and ankles (really they are wonderful for 60) quite easy.

30 October. Tiresome morning. No fire in Ernest's room because of the coal strike, so he sat in the drawing room and I couldn't settle down and my morning is spoilt. Got on both our nerves . . . we could never share one sitting room and as to sharing a bedroom I'd cut my throat first, and so would he! Yet for 20 years we wallowed in one bed!

24 November. Young 'Mr Charles' [21] Wycherley arrived. So nice and intelligent and very interested in all we have done to the house, as he took a hand in it at the start . . . Interview in *County Magazine* [22] arrived. Quite good.

8 December. Sent biscuits to Philip. We have been friends for 10 years.

11 December. From Philip a lovely evening shawl 'which I bought for you in Spain'. And will I lunch and go to a matinée on Jan 5th?

13 December. . . . to Evelyn [Fawssett] and stayed till nearly 7. She says their home is haunted. A gentleman – Jeannette the cook insists that he's a gentleman – in a tall silk hat and carrying an overcoat appears in the scullery. And once the housemaid went into mad hysterics and would never say *what* she saw.

21 Son of Alfred.
22 SCM Dec 1926, Vol 1, No 1, with photos of CPH and dogs.

14 December. I'm very fond of Ernest but I do feel that, always, he's been years too old for me. How lovely to be young so that Philip could be in love with me. And there is nothing really so outrageous in the idea, because if I were young he certainly would be. But then where does David come in? And what sort of person am I?

15 December. The Mrs Christie[23] mystery solved. The tiresome woman found at Harrogate. If she is mad she should be sent to Bedlam. If she is sane, she should be spanked. No patience with such people.

22 December. I was so happy. Lots of letters and little presents: wrote lots of letters back. But the letter and gift was from Ida who sent me a photograph of David's ship: 'We think you would like it.' She speaks of coming to call on me. Told Ernest who received this revolutionary suggestion with passivity – wonder what he felt.

25 December, Christmas Day. [Joan is staying] Communion at 8. Bitter cold and the church half empty. As I said to Ernest, with so many services there are really not enough Christians to go round. At 10.30 we all went to the Sung Mass, then home to turkey and plum pudding and all the rest of it. After tea we played 'Suggestions'.

29 December. Letter from Ida which I judiciously burned. Not good for Ernest to have too frequent doses!

31 December. Rather eerie to write the last words in a diary – have written to Philip for the New Year as I'd promised and sent a cheque to Emily, which I'd forgot. Also offered to pay to have her her shingled and suggested a meeting at Fulgens on Monday at eleven. Lots of things I've forgotten, that I went to see Mrs Batup and what she told me about Batup selling her cat for £2 . . .

23 Agatha Christie disappeared from her Surrey home for 11 days and said she had no recollection of reaching a Harrogate hotel.

1927

3 January. . . . took Emily to be shingled. Vast improvement to my amazement . . .

16 January. See in the *East Sussex [Gazette]* that Rosario[1]'s lodging house is to close. Comforting – very – the way things do come to pass.

19 January. [London] Went with Philip to *Trelawney of the Wells* [2] after lunch. And after the theatre to tea with Mrs Gubbay. I thought Philip looking very thin and ill (he delighted me by saying that Margery had sent him a Christmas card. So glad she did). Home by the 6.40.

22 January. Philip – at The Metropole [Brighton] – 12.45. An awful day and I got so stone cold in the bus. Philip very charming: in a private suite and with his valet in the lounge waiting to take me up to him, Lady Edward Grosvenor and Evan Charteris also there. Lunched with Philip's aunt and cousins at Hove. Then walked back to the Metropole and all drove, in an open car which made me colder than ever, here: then they motored back and I went off to Miss Gabell Smith's, a very tabby cat sort of affair.

26 January. I started off to lunch with David Sassoon (Philip's second cousin and the man I met on Saturday) and go to the theatre with him afterwards. Not looking forward to it. Elderly man I hadn't cared for greatly. To my surprise and relief a very grand home [3] and the usual flunkeys, 2 footmen and a butler. As a matter of fact it was at this house as the guest of David Sassoon's father, that King Edward used to stop. Eight people to lunch and

---

1 The Old Poor House, Castle Banks, built in 1633 as a Workhouse.
2 By Pinero.
3 7 Queen's Gardens, Hove. PS's grandfather owned a mansion at 1, Eastern Terrace, Brighton, where he built a domed family mausoleum, an air-raid shelter in WW2, now The Hanbury Arms.

four of us to the theatre afterwards. But I was really feeling seedy and was thankful to get home.

28 January. Lady Boyle and Mrs Hyeem [4] turned up. Very cordial, yet somehow Jewesses are different. You don't, or I didn't, feel quite at ease with them. For one thing, they are excessively curious.

1 February. Yesterday I just managed to happen on the exact moment when Rosario made his exit. He was locking the door. Signora Rosario was sitting in a motor van on top of the family sticks, her shawl over her head, her aquiline face quite immobile. Rosario has left his pigeons behind and they flap their wings at the closed windows and coo round the chimneys.

9 February. He [Ernest] is very anxious to please, do his duty and give every satisfaction, poor old thing. So I lick my wounds and wonder why never can I be philosophical . . . Took Emma on the hills . . . I am her slave as I was Nelson's. And the God of them both.

4 March. Winifred Fawssett came in after tea and stayed a nice long time. Very full, for one thing, of the ghost or ghosts in their kitchen. One, a rather jovial 'Johnny Walker' sort of gentleman who stands by the sink and doesn't frighten Jeannette the cook at all. The other – simultaneous – nothing to be seen but simply an *effect* which drives you mad with terror.

10 March. Mrs Hyeem 1.30. Went off – the Chinese cousins there. Also a Sir John and Lady Hall; he one of those anomalous men, great big creature with a tiny squeaky voice. She the type of party I had thought extinct, talking of "my cook", "my kitchenmaid" and "you always on visits tip the butler and the housemaid". Walked there and back: partly enjoyed it – don't want too much of Philip's 'Auntie'!

---

4 Mrs Hyeem, elderly aunt of David Sassoon, and his sister Lady Boyle, widow of former governor of Mauritius.

14 March. At night the man brought Ernest's wireless and I do hope it will be a joy to him. Listened in myself for a little, but it bothered me, 10,000 times rather sit by my fire and dream. Funny when I went in to say good night to see him with the evening paper on his knee, ear-phones on his head and he was doing a crossword puzzle in a second paper. Nothing like keeping all the senses going at once!

23 March. Keeping a diary is an awful bore: haven't touched this for a week. But a valuable record and I've never quite forgiven myself for dropping it through 1914–15 (dramatic years!) and burning the 1920 one because it was ugly and full of Burbidge.

25 March. Long talk with Innes[5] about Newcastle House[6], which he says is certainly coming down. He personally regrets it, but has no power. At night I listened in, as Ernest has now got his Frame Aerial, a Beethoven Sonata. Very clear and good, but I don't care for wireless.

26 March. Welfare tells me that Rosario's house could be got for £200 and that Blaker is the lawyer. Wrote to Harold Blaker.

6 April. Went to Brighton. Got at Woolworths 70 candles to put round Ernest's birthday cake.

30 April. Somehow, just now, everything is happy and beautiful. Letter from Collins saying *Seed Pods* is going very well. And I, faithless one (yet I know it isn't one of my best books), was afraid it wouldn't.

2 May. Letter from Ida – told Ernest she was coming! On the hills with Emma and she heard her first cuckoo! Very thrilled and a little bit frightened.

5 Mayor of Lewes.
6 Transformed by Duke of Newcastle in 1717 into a centre for his Whig supporters. AD fought a strenuous campaign each time it was threatened with demolition. The building remains next to the High Court in the High St.

18 May. Ida. [Ernest is diplomatically away] I was feeling really very 'cited and at 4 went off to the station to meet her. Had arranged for Dorothy Elliot[7] to come to tea as she, from childhood, has admired David's black and white work. Also it gave an excuse for using the Rockingham tea service; I wanted Ida to note – and to report! – how beautifully I have arranged myself in every way and how funny it all is, and how sad! After Dorothy Elliot had gone, took Ida all over the house, then we changed our frocks, had our evening grub and talked like mad. She really is a dear, but of course I realise that this visit is a special effort – both sides – and that the crust is too thin for us to walk far together without crashing into a crater!

15 June. Went to Park Lane. At 11.45 off I went for my little razzle-dazzle. Didn't want to, which proves how necessary it has become to go. Taxi to Park Lane. Miss Boyce was sent to entertain me till lunch time. Neither like nor trust that woman and she has eyes like a goat. After lunch to the House of Commons, Philip driving in a little open car. I was put into the Speaker's box and found the whole affair dull though Buchanan, one of the Scotch Labour members, was suspended – entirely, as Philip said, for my benefit! However he went quietly. I had wanted a scrimmage and some policemen. Tea on the terrace where the wind was polar. Lady Cholmondeley turned up, very pleasant and looking lovely – an indigo blue dress, very plain, a large indigo hat with pale blue feathers. Round her neck lots of pearls, real and wonderful. Later I went to see Mrs Gubbay who is ill in bed, also pearls and a lace nightgown and point lace coverlet and pillows! Philip drove me back. We dined and then went to the theatre *Marigold*. Very amusing. He came to my room to bid me goodbye as tomorrow he is flying. *Such* a room – part of my 'Suite' of bedroom, dressing room, bathroom. Funny little me! Once lying on my brocaded sofa by the big window overlooking the Park it occurred to me as quite comically fairytale-ish.

17 June. A little note on my breakfast tray, just saying goodbye. Got up and went out in roasting heat . . . Lovely to get home, lovely to have gone away!

7 Local artist who executed woodcuts of AD's properties.

25 June. After breakfast looked out of window and saw the dear old road-man, clinging desperately to the railings and apparently dying: acute asthma. Got him a chair and some brandy, then fetched Dr Nicholl who inoculated him in the hall and after some tea and a rest he was better.

28 June. Everybody talking about the eclipse [8] and apparently St Anne's churchyard will be full not only of the dead but of the living at 5 tomorrow morning. I really did work jolly well.

29 June. Letter from Lady Bryne [9] of all people. She is divorcing her third husband; some people have all the fun. Wrote and said I would lunch with her on Wed 13th as she wished. She suggests that I turn her 'tragic life story' into a novel!

2 July. Lovely walk and returning met Mr Spokes [10] who came in and gave me a most enthralling account of the anchoress cell, squint and skeleton they've found in the wall [11].

6 July. London. Car met me at the station. Philip as – well, what he always is. A man at lunch, Lord Lee of Fareham [12]. At 2 off to *The Constant Nymph* [13] which I enjoyed very much. Out at 5 and just caught the 5.20 home.

11 July. I got Rosario's key, then I worked like mad till dinner time. At 2 Mrs Miller arrived and, with our frocks tucked well up round us and keeping a sharp look out on our legs, we went over the place. It is vast, filthy, fascinating. She came back to tea and after I went to Harold Blaker's office and told him to offer £200.

8 First time for 200 years a total eclipse of the sun visible in Britain.
9 See 1920 diary, 2 July.
10 Sidney Spokes, surgeon and archaeologist, lived at Castle Place, High St.
11 At St Anne's Church.
12 A great collector. Gave Chequers to the nation in 1920. Uncle of Tam Dicker, see 1936 diary.
13 Dramatisation of Margaret Kennedy's bestselling novel.

20 July. Lady Cholmondeley. Off to London by the 10.49. Streaming rain, naturally in July. Taxi to Kensington Palace Gardens. A delightful house with a big garden and it might as well be in the heart of the country. To lunch Sir William Orpen the painter and also the Marquis of Cholmondeley who proved not only extremely handsome, which I knew, but most charming and interesting (although Mrs Gubbay told me he was stupid and good for nothing but playing games.) After lunch we drove to St James's Theatre and saw Gerald du Maurier [14] in *Indeference,* a play neither of us cared for, tea at Rumpelmayer's and I came home by the 6.40.

22 July. In the morning I went over Rosario's house with Fuller, the surveyor. It will cost a power of a lot of money to do up and something more than money to get rid of innumerable live stock which, without doubt, lurk in the woodwork. Don't feel quite so happy about it. However I suppose creosote and fumigation would do the trick.

27 July. Lady Bryne. Got to South Audley Street. Alice's face is a mask. She talked incessantly under her breath through lunch, hinting at horrible acts on the part of Sir William whom she means to divorce. These acts she elaborated later on in the smoking room where we were alone. I came away quite dithery and not sure whether she is mad or he is a Monster!

28 July. Letter from Harold Blaker. They will take £190 clear for Rosario's house! . . . I was so excited and my heart won't leave off beating or, rather, I'm afraid it will.

10 August. Emma caught her first butterfly and I couldn't get it away from her wicked paws. I really am just now enjoying my life like mad! . . . Yesterday I met Mr Beard [15], a silly little A-ar-ar-ss I don't care for. He said: "You'll have a row of cottages where the Malt House [16] is some day".

14 Actor Manager, son of George Du Maurier who wrote *Trilby*.
15 George Beard, tenant of Brack Mount and owner of Beards Brewery, which closed in 1958.
16 The Maltings, next to CPH, used by Beards Brewery and now the County Record Office where these diaries are stored.

15 August. I go to Lympne. Off I went feeling it a bore to go (there or anywhere) but knowing I would enjoy myself like mad . . . Heaps of people: Sir Louis Mallet, so nice to see him again; Lord and Lady Stanley; he quite nice but with a nervous twitch of the face, she with a face like a mask. Also a man I later rather liked – a Colonel Cooper (he had just lost a Dalmatian dog and that was our link), also a rather mystic and fragile young man Lord Ivor Churchill [17] (he was so disgusted with the weather that he flew to Paris next morning and was seen no more). He has taken The French House and Philip is doing it for him.

16 August. Heaps of Air Force men drifting in and out, a Mrs Clive Wigram, her husband private secretary to the King, came to lunch. I forget what happened. The whole thing, especially at night with everyone dressed and never less than 15 or 20 at dinner, was very decorative. Sometimes we sat at 2 round tables and sometimes one long one. I again met Lord Edward Grosvenor [18], a vast and very nice person.

17 August. A perfect day for a wonder. In the morning Philip, Sir Louis and I sat in the garden (never saw much of Mrs Gubbay who is always playing either golf or tennis). Lunch out of doors and lots of us as usual. Afterwards Philip and I alone in a little Essex – he driving and the chauffeur behind – to Folkestone, where there were water sports and he was giving the prizes . . . Back to Lympne, then off in 3 cars to see Leeds Castle. A Mrs Charles Kimber, one of the party, was a great friend of Sargent's. Old but still beautiful. After Leeds Castle went to see Otham, a lovely old house where Sir Louis once lived, and which he redeemed, originally occupied by 6 families of peasants. Very cold driving home, but I had a hot bath and felt better. The boxing Marquess of Clydesdale to dinner, a quite speechless young man.

19 August. Philip went to London, taking Mrs Hunter with him. Quiet lunch, just the four us, Gubbays, Sir Louis, me. After lunch she golfed at Sandgate,

17 2nd son of Duke and Duchess of Marlborough (Consuelo Vanderbilt.)
18 Died 1929, his widow married Evan Charteris in 1930.

Sir Louis and I motored on to Folkestone, where he wanted to buy a house-wife as he's going to stay in some remote place without a man-servant. No luck: finally got a wretched thing with neither buttons nor needles. Dead tired when we got back and found a whole new bunch arrived for the weekend. Miss Grenfell, very pretty; Mrs Dudley Coats, supposed to be a beauty but with a face like a doll; Lord and Lady Westminster, both simple and nice. Mrs Coats only buried her husband 10 days ago, after behaving devilishly to him. Also a Mrs Montagu, widow of the Secretary for India and a daughter of Lord Sheffield. She renounced the Christian Faith on marrying a Jew, and part of the rite was to spit on the Cross. I went up to my room, dizzy with people and hadn't been there long before there was a knock at the door and – to my joy – Philip walked in. At dinner met Maurice Baring again.

20 August. Raging, pouring day, so I was glad to be going home. Sat by a big fire reading all the morning. By the way another nice man, Sir John Ramsay arrived . . . Every evening as you dress for dinner a footman brings round cocktails, which I take to as a duck to water! Motored to Ashford with Lord Westminster whose aunt, Lady Londesborough has a bungalow at Kingston Ridge. Home, to my exceeding joy, in spite of the fact that I enjoyed myself enormously.

21 August. Mrs Miller to tea as usual, and a very piquant contrast after all the 'lords and ladies'.

22 August. Wrote to Philip and sent him the books I'd promised. Sent Sir Louis Mallet needles, pins and buttons for his housewife.

7 September. Ernest came home [from London] tired but successful. He is to have £100 from *Tit-Bits* [19] for a book on puzzles. Only a compilation – old stuff.

19 Weekly magazine, founded in 1881, closed 1989. The name survives as *Titbits International*.

3 October. [To Worthing] . . . Ida arrived with plants for me and also sandwiches, with the suggestion that on such a heavenly day we should lunch from the end of the pier! She told me how hard up they were and that it was just on the cards that Mond [20] might find a job for David in Canada! I said in that case, as it amounted to death at our age, David and I would have a whole day out and she and Ernest be damned! And we agreed that in view of everybody being over 60, this keeping me and David apart was becoming absurd. Yet I'm sure Ernest would be miserable.

29 October. Ghastly letter from Ida. They are literally on their beam ends. I wrote at once suggesting that David should apply for a Civil List pension [21] telling him, or rather her, how he should do it.

1 November. After tea Mrs Miller and I with Miss Falconer to the re-burial of the bones of the anchoress at St Anne's. Simple affair: just a bishop in cope and mitre, a few prayers, then "May she rest in peace" and "May light perpetual shine upon her". Moved me profoundly. Before that, after church in the morning, Mrs Innes said: "But she belongs to the R.C's. St Anne's Church was [Catholic] before the Reformation". Wrote to Fr Rawlings – couldn't he preach a sermon to convince these idiots that she is not the R.C's?

21 November. Every morning I wake to the delicious sound of workmen hammering away at my Poor House! Am living through one of the several thrilling times of my life . . . the whole affair is going to be lovely, so lovely that I want to live with one leg in this house, one in that. Makes me wonder whether, at the last, I shall go back to my old love, oak rafters and furniture yet the lofty airy Georgian effect of this is so gay and wholesome. If I were left a widow perhaps I would sell this and retire there? Who knows!

23 November. Just – 11 – been down to the 'Old Poor House of St John's'. It's too exciting for words. I must get to work and make money to pay for all this delirious fun. I did work quite nicely and I was so happy in a sleek, whisker-washing way all day long.

20 Mond Nickel Company, who had commissioned David.
21 Granted by royal bounty to those who had rendered service in science or arts.

7 December. Philip. To London, and oh so cold all day except when I was in Philip's house: a great big wood fire, footmen in red waistcoats, an enormous jar of white lilies and all the rest. He gave me a charming brooch for Christmas from Cartiers, jade and a great topaz. I came home by the 4.30 and oh so glad to get away from London.

21 December. I went in the morning to Brighton taking my mother a pudding, a cake, some chocolate and some pears. And all the time feeling downright ill, longing for bed . . . Also, feeling a sad, dim excitement, went and bought a toy boat for David. Told Ida I should, but no letter! And Ernest I do not tell at all. Wiser not. I wrote on a card the Provencal fisherman's proverb, 'Lord be good to me. Thy sea is so wide, my boat is so small' and put in the boat a toy sailor.

22 December. Vere came . . . I shopped, Christmassed and felt awful.

27 December. And now the fun begins! My temperature early in the morning over 103. Dr Vallance sent for. Acute capillary bronchitis and (although I was not told this until afterwards) penumonia. He told me I should be in bed 3 weeks, but he told Vere 6! A nurse, plasters on my back, Vere in the room all night. I, unable to breathe, and then ghastly pain in my side.

29 December. Everyone very kind, leaving cards, bringing flowers. Vere most adorably tender. Poor Ernest desperately anxious.

30 December. So there I lay choking but with just life enough left to like to hear the tapping and hammering at the Poor House.

31 December. And so the year ended . . .

1928

3 January. At 10 the Nurse came and got me out of bed. The sofa was pulled up round the fire, but even then I was too weak to walk alone to it . . .

7 January. Philip sent some pheasants, also he offered to lend me either Trent Park or Lympne to convalesce in. But I had decided to go to Hastings with Charlotte.

1 February. And now I really *begin* my diary! . . . At 10.30 just as I was trying to work, and it's so hideously hard to get back, who should arrive but Mr Sotheran – nervous long hands, flowing tie and cape, luxuriant brown mop (sure it's a wig!).

3 February. Again for a walk in the morning . . . as I said to Ernest when I got home, the High Street is strewn with potential corpses! Everyone seems mad, ill or dead.

6 February. At 4 old Mrs Grant arrived and stayed till 6 talking of the lost tribes of Israel. She is quite rabid on Joanna Southcott[1] and she also said that the late coal strike was prophesied in the Bible. Isaiah 47, verse 14[2]. She told me that years ago she went to a Salvation Army meeting and that a man there testified to his conversion. He was once a wife beater, but his wife cut up small the strap he beat her with and put them into a pie with a few bits of steak. He ate some, was very ill, and repented and 'found Jesus'! (Might make a short story). While I was trying to recover from all this, Evelyn Fawssett arrived . . .

1 19th century religious fanatic who left boxes containing 'revelations', one to be opened on 11.7.27 in the presence of a Bishop. The contents consisted of a pistol, pamphlets, trinkets, a night cap and a book called *The Surprises of Love*.
2 'Behold, they shall be as stubble, the fire shall burn them, they shall not deliver themselves of the flame, there shall not be a coal to warm at, nor fire to sit before it.'

'13 February. Went to Mrs Sotheran, as it cleared up. She quite loving and a very pathetic figure: lying beneath a wonderful quilt of silk patchwork wrapped in beautiful lace and looking absolutely transparent.

15 February. Letter from Margery ... such a wonderful letter of devotion and anxiety that I sat and, more or less, blissfully howled. Also Jamie wrote and Barney sent a drawing and Christopher sent a picture of the house they are building and Margery sent a scarf. Margery is like her father: full of profound tenderness, but it takes a devil of a lot to bring it to the surface ...

5 March. Such a day of rush, joy and brilliant sun. At 9.30 to Mass, then to Mr Gale's letter box dropping in a packet of chocolate, it being his 71st birthday. Then to Poor House ... the whole home including everything (even the housewarming) works out at £530. So whether I let for £60 or sell for £1,000 I've done well.

12 March. ... then off with Emma delivering notes of invitation, then home to a pile of letters, most of them acceptances.

13 March. After dinner interviewed Mrs Holloway, the new owner of Stevenses (an unpleasant saturnine person but capable) and arranged with her for the tea: "a dainty tea", 1/6 a head with buffet, 2 waitresses and silver vases filled with daffodils thrown in. Also thrown in some forms for the aged and infirm to sit on and "upon them I will put my yellow brocade cushions"!

17 March. At 4.30 they turned up ... Mrs Miller before Joan was helped out of the car whispering to me: "Of course you know that Joan can't stand". [Joan Fulleylove has been in hospital]. This sent me mad with terror, for I am still as weak as a rat and quite incapable of one bit of extra work. Then tea, Joan poor dear flopping like a walrus on the sofa ... at 8 Dr Nicholl came. At 9, thank heaven, I filled 3 water bottles, gave Joan her medicine, had a raw egg myself and we got to bed.

18 March. Joan in bed all day. The Nurse says, as the doctor says, "nerves" and with nerves I have so little patience. Brutal – perhaps? Not sure.

20 March. She [Joan] comes down at dinner time, all her meals are taken up into the drawing room and she either rolls on the sofa, rolling my best cushions into balls or squats before the fire on her elbows and knees like a four footed animal. I have the *greatest possible* difficulty in keeping my temper. Rushed to death, tired to death, knocked off my work, turned off my own sofa and that great hefty woman with *nothing* the matter with her – having a nurse to wash and dress her, even giving her a bath, which is disgusting.

22 March. Met Dr Nicholl. He says she is neurasthenic, (modern word for hysteria) and must be shaken out of it. I told him I could do nothing and that I really could not stand much more of it.

23 March. Meanwhile my sweet pretty Poor House is being dressed for the party! Fenders taken down and chairs hired (in addition to the forms) and I've put heaps of daffodils and hyacinths. And dear Mrs Bates brought me a great big bunch of wild plum blossom. Insisted on Joan coming down to have a look at it. But she won't come to the party.

24 March. The party was an immense success. I had asked 80 people and 70 came[3]. I wore my figured crepe de chine frock with Philip's brooch and over it the pink coat. A black hat. My reward was afterwards, when Ernest said, taking my hand: "You do these things so beautifully".

26 March. Reeves[4] the photographer came. Thank goodness she [Joan] goes. Somebody else can take it on. I'm exhausted.

6 April, Good Friday. Mass of the Pre-Sanctified at 10. What a relief that no Three Hours. Too emotional. And religious emotion good for none of us, especially bad for Ernest.

3 *The Sussex County Herald* of 31.3.28 reported the party and guest list on its front page. Joan Fulleylove, it revealed, made the 8 stained glass windows for Khartoum Cathedral.
4 High St. photographers founded by Edward Reeves in 1855, oldest in the country, if not the world.

26 April. Poor House to be blest at 11 o'clock. It was such a lovely service . . .
it was a lovely morning too and all the windows open . . . all day long I was
happy: you always are if you practise religion. Went to see Mr Gale and told
him he must dig himself out.

1 May. Poor House article out in the *Sussex County Magazine* [5]. Met Arthur
Beckett [Editor] in the High Street and he gave me half a dozen copies. Sent
one to Ida – for David. So silly not to send it to him direct. For what the deuce
do I care for Ida?!

7 May. Quite beset and have been since Saturday by awful terror. Those
brown marks on the Poor House wall in the kitchen near the skirting board
may be splashes of creosote or they may be --- [6] . . . Kent says his men never
complained even of a flea. Went there: thought I'd count the marks but didn't.
No electric men there. The place has been blest and I ought to have faith
'nothing wavering'. But then my common sense says to me (drat it!) does
incense and holy water do away with --- ? I wish Kent would come.

22 June. . . . a nice young couple called [Mr & Mrs Hill]. Enchanted with the
Poor House and it really looks as they would take it.

1 July. Quite a peaceful day and Mr Gale turned up after 5 weeks interval. I
think he looks very ill.

6 July. Philip . . . to Trent. It was an Air Force party so only aerial folk got
presented to the Prince [7]. He is rather insignificant and awfully nervy. Lady
Cholmondeley looked lovely, Mrs Gubbay in widow's black, poor dear, very
tar-brushey. Back to London . . . I felt it wasn't worth it.

5 Vol 2, 1928.
6 Vermin, AD's terror. There were none.
7 Prince of Wales, later Edward VIII.

7 July. Wire from Philip. When am I coming to Lympne? S'pose I will go, but it shall be 2 nights, not a week . . . Called on Mrs Sotheran. Didn't see her, only the nurse. She is very ill[8].

21 July. Winifred Fawsett came at 9 and stayed till 10. Such a pretty creature and full of humour. I wish she'd marry.

25 July. When I was in my bath, the whole plan of my book *By Consent* fell into shape and now I can enjoy doing it.

3 September. Great day in my simple annals! The Hills come into the Old Poor House. And a thundering headache as the result. They, the tenants, arrived at 4. I ran down and asked them to come and have some tea, but she was so tired, so I sent Winnie down with a big pot and some cake. What moments one lives! As I got into my bedroom at 7 to change my frock, a huge furniture van went perilously past the garden wall to the Poor House. And when I went to bed at 8.30, (a nervous wreck and dosed with aspirin) looked out again and "all of a sudding" lights broke out from all the windows and my Poor House looked as big as a palace.

4 September. Saw the Hills who insisted on my going over the Old Poor House. But with other folks in it and their furniture it is lost, gone. However I had my bit of poetry out of it. And I am now to rake in solid cash.

8 September. Did a lot of odd jobs: going to stay with Philip to meet half the peerage does make you pull yourself (which is your clothes!) together. Went for my Dutch clock. Clockmaker [Peskett] very contemptuous. Quite worn out and raised his brows sardonically when I said I'd have it back anyhow as it was old and pretty. "Did I *think* so?" I do like a tradesman to be a tradesman. This one did not go behind his counter, but leaned over me gracefully, his elbow on a show case. Moreover he wore a blue yachting sort of coat with brass buttons. Only wanted a cocked hat to turn him into an admiral.

8 She died in August. In October AD hears that Mr Southeran has been run over and killed at Hyde Park Corner.

10 September. I go to Philip. Arrived at Lympne. Sir Louis Mallet there with a patch over his eye: shingles. Lady Westmorland [9] also there.

11 September. Off we went in 2 cars: men-servants and the grub in one – and lunched on the beach near Dymchurch. Then motored to the leper hospital at Harbledown and afterwards to Canterbury Cathedral. (I am writing this a week after and am hanged if I can remember all the people I met.)

12 September. In the morning Sir Louis and I motored to Folkestone . . . in the afternoon we all went to see Lympne Castle: tenanted by Sir Thomas Beecham's brother who some years back got 3 years imprisonment for manslaughter – ran down some children and then motored on. In the afternoon an enormous garden party to constituents – about 200 – and a band.

13 September. Philip's agent from Trent came to lunch . . . Others came, but who – Heaven knows: lots. The weather was lovely. We were out of doors all the time and I read two wonderful books *The Bridge of San Luis Ray* and *Death Comes for the Archbishop*.[10] At teatime, by the way, David Sassoon arrived.

14 September. Lady Westmorland left. She was so nice and asked me to stay with her. But life isn't long enough (nor income large enough) to do much of this aristocratic, plutocratic stint. Philip is different and our relationship is now quite defined and delightful. Lots of people to tea. Captain and Mrs Herbert, Lady Victor Paget and at night Wing Commander Louis Grieg and his wife. She and I instant friends. We both love the Isle of Wight, both have a Dalmatian dog and are neither of us very musical.

15 September. Noël Coward to lunch. He brought with him (as Philip said) "a woman" and she was a specimen. Orange coloured lips and an evil face. Poisonous creature, so Mrs Gubbay said; but probably the only kind of woman who will be seen with Noël Coward. She hinted that he was of an unspeakable viciousness. Seemed frank and simple enough: she says they

9 Countess of Westmorland, wife of the 14th Earl and mother of Julian Fane, the writer, who lived in Lewes.
10 By Thornton Wilder and W Cather respectively.

always are. Horrible! At 3.30 left, travelling with David Sassoon which meant taking a 1st class ticket! Heavenly welcome from Emma, who gave one hard sob. Ernest also delighted to see me. Winnie too.

18 September. Just 3 years ago since my precious sweet Nelson died and 4 years since Winnie came. She is to have a rise!

21 September. Go to Freshwater Bay. The whole affair was a great success. Weather perfect, situation perfect. Hotel very comfortable and Ernest too amiable to be true!

26 September. In the morning Ernest actually went with me on the Downs to see Tennyson's monument.

4 October. Miss Doyle died. Dear little Miss Doyle.

8 October. Very thrilling going to tea at The Old Poor House. It looks very nice. I sat eating and drinking and conversing politely in that room which once was labelled 'for married couples only' and could not believe myself. At 6 I went to Vespers of the Dead for Agnes Doyle . . . At 9 to 9.30 I go to the church and watch by Miss Doyle's coffin.

9 October. At 2.30 Agnes Doyle's funeral. At the back of the church, later, saw Mrs Burbidge alone and said if she was going on to the grave might we go together? She was glad to and so was I. And we actually laughed over what I called "our historic row".

12 October. To tea with Mrs Miller and her sister. Two such incorrigible pieces of the coarsest sandpaper! For instance – on prostitution . . . "Why not take money for it? The labourer is worthy of his hire, and after all it is a way of making money."

18 October. Most lovely photographs from Lenare. Didn't know I was so handsome! After tea little Mrs Hill turned up complaining of smoky chimneys. I perceive that I am not going to get my £80 a year without a certain amount of trouble and expenditure.

25 October. I feel perfectly awful, lost, bereft, left hanging: Vere writes that she has married Sullivan! Of course I'm glad for her, if he treats her decently. Wrote her, sent her a little Tunbridge box . . .

7 November. Ernest off to London. A most successful day. *Daily News* contract renewed for another year.

12 November. Really very amusing writing to Ida which means writing between the lines to him. Wonder if he's subtle enough to get me? Men are a blunt lot – except Philip.

14 November. Another thrilling day. The electric men came to put electric light in the drawing room.

15 November. All the morning I sat trying to persuade myself that I liked it . . .

16 November. The beastly temper of the last week came to a head at breakfast . . . at supper I was treated to a pat on the head: his way of saying he's sorry! So – for the sake of peace – wagged my tail.

20 November. Sent off a photograph to Ida, by request (but not for her, as she jolly well knows).

3 December. Went for such a lovely walk on such a haunting dark December day. Emma kept running back and licking my hand, her eyes saying plainly: "Isn't this beautiful?"

5 December. Ernest to London to see Tom . . . gave a most amusing report of Tom's mistress: "Quite presentable: as much a lady as Mrs Miller". Short skirted, shingled, plump and podgy. Came into the room, was introduced and put up her cheek! Poor Ernest (with the air of confessing a minor infidelity) "I had to kiss her. What else could I do?!" After this she subsided, joined in the conversation and called him "Mr Ernest".

20 December. . . . at night the north wind blew, with a moaning, musical sound, like Paganini playing on his one string. I sent Philip biscuits, Vere baby clothes . . . Ida some chocolates, David a magazine . . .

24 December. At night Philip sent a turkey. That's 2 turkeys to eat. Very busy day. Cards, letters and flowers kept pouring in ...

25 December, Christmas Day. Communion at 7.45, then breakfast, presents: I gave Ernest a walking stick and he gave me a bag. More church! A little dim walk in the afternoon by the river, just me and Emma. Basement rooms and front parlours all lighted up and curtains drawn. Doleful sounds of festivity – mouth organs or gramophones – stealing out into the mist.

28 December. Ida wrote. A great deal too much of the 'we' and 'us'. I wonder if David feels the same; a resentment at her standing between us! What did she say once: "You two would step over my dead body to get at each other". It was true then, hideously. I expect that now poor David is too ill, worn, old, to feel very fiery!

All through Christmas Ernest was seedy and kept to his room . . . he feels the nervous strains of a visitor [Joan] in the house, so it becomes a strain, however fond you are of the visitor. I do love Emma so much. And I may, therefore, be laying up heartbreak for myself.

1929

Why do I bother to make notes when I don't mean to write any more?

2 days after this came Pinker's contract from Collins: 5 books, instead of the usual 3 and much better terms. Signed it, being human. So I am not to 'retire' and need not badger Philip to get me on the Civil List, unless I go 'dotty'.

3 January. He's [Ernest] quite all right now that the home is empty [Joan has left]. So to placate myself for all my unkind, dangerous thoughts I went and bought two red herrings for his breakfast – he adores them . . . Charming letter from Philip offering to take me to a matinée.

5 January. At night went through my 1923–4–5–6 diaries trying to find some entry about Tom's (alleged) sons 'Douglas, Renée, Kenneth'. I feel sure that when first we were told of their (presumed) existence that there were 4. But I found nothing. Very provoking how in a diary one always seems to leave out the essential thing.

18 January. *By Consent*[1] proofs came . . . Pouring day and the greengrocer's daft errand boy arriving at the back door dripping wet said joyfully: "This rain will make the grass seed I sowed on my mother's grave come up."

6 February. Oh my goodness! Have just, at last, done the first thousand words of my new book! Ernest goes from bad to worse, and can anyone wonder. All day and every day he sits doubled up in an easy chair, except for one move when he comes out to dinner. Tea he's given up: but I insist on a glass of hot milk. This is taken in to him. And (also taken in to him) a bowl of Benger's at 7. And then, still all huddled up in a heap by the fire, interminable wireless. Sometimes I feel that the gloom and the lack of heart that there is to everything will send me crazy.

---

1 Published by Collins.

9 February. I was thinking so very much of David all day and dreamed of him at night. Wonder if he was thinking of me! Probably not. These emotional things do not, as a rule, go in pairs.

22 February. *What* a lovely playful life: when one feels well and when the Dudeney Black Dog is so far in his kennel that you can hardly believe he's there. Air like wine and golden sun – I struck work and have put in a whole morning . . . sent 3 articles to *Morning Post*.

6 March. Winnie brought up a note from Mrs Harvey: Mr Gale had 'passed away' and, quite to my own amazement, I turned round on the pillow and cried. Went down, found Ernest in such a mad tomfool state that I went off for Dr Vallance. Nothing wrong that the idiot couldn't put right himself by taking a dose instead of pestering me with endless information. Dr Vallance suggested castor oil which I had to give him in coffee.

7 March. Worn out, right through to the bone. I told Ernest that if he had a whole hospital full of nurses I should go to London [to Philip] just the same – and I did, but it was no good and I would rather have been at home in bed. Even my vitality is giving out, and that's saying a lot. Saw the silver exhibition [2]. After lunch sat on the balcony: quite a hot lovely day. Mrs Gubbay very regal in black velvet, pearls and some diamond bracelets: as the Duke and Duchess of York were coming to tea and to see the silver. I came home by the 4.35. Two nice things have happened. Pinker has sold *The Permanent Way* for £30 and – of more import – the *American Saturday Review* has Putnam's full page advert of *Brighton Beach* [3] with some very good notices.

9 March. Went to see Mrs Harvey to find out when my dear Mr Gale is to be buried . . . [wrote] to Lady Demetriardi's [4] kennel man about mating Emma with 'Odd Trick'.

2 Every Spring PS organised a charity exhibition at Park Lane.
3 Published by Collins 1928, story of a woman of 40 who lived 'backwards' and became a child of 8. Later dramtised in West End.
4 Elder daughter of Mr & Mrs Bates, married to Sir Stephen Demetriardi, influential business man and later High Sheriff of Sussex.

11 March. Mr Gale's funeral at 12 . . . a great trial, and really to see [Ernest] standing at the edge of the grave taking his last look and so tottery that I was afraid he'd fall in, was heart-rending. But I comforted myself by reflecting that some of it *might* be pose! He is always anxious to look the part!

13 March. I went in and he [Ernest] was on a chair utterly collapsed, unable to move or undress himself. I rushed down for whiskey, gave him a little neat and got him to bed. Gave him a kiss. The way he looked and the way he said: "Good night, my darling" wiped out every injury. I came in here, sat by the fire and an awful storm blew up in me. I felt that if he died then the world went out so far as I was concerned. But pulled myself together. Must. For heaven knows what lies in front of me.

25 March. Emma to be mated. At 10 Tingley the vet arrived and we motored over to Lady Demetriardi's leaving poor Emma in a loose box.

26 March. Off we went, Tingley and I at 10, to fetch the bride home! Everything very successful and no reason why we shouldn't have puppies.

31 March, Easter Sunday. Went as arranged to call him [Ernest] at 7.30 for communion. Found he had been violently sick in the night, looked like blood and [he] was in great pain . . . got Dr Vallance . . . He, from the nature of the sickness, told me it was cancer of the stomach. No cure, nor had he strength for an operation. I was absolutely crushed.

1 April. Vere's baby born: a boy. Such days followed! Kent [builder] promised to come today which he nobly did, Ernest's study being filthy and Dr Vallance is anxious to get his bed in there, as he'll have a more cheerful look out and also it will be easier to wait on him and he can have a bigger fire.

5 April. Nothing from Margery! Wrote her and told her how ill her father was.

10 April. Ernest's birthday, and his room is like a florist's shop with tulips and daffodils. They keep on arriving and Margaret Hill said grimly: "He'll think it's his funeral"!

12 April. Wrote Philip saying Ernest was ill and my visit to him, therefore, was out of the question.

30 April. Nice walk after tea. Emma's figure very robust, almost ashamed to go out with her!

1 May. And 24 years since David and I went to early Mass at Prestbury. Ah my darling. Yes I did (and do? love you) . . . Dusart came and clipped Ernest's hair and beard.

2 May. Philip sent his book[5] – wrote him.

9 May. My mother died. I came home from Mass and found Emily's letter. Went off at once. Saw her – my poor little ancient, *tiny* mother - in her coffin.

11 May. Funeral 11.30. Off I went, carrying a really lovely cross: tulips, irises, narcissi. Found all Emily's cronies there . . . and one room chock-a-block with wreaths. It was a most awful trial and Emily and I cried just a little, but not enough to lose dignity, when her very swagger coffin (too swagger) was lowered into the grave with her dear little wasted old body inside.

18 May. My sister: after 3 . . . Emily isn't lonely: she can feel nothing except that she is free after 10 years. We went through poor Mother's things. I've got her gold watch and chain: one of her gold bracelets and the little ring she had for her 18th birthday. Also we share the dessert service. Emily, quite properly, takes the rest. Then we went to the grave and I got home about 7.

23 May. At 6.45 Ernest's bell rang. Very alarmed and half asleep, rolled out of bed and downstairs. Emma had just produced – in her own bed and with no fuss – a puppy. Seven more followed and by 10 everything was happily over: 'Mother and children doing well'.

5 *The Third Route*, published by Heinemann. PS's account of his 17,000 mile trip as Air Minister in 1927 to India and Middle East. He met TE Lawrence who became a close friend.

24 May. Emma the heroine of the occasion. She has seen various visitors, but doesn't welcome them. I've put two screens, one each side of her box, so that she gets a little seclusion.

14 June. At 1 the specialist arrived. I sat, a very calm Victorian lady (to the eye!) doing crochet and waiting for the verdict. Got it: it is not cancer, thank God.

16 June. Took the puppies all out and put them on the little lawn in the sun for 5 minutes. They were delighted but poor Emma was worried to death.

17 June. Dr Fawssett died. Met Winifred going to church. She said: "My dear, it is all over and I'm going to church to make my thanksgiving". A perfect day: seems, to pagan me, horrible that any one should be dead . . .

19 June. At 12 off to Dr Fawssett's funeral. A most impressive affair as he was a Freemason and the police surgeon.

20 June. Rather a wonderful meeting: Vere [and her mother and husband] and the baby came up . . . Vere sort of threw the infant at her mother: "Hold it, and let me hug her". Darling Vere! A little mother, and it is a very sweet baby. Smiled at me and I think it was a really, truly smile. We all had tea in the garden; then the Sullivans went off.

1 July. Ernest went and got weighed. He has put on 4 ounces in 3 days. Now weighs nearly 9 stone. Grievously inadequate weight for such a big man.

2 July. Wrote to Philip, congratulating him on being made a Privy Councillor.
4 July. Letter from Philip: hollow, affable, airy. I expect Margery is right: he is unreal and a person of dreams. The realities are to me, now, so threatening that I can't possibly bother about fantasy.

5 July. Dear Ernest sat in the garden, very wan, but enjoying the look of the six puppies as they played about in their enchanting way . . .

6 July. It came on to pour at 1.30. Winnie rushed out and fetched the puppies in. And they've been screaming with temper . . . they love the garden. Emma goes to the top of the stairs and scolds them in high squeaks.

18 July. Ernest *actually played* Bowls. I started on the final phase of *Travellers' Rest* [6]. In the afternoon a wire from Philip: 'Alas – must postpone'. Was, beyond measure thankful: all this wealth and this dressing up oppresses me and I'd get out of the Lympne visit if I could.

19 July. Wire from Philip. Will I go on Friday? Suppose I must. Wired I would. Probably quite good for me.

26 July. Philip. At 3.5 departed. At 5.30 motored to Trent, from Park Lane. Philip and Mrs Gubbay on the terrace, and it appears I arrived half an hour after the Queen had departed. Philip very charming. We had a long talk after Mrs Gubbay had taken herself off. I feel certain that woman dislikes me more and more.

27 July. Most of the morning in the gardens with Philip and the gardens are lovely. To lunch, Lady Ancaster and I never saw a woman more made up (her 'face rent' to quote Isaiah) or with bigger pearls. After lunch to play golf Lord and Lady Cholmondeley and Mr Charteris (don't like that man, feel sure he isn't good). At 4 motored back to Victoria. So lovely to get home: so lovely to have got away!

11 August. At night I sat and cried by the window in his bedroom alone. He looks so thin and is so exhausted. When I bade him good night we both broke down, suddenly. Terrible! Yet a relief from dry speechless misery . . .

14 August. Poor Ernest consented to go [to a throat specialist]. Miss Parker telephoned and made an appointment for 12.30 on Friday. The Hills will very kindly motor us in . . . how it is I work, God only knows. Ernest in

---

6 Published Collins 1930.

profound and speechless gloom, poor thing. The puppies slowly departing – like the 10 little nigger boys[7] . . .

16 August. Dr Hutchison, throat specialist, 12.30 . . . Agonising wait. Saw the doctor after and he says the growth at the side is so immense that he simply cannot see the larynx. The danger is that Ernest may choke: in which case tracheotomy. I pray God he may die before it comes to that. Oh the cloud of horror that hangs over us! But I simply must not give way and cry.

21 October. Quite a happy birthday, yet so sad. Ernest so weak that he didn't feel he could get up in the drawing room, yet did, because it was my birthday. Signed the contract for 5 novels!

22 October. After this a peaceful feminine morning, machining the 8 table napkins cut off from the borders of the vast tablecloth[8] my father marked so boldly in 1873. There was his signature; as a young man – 31. And he's been dead 51 years and I, an old woman past 60, sit machining that damask.

24 October. Then I went to Mr Warren's[9] sale, the last day . . . fabulous prices, an Elizabethan oak table over £2,000, a Chippendale couch £6. 5. 0.

27 October. Dear Ernest came up to see me, so breathless, so thin. He gripped my wrist hard and said, lying tenderly: "Darling. Pull yourself together. I am getting better every day".

28 October. Ernest came up . . . he spoke of his steady wasting and said: "There is mischief somewhere. I am getting as thin as a consumptive". Is it possible that he doesn't guess or won't he admit it even to his own mind? He said "I'm

7 AD keeps one, called Spangles.
8 From her mother's effects.
9 Edward Warren died December 1928. The extraordinary contents of Lewes House, including Rodin's *The Kiss*, were auctioned by Rowland Gorringe but the sculpture did not meet its reserve of £9,000. It was privately bought by a friend of EW and loaned to The Tate Gallery in 1939. In 1955 the Tate purchased it for a nominal £7,500.

a doomed man". I said, as carelessly as I could: "We are all doomed, but the date varies."

29 October. . . . it is so difficult to hear what he says, he's so husky. I went to bed and cried, but not too much. Just a little. . . . it is plain to me now, as he slips away, that love for David was partly poetry, partly physical desire, all tangled up together. But with Ernest is my life and the tradition of 45 years.

12 November. Nice to get away from home . . . saw all the blinds down at poor David Sassoon's great chunk of a house on the Hove front. So I suppose he's dead.

27 November. So heart-rent, what with Ernest's long illness and Margery's 7 weeks' silence that I wrote to her, my 3rd letter since I heard – and more fool I! If she doesn't want to write and doesn't care enough to have to write, why should I care. Enclosed a cheque £1.10, ten shillings each for Christmas for the 3 elder children . . . Sale tomorrow. I must and will have that garden [10].

28 November. Have got the garden for £45. On top of that arrives Wycherley in Batup's car. Batup had bought the 6 [Mount] cottages [11] for £200 and offered them to me, through Wycherley, at £220. Won't take a penny less, but will pay Wycherley's commission £5. Ernest agreed with me and Wycherley that to let them fall into the hands of a rough character like Batup would very much injure the Old Poor House. So I've got 'em! Margaret Hill comes and plays Corelli duets with Ernest. Ernest enjoyed it and played beautifully.

3 December. Went over the cottages. They are all right, darling little born almshouses. But the tenants are an awful slum lot. No doubt shall be able to get them into line. *Must* and *mean* to!

10 Garden with lean-to beside Mount Cottages on edge of town wall. The lean-to then known as 7 Castle Banks, now The Trap House.
11 1–6 Mount Cottages, opposite OPH.

13 December. Met Kent who says the cottages (repairs) will be about £15 per cottage. More than I thought. Been frenziedly working out on paper how much I've got and how much I shall have to shell out. These material affairs destroy your imagination: but to sit by the fire and dream about how they'll look when done is most entrancing.

20 December. Philip sent me a lovely brooch. That cheered me up a bit – and what a lot of lovely brooches I've got . . .

21 December. Grimacing and groaning at dinner time. Got shouted at and called "A Liar" for protesting. Is it any wonder – after so long – that I'm worn out and (although I dread his dying) yet want this torture ended?

28 December. Every morning . . . I go to the cupboard and read bits of old diaries – at this date. Very foolish thing to do! Yet how glad I am that, all these years, I've kept a diary. Emily very sympathetic, I very responsive, yet both of us remaining aloof. Gave her the black flowered muslin frock, also the pink stockinette coat. She delighted: "Saves me the bother of thinking out clothes for myself"! Incomprehensible attitude.

31 December. Goodbye 1929. Not one good word to say for you.

1930

11 January. Bought Ernest a bunch of violets. Met him just coming down stairs about 12.30 incredibly weak and wasted: 'a frame of a man'. I feel frantic. I didn't know till now how much he means. And he is slipping away from me so fast: in a sense he has already gone. Too tired to come up to tea. So I sit here alone, except for the two dear dogs, and wonder what it will be like in this house when he never comes up.

12 January. Another frightful gale: 'worst in living memory' the newspapers say, but they always do say that . . . Mrs Miller told me of a widow – old – who had never left off 'weeds' and had a new rig made by the dressmaker. These she took without unpacking to Lincoln on a visit to her daughter. She opened the box and found a bride's dress, the dressmaker had sent the wrong box. This ought to make a short story.

14 January. Worked in the morning and how I work, through this time of agony, God only knows. No letters, but a wire from Philip: 'Am fetching you out to lunch on Friday'. Wrote him. I may as well go, but no heart in anything and feel a brute for going.

17 January. My 'dearest Philip' turned up in a Rolls-Royce with lunch which he proposed we should eat on the Downs. Took him first so see the Old Poor House and my six cottages. We lunched near Ditchling, the chauffeur driving up a sheep track into a little copse; then on to Brighton, then home. He had tea with me, chatted with Ernest, then departed. Joan arrived to supper. Before that Wycherley came about the cottages. He is to collect the rents.

28 January. When I was first married, almost the first time I made the tea, I put no tea in the pot. Did the same thing this morning, after 45 years, and regarded it as an omen! It was: at one o'clock, exhausted by the last touch to the proofs, I tottered out. Met by Miss Parker, Ernest had another shivering fit. Got him to bed. Went over ex-Finch's cottage with Kent who with courteous "excuse me going first, Madams" went ahead and squirted

disinfectant everywhere. I was gratified – and choked! He assured me – no bugs. This insect seems to have lost its vogue . . .

30 January. Went down to the cottages. They are putting down the bricks and cobbles in front, also little eunonymous trees, but oh those tenants! How they hate me, just for trying to make them a bit cleaner.

31 January. Letter from Philip. Rather wooden, so burnt it, first one of his I have burnt (and I see, by the way, that his cousin David Sassoon has left him £150,000, which means about as much to Philip as £1,000 would mean to me!) Fact is, everything and everyone they are *nothing* now Ernest is so ill. Went in to chat with Ernest, found him so utterly weak and vague that I persuaded him to let me help him into bed. And he did. And, suddenly, it overwhelmed me. I began to cry. He said, half crying himself: "I'm too weak to take you in my arms, my darling". And then we composed ourselves, agreeing that this emotion does not help.

4 February. After lunch Ernest and I came to grips. It was agonising. He said he knew he was dying and that I knew and that we had been bluffing each other, which is true. And he broke down and spoke of the garden and how lovely it was each summer: "I used, when you were out, to walk about and worship each flower. But I wouldn't say anything to you. Pride I suppose and wrong of me. I see it now." And then, holding my hand and weeping: "Darling, we've always loved the best things together". I said we had and, that being so, what else mattered.

12 February. To tea with the Howards. She – Mrs Howard – looking stately and most becomingy shingled. Usually elderly women, when cropped, look like witches. The daughter frightfully excited over the shed [lean-to] which she is to rent from me.

16 February. Poor Ernest unduly worried by his brother Tom who writes absurd letters reminding him to try an electric belt soaked in vinegar!

17 February. Mrs Howard. 1.30. It was a heavenly morning, cold, sunny , as I walked by the sea to The Grand. I felt I had never been happier! And this

seemed monstrous, when one thought of that poor dear at home . . . Charming lunch. Mrs Howard told me of a friend of hers who, adoring her husband, yet said to him during a long illness: "You really must get better, James, or I shall dislike you". This consoled me and explained my own occasional mental attitude which I have felt was so devilish.

18 February. Letter from Margery about 3 lines long, after 7 weeks.

19 February. Charlotte's coming and there is something about the very imminence of Charlotte which paralyses me! She is like a clipped privet hedge, neat, praiseworthy, and no quality. What a beast I am! But the truth is I am dog dead tired and would give worlds to go to bed for a week, my meals brought up by one to whom I need not speak, barely human – say a black eunuch . . . Charlotte came, not in her best mood. No doubt I annoy her. I looked up suddenly at tea time and saw satanic temper and Christian forbearance fighting a pitched battle on her face! And kind as she is and invaluable in crisis, one isn't always in a state of dramatic collapse but very often gay and joyous, for which mood she has no use.

26 February. Mended the chair in Ernest's room which that wicked little Spangles disembowelled. Then got on quite well to my amazement with Chapter I . . . After tea went off to a Miss Curtis, a sort of semi-nurse who will come and help him dress, 1/- an hour.

5 March. Very nice letter from Philip which enchanted me. Surely I can't be fool enough to be half in love with him? But no harm done: nobody knows, nor will! And I expect it is only just reaction and because I am, really, so dull and sad.

10 March. Absolutely sick with misery and dread, visualising the lonely life I shall live (and die) in this house. Yes, I hope this house. And then I thought of him and all the young, so very young, days and so long ago. And I felt I could not go through with it. Yet there it lies before me, coming so close – his death.

18 March. Ernest said yesterday with a broad cold stare when I said I was tired: "Why? You are leading a perfectly normal life, aren't you?"

20 March. Shall I ever forget the horror of these terrible 'puttings to bed'? Getting the poor dear up those stairs, so dreadful as if he'd die at every step. And then the undressing, which *physically* revolts me. Can't help it. May be a beast, but anyhow he never guesses and that is all that matters.

31 March. Went down to the lean-to. Miss Howard moved in and the place looking quite charming.

8 April. How I am going to remember all the sharp details of this time. How every morning I put a fresh little jug of flowering currant in his room, because he loves flowering currant. And how, this very day, I have folded up and put his suit away, for he no longer gets up. And locked away his ring, which for months he's kept in his waistcoat pocket, because his finger got so thin.

10 April. Ernest's birthday: 73. He had communion. I'm so glad that he had heaps and heaps of flowers, the room like a florist's shop . . . Emily came. Very loving and sweet, very moved by Ernest's terrible condition. I gave her those strap shoes and two cotton frocks and that nice lace jumper.

16 April. The Rector called. Dear Ernest, talking of his death and how much money he would leave me! And wanted me to make a list of people I must write to afterwards! But I headed him off that ghoulish enterprise . . . went to Mrs Fawssett and borrowed a bed pan!

17 April. Rector 8. Ernest's communion and Last Sacrament . . . Mrs Miller arrived, but she proved a comfort. Stayed to supper and we, together, put together the original crochet pattern (Mrs Hubert's) of which I've done yards, but had forgotten. Helped Miss Curtis to turn Ernest in the bed. He so *frightfully* emaciated.

20 April. Easter Sunday. Easter Day and the second grisly one! Communion at 8. I returned and was met by the news that the nurse wanted my help in lifting Ernest. Went in that sick, warm room and the poor thing was wet and the sheets had to be changed and everything was smelly and I felt sick. In the middle of which she said cheerfully: "The breakfast smells good".

22 April. Weather perfect and I with a heavenly sense of freedom walked on the Glynde hills. So lovely up there, tranquil and safe.

23 April. Vallance came in, saw a great change, thought him sinking and not to be left . . . A wet warm day, large green leaves, dead-white blossom, the blackbird singing. 3 p.m. Been sitting here all day. Dr Vallance came, thinks him unconscious. I feel sure he doesn't know me. Now and again I go to the bed to cover up his poor sticks of arms which he keeps flinging out. He stares at me, with those large, brilliant, unseeing eyes. When it is over, how am I going to bear it? 8 p.m. And it is. At quarter past 7, he gave one last breath and was gone. I sat beside him, crying and crying and crying without stint. Winnie and Olive were angels of sympathy. Olive went off for Miss Curtis and her helper. I sat there by him alone, until bundled out. Came up here, wrote heaps and heaps of letters till 11.30. The Rector came. No sleep or very little.

24 April. Saw the undertaker, arranged everything. More letters. At 10.30 Emily came. At 12 Tom. It seems so ghastly to eat and drink and move while he lies there so still. The day is perfect. Two or three times I've walked about the garden. Oh, my *dear*, how lonely I am and shall be . . .

25 April. I want to put down all that I can remember, but it will be just agonised impressions. His coffin coming at night and the stealthy stepping, scraping, rumble underneath and then we went down to see him. Oh my dear, your poor loved face incredibly thin, hardly knowable, but your hands adorably beautiful and holding the crucifix I told the undertaker to place there. At night they carried his coffin away – so lovely: the sunset wonderful: surplices, acolytes, the lovely lime trees all fresh and green. Past the Bowling Green he was carried, away from his home for ever. Goodbye, my dear.

28 April. Ernest buried. At 8.40 the Requiem. Emily came with me. I went up to the altar, past that coffin. Didn't cry or even flinch, and I'd dreaded that I would. The rest of the day was all wreaths coming and people coming . . . In exquisite weather – blossom and birds and sun – we drove to the church and then to the cemetery. It nearly broke me up when somebody, Charlotte I think, took my arm and led me to look down into the grave. But not quite. For months I've dreaded making a fool of myself and I didn't!

29 April. Stacks and stacks of letters. Can't remember what happened . . . letters, of course, and people leaving cards.

5 May. Paid every sort of bill including the funeral: £31 odd . . . just now – 4 – seen my sister off, dear good little soul, with Ernest's wireless. So glad she's got it and not some stranger.

7 May. Yesterday I wrote to Kate, like the fool that I am. Might as well expect sympathy from a black panther. Darling Margery sent a cable. She's got the letter and knows that her father is dead.

8 May. A steely cold evening, the house all unpicked, for the workmen come tomorrow and the spring clean starts. Will turn to the fire and smoke a cig: I smoke too much – 3 a day. And always I am wretched, wretched, wretched. Oh my dear! I did love you so, and nobody else. All the rest – and every other – is sheer fantasy.

21 May. I have been turning out papers – innumerable – in the study. Various old things and photographs connected with his family, which should interest Margery: old early letters I wrote him in 1905 . . . Tore 'em up. They didn't seem me, nor were they the me which now is me. So childish, verbose, passionate. Anyhow, all this turning out is heartrending and it seems everlasting. Perhaps, when I've burnt his overflow, I ought to burn my own diaries and letters.

24 May. I went and raked out my tin box of papers in the attic and found the letters he wrote me – answering mine – after Margery sailed for Canada. A wonderful letter, prudent yet devoted. Makes David seem a poor thing! I think David, poor dear, was only a bit of fringe on life's garment!

30 May. . . . the home was sort of vast, with an echoing silence. And he upon the wall [Ernest's photograph] looked so real, so alive. A little smile, cynical and fond. Well! Serves me right. I was worn out. I wanted rest and peace, nothing else. I've got this freedom and my heart is broken.

12 June. Feel I must write letters, which is next door to talking. Feel why not instal a telephone. But poor – equally desolate – Mr Gale did that and nobody rang him up!

17 June. My dear darling Ernest's will quoted in the *Daily Mail*. He left £5,000 and a little over. All by his own brain and saved up for me.

18 June. Letter from Margery. Will I go to America? Felt I couldn't, yet must. Charlotte came. She thinks I ought to go.

20 June. Wrote Margery saying I'd come. Emily came. Very helpful, affectionate and quite excited at the American [trip]. I'm not: afraid of being drowned and don't want to be! Lovely to see Margery and the children but the idea is so stupendous that my tired mind hasn't quite got it yet.

25 June. Today for the first time since I was left alone I've been – in an abstract sense – happy, realising what a lot I've got left and most valuing the deep spiritual side of our love for each other: and that we've got without any bodily hindrance or ugliness through all eternity. So I won't fret, cry and be dark.

26 June. Letter from Philip. Lunched with him which was a mercy because not only did he send me to the Consulate in a cab to get my visa but he promised if I sailed from London to see me off. Later had tea with him on the terrace of the

House of Commons, and got introduced to Lady Astor[1] and Lady Oxford[2]. But the whole thing was hard. I felt extra desolate. I don't mean Philip is hard, only the life he leads. He came with me in the car to Victoria . . . I dread America, the getting there.

28 June. Naughty Spangles killed a lark on the Downs. I do so cherish my pretty spotted beasts. God keep them when I'm 3,000 miles away.

11 July. Most ghastly shock. Note from Harold Blaker, Charlotte's lawyer. She died the day before yesterday [on holiday in Yorkshire]. My faithful loyal loving prim little friend for 30 years: and never once failing me.

12 July. It's amazing, somehow, that Charlotte – so lacking warmth and colour in life – should at death leave me with such a passionate sorrow.

17 July. [Park Lane] I arrived very excited and sad and frightened, in a kind of trance, as I had been ever since Ernest died. Very chilling to be met by Miss Boyce, the Secretary: "Sir Philip has to dine out. He thought, as you would have a tiring day tomorrow, that you would prefer to dine in your room and go to bed early"! That gave me an awful setback, to begin with. The "room" being one out of a suite of four, had a big wood fire and my grub arrived! In the middle, in comes Philip. Very restless, as, once at Lympne, and once at Trent. Finally, swung me round: "I'm one of those people who can't *say* things. I want helping out". A little pause and then I said: "Not in the mood to lend a helping hand". Then we laughed, as always at these moments. And off he went. He returned later in evening dress with decorations[3], looking very handsome and just like Sargent's portrait[4] of him. Stood over my low

---

1 Nancy Astor, first woman MP.
2 Wife of Asquith, former PM.
3 PS's decorations included the CMG, GBE, Croix de Guerre and the Legion of Honour.
4 Left to the Tate Gallery by PS.

chair, as I sat by the fire reading. "Hannah wants us to lunch with her tomorrow". "But I sail tomorrow". "Oh, we can get down to the Docks in plenty of time *after* lunch." He spoke as if it were nothing of an affair. But my longest voyage so far had been from Portsmouth to Ryde! He didn't seem to realise anything. These rich people are heartless devils. "When you return in September promise to come *straight* to Lympne. I know what you are once you get to Lewes and your Castle; no digging you out." I said I was all in a fog and could promise nothing. He just laughed and, stooping, kissed me – for the first time. I was very much stirred and so – clearly – was he. But we finished off with a laugh, as always with any tender emotion. And he went away. I was left to my own bewildered, sad thoughts, alone by the fire in that great rich room. I thought – realising it fully for the first time – "I'm a widow".

27 July. Arrived. Margery met me.

28 July. Went to Detroit. Christopher met us. Then on to Birmingham. Dear Christopher, very tall and unchanged. He said at once: "To hear you talk, after the voices out here, is like listening to a blackbird".

11 August. Had my hair shingled.

20 August. Said goodbye to everybody and went from Detroit to New York.

21 August. I sail for home, unless I drown on the way out! Didn't drown and did sail for home.

11 September. At 2.30 Bridgman [stonemason] took me in his car to Ringmer where we saw a charming old stone tomb – 1727 – in Sussex sandstone. If it isn't too much money he will copy it for Ernest's grave.

24 September. I thought I'd turn out Margery's letters and Philip's, all gloriously jumbled together, and give them a drawer each. Amongst them found one from Ernest, written in 1921 when he was at Edenbridge with Maurice[5]. So

5 Pockock, Kate Dudeney's late husband, an architect.

precise, so tender and faithful; saying he'd got work on *Sunday Express* but didn't know where the ideas were coming from: "I know you'll be patient with me if I'm cross".

1 October. Letter from Margery . . . I'm so distresssed and worried. She asks: 'Is there any chance of my getting any of my inheritance now?' Apparently quite oblivious of the fact that if I gave her a sum of any significance now it would reduce my small income. And, as it is, I can only stay on here by keeping on working. Pointed this out, but was worried and never slept till 1. I'd *love* to give her a house, but I can't even *help* so far.

4 October. Such a nice little weekend with Vere. Presented my parrot to the infant and he instantly made friends, which was lucky as Vere says he sometimes takes violent dislikes. A very handsome, sturdy little child and so good.

21 October. What a birthday. Not likely to forget it. Assessment £500: 'Earnings as a novelist'. Saw the Inspector, an infernally sceptical and beastly man. Wants to see the publisher's accounts! Wrote Pinker about that. Came away, feeling so angry and insulted, so *alone*.

24 October. I went out of mourning. So depressed by black necklaces. Put on a lace collar and Philip's jade brooch. Miss Hardy[6] is a quite plain but rather attractive creature, who trades on her plainness and succeeds! Very large, bald face, bobbed hair quite straight, age 48ish. Colours: magentas and crude blues, both very trying, but she succeeds.

26 October. After church went to the cemetery and saw the tombstone, a little hard and new, of course, but very dignified. In 20 years time (when I'm dead) it will be weathered, time-stained and lovely.

5 November. Ida arrives. Winnie was out – Bonfire Orgies[7]! I was afraid Spangles would go mad with terror but she didn't. Ida and I sat over the fire

6 Muriel Hardy, an artist, lived with her sister Winifred at 18 Keere Street, then known as Dale View (now House) and a former home of the editor.
7 The famous Lewes Bonfire celebrations.

talking hard. They are desperately hard up and I feel so dreadfully sorry for her. As for him! Hanged if I know what I feel. She is – as of old – fussy and peevish. Bedroom so cold. Might she brush her hair in my room by the gas fire?

7 November. We went off to the Iron Works and saw Mr Every's[8] wonderful collection. She enthralled: "*How* David would revel in this". I said then why couldn't he come and that really this rigid parting – at our age – was ludicrous. She didn't mind but wondered if he'd want to. This made me furious inside, which was silly, for of course he wants to. Question is – do I?? At 3 she went off . . .

11 November. Ida wrote that she told David what I said about a meeting . . . "He was amazed, said nothing, but I could see that the iron entered his soul". Do I want to see him again? Do I? Don't I? Shall I? Shan't I?

14 November. Finished and packed up my novel: Miss Cordelia Birtles[9].

19 November. Saw in the *East Sussex [Gazette]* a notice of Mrs Fawssett's death.

22 November. Met Evelyn [Fawssett] in her car. She stopped. We had a talk and she asked me to go in to see Winifred. Poor Winifred broke down a little. She was in the middle of turning out her mother's things. She told me an odd thing. Bubbles, Mrs Fawssett's cat had been curled asleep on the rug, very much à la cat. Then suddenly he started up, his eyes glaring, his fur on end, made frantic efforts to get out and when he did rushed to Mrs Fawssett's room which was empty as she'd been taken to Dr Helen Boyle's. Cecil was so impressed by this that he made a note of the time – a quarter past four – and this, as they learnt later, was the exact time that Mrs Fawssett died.

8 John Every of the Phoenix Ironworks, 1832–1951. His collection of firebacks is now at the Anne of Cleves Museum, Southover High St.
9 The heroine of *The House in the High Street*, published by Collins 1931. Set in Lewes.

3 December. Thank goodness I haven't heard from Philip, I don't want to be bothered by him, by David, by anybody. Just to keep well, to keep here, to have enough money and to work is all I now want.

6 December. I don't want to be alone and yet alone I am and must be, everybody is dead, across the sea or otherwise occupied, getting on quite nicely without me! I must face it. And as for David, he doesn't write or come. He is wise. I begin to feel that any resurrection of that affair would be disastrous.

18 December. Very depressing interview with Skues. It really looks as if Ernest had made false income tax returns and I may have to pay up hundreds. But I'm quite sure he didn't mean it. So much mathematical juggling with figures bemuddled him for practical accounts. Skues took me out to lunch – glad he did, for I was exhausted and on the point of tears.

22 December. Got on silk stockings, my best shoes, clean cuffs and collar ready to be gracious to Mr Travers. [10.] An explosive charming Irishman who never once left off talking. At once, in dear Ernest's study, turned on electric light, sat by a big fire surrounded by mathematical books and ministered to by Miss Parker. It was uncanny and heartrending to sit up here and, once more, hear someone poking the fire underneath! The dear dogs mystified. They went in, stood close to him, stared at him, with a dim fond feeling that 'Master' although so changed, had come back. He sat up till 12, read in bed till 4 (sleeping in Ernest's room, and jolly for my electric light bill). But Miss Parker says he will be a great help to us with the book, which is the great point. He does not eat butter, cheese, vegetables, fruit or eggs. Has when at home from ten to twelve 3-cornered jam puffs a day and for dinner a little lean meat and sometimes pudding. At 12 on Tuesday he departed, after an early lunch of jam tarts which Miss Parker fetched from Holloways (no puffs to be had) and lots of tea.

10 James Travers, headmaster of Peterborough College, Harrow, compiled ED's writings for posthumous publication.

25 December, Christmas Day. At 10 to church again. The departed were prayed for, including "Henry Ernest Dudeney," and, for it's always the slight and the unexpected that bowls you over, I who went through his Requiem and his burial without a tear suddenly began to weep.

31 December. And so the year ends. Sad and disastrous for me. Must pull up my socks for 1931.

Alice Dudeney by John Russell & Sons,
about 1916

Ernest Dudeney, frontispiece from
Puzzles and Curious Problems

mean. That poor pretty Mrs Wood has a great niece in our early. After Tea we talked of it

31 DAYS | MOON SETS 11.30 a.m.
32ND WEEK | MOON RISES 0.55 p.m.
AUGUST, 1933
SUN RISES 5.37
SUN SETS 8.33

appears that Miriel Nandy knows Lady Wolseley & Mary Musgrave (Antony's niece). And that she — M. M — "can't bear Mrs Dudeney!"

In the morning off I went — by invitation — to Miss Seymour's

MISS Hardy
4.30
no letters

10 THURSDAY (222-143) *garden. They sister, an extremely nice woman, staying with her. Lots of loose lies. Bleeding — I they didn't even know the name of it. The gardener cut me such a hefty bunch that I reeled under it. Met Mrs Briggs look who says that Mrs Perceval has had a bad operation & that. Miss Lunshawe is "rapidly losing weight". Makes you feel grateful for whole limbs and well-regulated "innards." Nothing much more to say. Very dull, but feel better.*

A typical extract from Alice Dudeney's Diaries

Mrs Dudeney sewing at Castle Precincts House, April 1928, by Edward Reeves

Emma at Castle Precincts House, April 1928, by Edward Reeves

The Lean-To, Castle Banks

Castle Precincts House

Castle Banks

The Old Poor House,
Castle Banks

Woodcuts by Dorothy Elliot of Alice Dudeney's properties in Lewes

Sir Philip Sassoon
by John Singer Sargent, 1923

Port Lympne, 1923

Trent Park, 1931

1931

2 January. I am dreadfully hurt both by David and Philip, not that the latter matters much. But it is clear that neither of them really cares twopence for me. The only man who did care, vitally, wholly, always, is dead: and yet we could do nothing when he was alive but starve each other out! Queer creatures, men and women.

6 January. After tea Margaret [Hill] came in, which was nice. The poor little soul seems to be more and more unhappy. What fools husbands are: he loves her, yet starves her out. Not the first one to do that! I tried to say a few wise words!

14 January. Called on Lady Cust [1] who was in and I liked her better in her own house and with her hat off. Dark thin woman, small features but not mean . . . very quietly vivacious, with much movement of her hands. Quite attractively dowdy. A black frock with widow's collars and cuffs, greyish hair taken straight back in a bun.

17 January. Proofs of *The House in the High Street* came. So no diary till they're done.

20 January. I do feel that the speechlessness and motivelessness of this life is impossible to endure. Yet, endure it I must and I may live to be 80 odd. And I don't want to die. What I want is love, laughter, affection, warmth, and there is none of either of it.

6 February. Philip [Park Lane]. Found he'd got a big lunch party and the only one I knew was Lord Hugh Cecil, who has had pernicious anaemia and is living upon liver. The other people quite pleasant; the usual affable, artificial crowd.

1 Lady Cust lived at Glebe House, Rotten Row.

7 March. A letter from Philip *and* David which amused me. But when I had read both – inconsequent creature as I suppose all women are (except those who are half men) – went to my bedroom, looked at Ernest's photograph, met his kind, cynical eyes, put my cheek against the cold glass and cried . . . wrote to them both.

10 March. At night my six copies of *The House in the High Street* came. It appears on March 23rd, not one of my best, not in the same world with, say, *Quince Alley*. But sprightly, and how I did it in the midst of such agony of mind God alone knows. Letter from David.

25 March. Lovely notice of *The House in the High Street* in the *Sussex Daily News* and no one to show it to: the study empty, no turn of the head, loving smile, outstretched hand . . .

26 March. Bedside table came, put it in his (once) bedroom which is being got ready for David. If he comes. I never trust him. Never can. Altogether am bewildered and not happy.

27 March. Philip. The Georgian Exhibition[2] quite wonderful. After that, lunch. Lots of people as always.

28 March. David for the weekend. Well, I can't say a word about this day, here anywhere or to any one. We met in the middle of the drawing room and – quite instinctively, not knowing that I would – I put up my cheek and he kissed it. Yes, wonderful but all through I was troubled and thought of Ernest: and somehow it didn't seem right that David should come to this house and sleep in Ernest's room. The whole thing emotionally is an awful mix up for me. Not for him. Men are neither so sensitive nor so analytical. He adores me as he always did. But I feel only a very tender, maternal sort of affection. And when he *would* kiss me, I wished he wouldn't.

29 March. A very peaceful strange day.

2 Exhibition of Georgian furniture at 25 Park Lane.

30 March. In the morning I took David down by appointment to Every's iron works and left him there, where he stayed for hours, gloating over Every's collection. After lunch off he went (he thinks Ida won't let him come often!).

6 April. Another whirling letter from David. So once more after 17 years I lock letters up . . .

10 April. Letter (like a mill race) from David . . . Dear Ernest's birthday. He would have been 74.

24 April. Requiem for Ernest at 8.30. Managed to get through the Requiem without crying, but felt like crying.

28 April. Wrote Skues who proposed to 'consult Counsel' over this Income Tax infamy. I shall be ruined for sure . . . And it is dreadful to have no one to speak to or share one's life. David's love letters are all very well but sort of twilight-ey and unreal, just a queer recrudescence of 25 years ago with the motive (so far as I am concerned) dead as a door nail.

29 April. Tried to work and did, in a way . . . Took Emma for a walk. Met Mrs Bates and Zeb. And she took me over the Shelleys [3] of which she'd got the key. Wonderful, vast old house with more than one hideyhole. Tradition is that 200 Royalist soldiers were hidden here during the Civil Wars.

4 May. David's letters are such uncanny replicas of 25 years ago. At first they thrill, then they strike me as tinsel-ish. Quite beastly of me, but I'm a cold and critical old woman. He seems as young as ever.

12 May. To my bewilderment no letter from David. I begin to miss him.

14 May. And I did enjoy writing that letter [to David]! He says – for safety's sake – write him a 'dear David' letter now and then that can, if necessary, be handed across the breakfast table. So did!

3 Shelleys Hotel, St Anne's Hill, an historic Georgian building on the site of the Old Vine Inn.

20 May. Worked very well finishing that chapter which concludes with the kiss in *The Treasure Field*[4] . . . piercing brutal north wind and a sky of slate. . . . saw through the bathroom window Margaret, Father Flannagan and the little dog go by. Disgraceful of them both, with things as they are, and if Hill knows then he ought to punch the priest's head.

2 July. Very unpleasant affair at Pallants. I'm sure the dress was marked in the window £3 3s but they said "No, Modom, £4 4s" and I had no proof. Shall never enter the shop again.

25 July. This doing without a servant really is the very devil. You have neither mind nor soul, simply hands to wash up dishes (and my sink any mother might be proud of!) and legs to trot about. I was feeling absolutely sluttish and greasy (mentally, only!) when in came one of David's fervid letters, which "cheered up me".

3 August. Poor Spangles shut up in the basement with hysteria. Can't of course think of leaving her and have written to Philip preparing him. Expect he'll be furious. Can't help that. For me I feel a curious emptiness but, first and foremost, intense relief. I simply can't mix with that 18 carat crowd any more.

4 August. I woke with the feeling that something lovely had happened, and then remembered that I hadn't got to go to Lympne. I really am too old to be bothered with all this dressing up and being at your best. But what a fool to have bought so many clothes, but they'll come in. Have been peacefully correcting Chapter IX. So odd to write by the same post to David and Philip, each letter with its own mode. Who would have supposed things would turn out so! (What a silly old woman I am). . . . All the time I am peacefully grinning with relief because I am not at Lympne with a footman and a butler coming round (six or seven rich courses, not one of which I enjoy). To say nothing of strange 'lords and ladies' and Mrs Gubbay with her brassy laugh.

4 Published Collins 1932.

10 August. Letter from Lady Gage. Will I go to lunch on Wednesday?

12 August. Lady Gage 1.30. . . . They were most kind and she is lovely and the house is wonderful but, somehow, I felt miserable and lonely. I can no longer stand this young society people, of a quite different age and tradition. Perhaps I was just tired.

18 August. [To Ida and David]. Dear David met the bus: not altered in figure a bit. And in country clothes which made it all so real, so joyful, so poignant. When he came to Lewes that was just romance: wonderful but a little unreal. But now, this time, it was love come back; just as overpowering as when I was 31 and he was 35 . . . And Ida herself very affable. She's an excellent hostess but a very so-so visitor.

19 August. After dinner David and I walked up the lane towards the Downs; yes, once again, my darling, up that lane. And he kissed me there, which was most imprudent and quite heavenly.

29 August. Proofs from Nelson of dear Ernest's posthumous book[5] . . . Wrote to Travers about correcting said proofs. What manna from Heaven said Travers is!

1 September. A year today since I came home from America. Interviewed and engaged typist at 3. [Ellen Hayward]

12 September. Had innumerable chats about the Budget and increased income tax. Miss Smythe has had no dividends, Mrs Vallance says Vallance is furious because doctor's panel pay is cut, Newington the coal merchant predicts national ruin and worthless Arkwell[6] who with his 9 children lives on the Dole, hanging about the street as usual, called over his shoulder to a pal about the odds on a horse!

5 *Puzzles and Curious Problems.*
6 Feckless neighbour living near OPH.

14 September. In the morning I took the dogs out – oh and I was happy. I was going to have David with me for days and nobody else. He was here when I got back, looking so effective in country clothes and to me hardly changed except that he is thinner and his hair is white. After dinner and after the first loveliness of meeting we took bus to Firle, walked through the Park to the church, saw the Gage tombs, tea at The Ram, then home. A lovely fire-lit candle-lit evening. Oh my dear! We have loved each other for 33 years and for 21 of them we've been parted.

16 September. We went on the Glynde hills with the dogs: the look of the world and the joy in our hearts as near Paradise as possible. And I bought at Freeland and Geering what I didn't want, can't afford and couldn't resist, a charming looking glass in a gilded wooden frame £1 5s . . . David hung it up in the ante room. Same sweet evening, but not quite so perfect because we knew it was our last.

18 September. Margaret came in at breakfast time and said I looked "so well and happy". And so I am, my darling, because we have met again.

25 September. Winnie took the dogs out. I don't think I could do without Winnie. Paid her wages and gave her the promised £2 rise: that's £34 a year and Olive helping and Insurance brings it up to more than £40.

5 October. Ida's letter full of grizzle-drizzle: when doesn't she and hasn't she. Don't want to be spiteful but what a woman for a sunny creature like David to be chained to.

7 October. . . . to Evelyn Fawssett[7]: she really handsome in cord breeches, a blue jumper and a silk handkerchief round her head. Gardening get up. But when a woman gets into breeches what an enormous behind she displays!

7 Evelyn, a garden designer, and sister Winifred, a social worker, had moved to 56 St Anne's Crescent.

23 October. Lady Gage 1.15. Such nice kind simple people: no glitter as at Philip's. Miss Stead drove me out (5/-) and Lord Gage brought me back; he having a political meeting at Lewes. Lady Desborough [8] there – talkative (but so am I!). Has been trying for 27 years through Bumpus to get a copy of *The Orchard Thief* [9] . Sent her one.

28 October. Went out at 12.30 to hear result of election: Conservative 25,000, Socialist 5,000. Conservative winning all over the country. No parallel, the papers say, since Monk's Parliament in 1660.

30 October. Again nothing from David. David might be dead and I'd never know unless she wrote and told me. That's the helpless position I'm in, and with no right to expect any other.

31 October. David's letter nothing but a struggle and a pull to come to me. So futile and yet we both do it, all the time and nothing else . . .

1 December. . . . came down to find Skues horrifying letter enclosing all the figures of the income tax people over Ernest's estate: 'H.E. Dudeney, deceased'. It breaks my heart and yet so angers me that I'd like to take the Inland Revenue – collectively and individually – by the throat. I can't understand their figures but, at the best, I shall have to pay out (as far as I can see) the £250 I've managed to save since he died. And that with Margery being hard up and parted from me!

8 December. Letter from David, from Margery . . . I love getting their letters together – David and Margery, the two I love best in the world ...

17 December. Philip sent a chest of china tea. Wrote him. Very frosty and hateful Xmas weather. Butcher running along with a well-scrubbed tray full of red meat and singing "Good King Wenceslas" at the top of his voice.

---

8 Mother of Lady Gage. Held a salon at Taplow Court, Bucks, for the Souls, a coterie of wits and statesmen.
9 Novel published 1910.

18 December. Lord and Lady Gage, Lady Cust, Mr Spokes [to tea]. It went off very well, except that Lady Gage had a bad cold in her head which didn't make me any happier! Gargled and snuffled well as soon as I got the chance! Mr Spokes stayed till 6.

23 December. Bought little presents for Auntie Miller, Margaret, Emily and Winnie (in addition to her usual 10/-) Tipped the road sweeper 2/6d: distributed various grins and Merry Christmases.

31 December. Proofs, Proofs, Proofs!

In my leisure moments – so many – I sit by the fire and make limericks, some very silly, some not so bad:

> 'There was a young Curate of Ealing
> Whose manners were mildly appealing
> But his Sermons were just –
> Well! – the Last Word in Lust –
> And devoid of all delicate feeling.'

1932

2 January. I do miss David horribly and Heaven knows when we shall meet, or even to write – to call it writing.

19 January. I was fairly tragic going alone to this doctor (though I'd rather be alone) not knowing what she would tell me. I'm glad she was a woman considering the examination, outside and in, I got! To my absolute tragic crushing (being the sort of fool that I am) she said there was a "lump" inside. Not a wicked one, she assured me of that. But said I'd had it a long time and it must be treated, perhaps by operation. I got home feeling doomed. So silly of me.

20 January. Very little sleep. Felt I could bear anything if only Margery was in England. As things are shan't even tell her, of course.

23 January. After dinner the discomfort and swelling so awful that I was quite desperate and went off to Dr Vallance, told him all and made an appointment for him to come and see me at 7.30. I feel so *frightened* and so alone . . . *Never let anyone say one word against Vallance.* That ass of a lady doctor frightened me to death. I go to Vallance, he examines me as she did, assures me that there is nothing wrong that a certain treatment won't probably put right, and if it doesn't, at the worst, it only means a very simple operation.

26 January. Henceforth nothing but indignity and futile effort. Drugs down my throat, humiliating injections every morning, and always in bed. The one ray of light was the loving friendship of everybody, the Howards, Mrs Bates and the rest, flowers arriving and fruit. And these dear things, including Auntie M coming in to chat and cheer me up, which they didn't. Nothing can, I'm frightened to death.

30 January. The 'home' treatment over and a failure . . . so nothing for it but an operation.

153

2 February. Hospital 9.30. Shall I ever forget it! Going off in that car rolled in blankets, the operating theatre, the chloroform, the hellish, sick-unto-death coming to. And then, hours after, the heavenly return home and being got to bed: and the kindness of Nurse Berry and Kitty and the sweetness of Winnie and then Vallance coming – angel that he is! and saying "nothing to worry about". But a little trouble there certainly is and I must bear it, or submit to an abdominal operation which would be 10 times worse and which neither he nor Beresford the surgeon advise at my age.

8 February. Worked a bit, concluding Chapter II, but it goes heavily after such an interval . . . See in *The Observer* that Collins brings out my *Treasure Field* next Monday. The whole of the royalty advance and a £100 more goes in Ernest's income tax and lawyers' costs. In fact, a year's income and savings wiped clean out.

2 March. The sun was out, the bitter wind gone so up I went – and out! Down the High Street with the dogs, suddenly remembering that I must have ginger biscuits and some new stays, preferably pink satin . . . then to Auntie M who amused me enormously by asking: "Are you thinking of marrying again?" "Who to?" She said: "Mr Spokes." And then told me that as he was here to meet the Townends and stayed on after they'd gone, Mr Townend said: "We met a man called Spokes. Is he sweet on Mrs Dudeney?"

8 March. Great news. David's got the Civil List pension: £80 a year. Ida says she did it, which riled me extremely considering that the suggestion and all the information came through me, they never even having heard of a Civil List Pension. At least I've done that for David: and I'm damned if I can see what she's got to do with it.

10 March. Ida sent a handsome apology, admitting that the Civil List pension was 'entirely owing to me'.

19 March. David. He came – tea time, as last year. What else is there to say, here anyway. Looking what he is, an old man, but his figure unchanged. Sprang on me the fact that he must get back on Sunday night, so as to be fresh for work on Monday morning. I understood and, in a way, was glad.

20 March. To church together and then took the dogs by the river. At 5 he went. I was so unsettled and unhappy that I was in bed by 8.

5 April. Letter from Ida. Quite stunned. Ida said that on Friday David might have died. Penumonia, out of danger now. Couldn't dream of working.

8 April. Feel better and have gone up like a kite. David is better. I now realise that I can't *bear* him to die. Sent to Ida for them both (so I said) a bottle of Red Bone Marrow which did Ernest so much good.

11 April. Ida wrote: 'You are Not going to take David to Hastings or anywhere else, till I am well and strong'. Wrote back that I was only 'playing about' but that through all my playing about I was intensely practical and that as David was the breadwinner and the King's Pensioner it seemed only common sense to do everything possible to make him well.

29 April. Poor David still in his room and hideously depressed with the after effects of 'flu. I went off to Brighton . . . then went on my romantic journey to St Ann's Well [1] where Ernest proposed to me in 1884. Found it quite unchanged.

2 May. My little operation and all the rest of it will run me in for £30! Bought a little birthday present for Elizabeth Ann.

31 May. The first glorious summer day . . . Finished sofa cover and cushions. Only one chair now to stitch up and 2 pairs of curtains to make. Then I can get back to work which is my real and only life. Went for a walk but so tired. Turned in to the cemetery and sat, actually and for the first time, on Ernest's grave. Oh my dear, how strange it seems that you are dead, that that is your grave. And some day it will be mine.

5 June. Auntie M. Bezique. What *should* I do without her and a pack of cards on a Sunday?!

1 Public gardens, Hove, which were purchased and donated to the public by PS's great-aunt, Mrs SD Sassoon.

15 June. Letter from David: his letter said that the 'nerves of the powers that be are in a very dangerous state' . . . Somehow I feel that there is more than David says and that he won't be coming here for a long time, if at all!

22 June. London. I went off so peacefully and meant to come back with beautiful clothes: £10 in my bag! And I felt rather sad and sentimental, when I was young and should have done justice to pretty clothes I never had any money. And today I never spent a penny! . . . So Brighton can dress me, as heretofore. And I never wish to see London again. In the bus past Philip's house in Park Lane, all the blinds down, so I suppose he's abroad. Very odd. Never hear from him now, wonder if Mrs Gubbay has made mischief, she's spiteful enough. Or perhaps he feels, as I certainly do, that the affair has flickered out.

24 June. Went to Hannington, saw a very smart coat and skirt, parchment and brown in stripes. But it occurred to me if I took out two spotted dogs in a zebra striped costume, the effect would be worse than funny.

13 July. Ida. She arrived, friendly, cryptic and fussy (as usual). The worst guest in the world. Might she have ink in her bedroom, she kept a diary and filled it up each night. Also – what, no books in my bedroom? So I went down, half undressed, and dug some out.

15 July. I terribly exhausted, lay full length in the summer house all the morning while she shopped on her own. At 2.30 she departed. I was terribly depressed. I hate the sort of domestic pictures she makes. They somehow destroy the David who is all mine and nothing whatever to do with her!

16 July. Pinker says that *Brighton Beach* is to be produced in New York, a trial trip by two different managers, one July 25th, one end of August.

27 July. Letter from Philip asking me to Lympne for the weekend only. Wrote him again saying how awfully good of him to give me another chance, but no I wouldn't.

31 July. Wrote David for his birthday. 70, my poor lamb!

3 August. My 'dearest Philip' (we seem to begin again after an interval of months) sent a box of scented geranium and verbena for my pot-pourri jar. Also a letter, not resenting my refusal to go to Lympne but suggesting I go up in October to London, which I'd love to do.

19 August. At 12 I was sitting in the lean-to garden having tea with the Howards when who should walk in but David! Introduced him. Also he thought it most imprudent to remain 'in hiding' so appeared at the tea party and got on awfully well with Mrs Topham, who was once a student of Sir John Millais. Miss Brigstocke departed with a wicked smile remarking: "I have been very much entertained". For a walk on the hills after tea.

20 August. We spent the afternoon in the garden and tea there and then went to the Castle. Peaceful, lovely evening together.

26 August. Letter from Margery. Wrote David. Forgot to say that yesterday Wycherley called: 2 cottages for sale in Westgate Street. Told him to make an offer for them. Darling Margery delighted with the clothes I sent but now says: 'We have taken to mending our own shoes'. Which shows how hard up they are and worries me extremely.

1 September. Met Mrs Topham, enthusiastic about David, so that's all right. I'm nervous of him meeting people in case he gives the whole affair away by his manner to me, poor darling.

17 September. Down the High Street little chats. Saw Wycherley, he has bought the cottages for £240. Saw Perkins the Bank Manager and sold out £150 Conversion Loan and £115 Consols . . . so the cottages, allowing £10 extra for law expenses will cost me only £225 and give about 9 per cent clear profit . . . At 9.30 went to bed quite charmed with the world!

1 October. After tea took the dogs out. Met Bates and had a rather touching little talk with him: both of us feeling so old and tired and so hating it. Came home and found the six copies of Ernest's book, which moved me very much.

6 October. David's letter very rhapsodical and up in the air. He is going to London and I am not to write till he gets back.

8 October. Saw Jackson about the disgraceful car parking in the Castle. He will do what he can and I am to write to the Town Clerk. Never did grudge drawing a cheque so much as I did the preposterous one for Vallance: almost a guinea a visit. *Done with him.*

19 October. Dusart did my hair beautifully. The tea party just as usual. Less and less do I care for Mrs Milne and I'm not sure that to an insular party like me nationality doesn't make a bigger barrier than class. She's Dutch, poor devil.

31 October. In the afternoon took the dogs for a long walk on the hills and returning met Father Flannagan and Margaret with the dogs. Close together and really quite cuddlesome (though I don't mean that they cuddled). But I can't imagine what his Bishop is thinking of or [what] his parishioners think!

1 November. Philip. Didn't want to go to London but ended by really enjoying myself. . . . Big lunch party as usual, but very nice: Lady Desborough, Evan Charteris and Lady Dorothy Charteris, Count Mensdorff, Lady Juliet Duff, Mrs Arthur Sassoon[2] and Osbert Sitwell[3]. Philip very affectionate at the last, pinning carnations in my coat and kissing me. And he sent me in his car to Holland Park where I called on Mrs Howard, who was out. So back to Victoria in driving rain

3 November. Hanged if I can remember all the nice little tiny things, and the only things worth recording.

24 November. Collins doesn't want the short story book! What a contrast to 1927 when they were 'delighted to welcome *Puff Paste*'. Also they say they have 'great difficulty' in keeping up my circulation. So that altogether I was dashed, not to the earth, but fathoms deep *into* it. But decided to keep my nerves to myself and not tell either David or Margery who have worries enough of their own. (Ended by telling them both.)

2 Edwardian beauty, close friend of King Edward VII.
3 PS's fag at Eton. Sitwell wrote a description of his 'magic' in *Dictionary of National Biography* 1931–40.

4 December. Saw in *The Observer* that it is Philip's birthday. He is 44.

7 December. Vere. It was so delightful to meet Vere and I never saw her looking prettier: a little black frock with a lace collar, a little black hat and a fur coat. We lunched at Harvey Nichols (3/- each and a glass of sherry which made it 4/-) But, as we said, our Christmas feast together.

16 December. David, after worrying myself sick and imagining him dead or dying has simply been 'rushed to death', calls himself a 'beast' and sends a little spotted dog in wood for Emma and Spangles. Shall not hurry to answer. Philip wants me to go to Trent for Xmas: failing that, soon after. I shall go. Shall buy myself all the clothes I want and be reckless. I'm really annoyed with David: and yet I am glad, because it frees me. I have been banking on him too much and I *ought* to have learned by this time that, in spite of profusely expressed adoration, he's untrustworthy. I suppose you can't have *everything*.

23 December. Pinker sent a wire, would I ring him up between 3 and 4? Got Dorothy Elliot to do it. They want permission for a fresh contract for *Peep Show*. Gave it, but get more and more faithless over the affair. And I do want it to go through.

29 December. Off to Philip's and never did I want to go less. Met at Victoria and conveyed to Trent, a palatial house which could put Lympne into its pocket. Found Sir Louis Mallet there; which was a comfort. Also a Lord Berners[4], quite pleasant, Mrs Arthur Sassoon – met her the last time I was at Trent – 2 rather chilly and dowdy old things, the Misses Du Cane, and a most delightful man the Marquis of Anglesey[5]. After dinner played Bagatelle with Philip, Sir Louis and Lord Anglesey. Got on so well with it that Philip promised to give me a Bagatelle board. I slipped off to bed later without saying goodnight as they all do and went to my lovely room, with a wood fire. And while I stood by it Philip came in to say good night and give me the

4 Millionaire, composer, author and eccentric.
5 Lord Chamberlain to Queen Mary 1922–47.

rather piquing little kiss on the cheek, in which we now indulge. Couldn't sleep. The room was so hot. The tip is as Sir Louis told me next day is to tell the servant to turn off the central heating at night.

30 December. Got up a little before lunch and talked to Sir Louis who is reading *Brighton Beach* and is enchanted with it. Lord Anglesey has gone, also the stiff old maids. Lady Juliet Duff has come and Mrs Harry Lindsey, who seems to be a vulgar little beast. Philip said after dinner, taking me round the middle: "Come and play Bagatelle with me and Louis. You're a man's woman". I said: "Oh but I've always considered myself very womanly and womanish". "Well of course, those are the men's women. So come along." He came to my room with the usual farewell, and I slept like a top.

31 December. Very peaceful luxurious life, for a little while. You get up when you like, always breakfasting in your room. This morning I went for a walk. In the afternoon you motor or read or talk and some of them play tennis. A luxurious tea at 4.30, 2 footmen in their scarlet waistcoats handing round the cups. After tea all separate and go to their rooms where there are big fires. Some of them get actually into bed as the housemaid, who waits on me, asked would I like a hot bottle before dinner. Then you have your bath and make yourself look as beautiful as you know how for dinner at 8, which is an extremely gay, prolonged meal with champagne. Then the women work – some of them do lovely needlework – and some play Backgammon and one (me) Bagatelle. Today a great big luncheon party. Rex Whistler[6], an artist, all of us staying in the house, Lord Ashfield, Sir John[7] and Lady Davidson, 13 all told. So Philip, instead of the one long table, divided us into two parties at 2 round tables. At 3 I left, motored to Victoria, got home in time for tea, had a lovely welcome and lots of letters, including (and most) one from darling Margery.

And so ends 1932: quite a gay, yet quite a peaceful ending.

6 Painted murals at Lympne and Trent Park. He was killed in action in 1944. In 1933 PS invited his second cousin Siegfried Sassoon to Lympne to see the murals. The visit was not a success.
7 Cabinet Minister, former Director of Mililitary Operations in France.

1933

'There once was a parson called Rawlings
Whose church was the scene of sad brawlings
For the Protestants stated
That they were quite sated
With the Catholics' creepings and crawlings.' [1]

1 January. Anyhow the year began as last year: proofs to do [*Trundle Square*] and awake half the night with a ghastly pain between my shoulders. So no communion.

16 January. Started on *Petty Cash* and, because it worked, it was a happy day. I quite like the topic and I would not 'retire' from writing for worlds, nor for fortune! After dinner took the dogs out and, as so often, met Mr Bates, always a little flirtatious which is rather satisfying as I subsist nowadays almost entirely on women.

21 January. I met Mr Bates. He's getting a little too flirtatious, even at our advanced age! And must be gently snubbed. . . . Philip says that the Tate Gallery has accepted the Rodin [2]. I'm *delighted*.

31 January. *Peep Show* (*Brighton Beach*) was produced in New York on the 24th. I wrote and asked why the advance 500 dollars had not been paid me.

10 February. Bezique: 3 to 6. It was such a jolly party: 8 of us and they all said how happy we were and what a good idea of mine to start the Club!

---

1 AD's limerick about St Michael's Church refers to accusations of it being 'semi-papal' in a town of strong dissenting tradition.
2 *The Kiss.*

21 February. Paid in the *Brighton Beach* cheque: 250 dollars, not 500. My mistake! The dramatist woman collars half according to the Agreement . . . In the afternoon the sun came out and I took the dogs on the Kingston hills. How *utterly* happy I am, and for years have been, on the hills with spotted dogs. Makes one understand immortality as just one perfect pause which goes on for ever.

28 February. Rather lovely every morning to see Wycherley ride by on his skewbald mare[3].

4 March. Well: I *hate* to see Ida. So long as I *don't* see her I can ignore her existence. However she came and we have nothing to say to each other. There is an implied enmity: a leaning on the lance.

9 March. I do pray I shan't ever die in the *middle* of a book. Early Spring with the new book printed and the proofs corrected is my time for dying.

20 March. Letters from these three [David, Philip, Margery] whose letters matter most. Philip wants me to go to Lympe for a weekend, London first. Said I would. I seem to be responding to him! After all, an old woman's clock is so fast running down. Darling Margery's letter worries me sick. But what can I do? Letter from Miss Hurlstone-Jones asking me to speak one evening at the 'Bookman Circle'. Declined explaining that, since my widowhood I spoke – nowhere! Funny! Can't be bothered. Should have been *frightfully* pleased once upon a time.

28 March. *Trundle Square*[4] appears. Very encouraging letter from Collins: the book already well subscribed for.

31 March. Philip and Lympne. At lunch a crowd as usual: The Mackintosh of Mackintosh, Lord Clevedon, Rex Whistler, an elderly woman – kissed on arrival by Philip so probably one of the tribe – a very smart and delightful

3 Jeannie, stabled in Castle Ditch Lane, was ridden by all three generations of the Wycherley family.
4 Set in Brighton.

American woman who runs 3 newspapers, and Miss Du Cane – the woman who was at Trent (don't care for her). At 4 off she and I started in the Rolls Royce for Lympne – oh yes, and also the sub-editor of *Country Life*. I in front with the chauffeur as that awful car makes me feel sick. Philip flew. Arrived. Very chilled to find the house only half opened, so all the pomp and colour which makes Lympne – to me – worthwhile, wanting. Everything shrouded in dust sheets, only one footman and one housemaid, in addition to a cook. It turned out that they'd all come down – Philip, Miss Du Cane and the *Country Life* man – to plan some fresh terraces in the garden. And directly after dinner Philip went out, so I went to bed.

1 April. I should have been bored stiff had not a most delightful Frenchman turned up, a decorator. The drawing room entirely changed. The ceiling painted out and the walls white.[5] The walls to be hung with some fascinating parchment coloured stuff, the chairs if they please covered in ivory *silk* velvet. After lunch to the French House and more everlasting talk of gardens. I took myself off for a walk.

2 April. Philip was going to Folkestone so dropped me at Lympne Church. Lunch also out of doors. At 2 off we went, stopping an interminable time at the tiresome French House. Then motored to London. They dropped me at Victoria and I never was more glad to get away.

3 April. Saw Wycherley who can now get me 6 [9] Castle Banks[6], owner dead and Trustee wishing to sell. . . . Sent Philip *Trundle Square*.

5 April. At 10.30 Wycherley arrived. He's got 6 [9] Castle Banks for me – that's 10 cottages, 2 large houses and a garage – all mine (and, if I live, I haven't done yet). Price £110, which ought to give me a clear 8 per cent. I was in bed when he came and as I felt he was the sort of man who'd be shocked if asked up to my bedroom, I descended in shoes and stockings, knickers, a dress over my nightgown, fur coat and hat. The effect quite decorous. Also he has told

5 The flowers at Trent Park were dyed to match the curtains in each room.
6 Next door to OPH.

Pilfold to get out of Mount Cottages and go into Kenward's empty one. Then we'll shuffle Mrs Verrall into No 1, and that decontrols the two of 'em! Very clever, if it works. That is if the damned Government and the new Rent Act doesn't put in some clause.

10 April. By the way 'The Sandstorm' in the *London Mercury* and 'Mrs Henry Dudeney' in a prominent place with Walter de La Mare and two others. Faithless Beast! I'd been dreading seeing myself just lumped in 'with other contributors'. Such a blow to vanity.

21 April. Emily – poor dear – not her fault, mine, on my nerves as usual. That awful way, furtive yet self indulgent, in which *constantly* she blows her nose!

22 April. At tea time Margaret arrived, for which I was thankful. She at last unbosomed herself about Father Flannagan. Great scandal, as I knew there must be. Someone has written to his Bishop but the Bishop takes no notice as he trusts Flannagan . . . Said what I could, but I feel that Flannagan comes out in a very bad light.

27 April. *Brighton Beach* now to be played in England at the Globe Theatre under the horrible title of *Champagne Supper*. Very excited and bucked, with all of this.

1 May. Dear David looking so nice with his youthful figure. The worst of it was that, just my luck, bad toothache started on Saturday (not had it for 12 months). In awful pain. So after tea he insisting on coming with me off to Beckley who said it was hopeless and he'd take it out in an hour. We then went for a walk and also into St Anne's church. Then I had it out with gas. Felt deadly sick when I got home, so that angel went to the public house and got me some brandy. Felt better and we played Bagatelle, also I looked very nice in my *real* evening frock!

2 May. Went to see Blaker by appointment. 9 Castle Banks is Copyhold, so I must free it[7]: but, even then, a bargain at £110. Slept all the afternoon and we had a peaceful, happy evening. David terribly hard up: got £10 of work coming in and no prospect of any more. His £80 pension doesn't help as it should because he's overdrawn at the Bank, so they lay hands on some of it! I asked him if he would, as a *professional* job, clean off the paint on the lovely Adams fireplace in the dining room and – after a great deal of demur and offering to do it "for love" – he consented. So it's a commission and will help him a little.

3 May. In the morning we went, and it was quite wonderful, to the little house in the High Street (now to let) where I lived for seven years with Ernest and Nelson! What an extraordinary affair life is and how little I thought through those 7 years that I should stand in that exquisite panelled room with David. We were both, in slightly different ways, very moved. He adored the room and it looked so very lovely. After dinner he went.
7
May. Great excitement. Saw in *The Sunday Times* that *Brighton Beach* under the title of *The Day I Forgot* is to be played at The Globe next Thursday. And asked Auntie M if she'd come, and she jumped at it.

12 May. Went up with Auntie M, Joan dined with us at Garland's Hotel where we stayed. . . . At Victoria bought all the morning newspapers, and all the notices of the play bad. (It was withdrawn after 3 performances!)

15 May. Dear David came and started on the mantelpiece.

22 May. The mantelpiece done and looking heavenly. We put on it only the two papier-maché screens and the Staffordshire 'Sportsman'. Divine weather and I was happy with him – happy. All the same I am now broken in to living alone and alone I'd rather be! Sounds heartless.

7 Copyhold tenure had been abolished in 1922 and existing copyholds enfranchised.

23 May. David left and he leaves behind him a curious blank.

4 June. Exquisite day, hottest Whitsun for 33 years! At night by the window saw an exquisite silver, green and red thing, like a wonderful swift serpent shoot across the sky.

5 June. See in this morning's paper that the thing I saw was a meteor and a very remarkable one. Pilfold [8] and his wife gone by in full Salvation Army rig. Winnie is of the firm opinion that Pilfold has washed his face!

8 June. Emily never enraged me more: can't account for these things. But suddenly while talking of altering her Will in Margery's favour, she flew off the handle: said she was and always had been "shut out" (quite true and quite inevitable). And we very nearly degenerated into a vulgar squabble. And when, at last, she went I could have cried and sworn! Feeling, as I always do, how I hate her nature.

15 June. Card from Philip: Garden party at Trent. Don't catch me going!

23 June. Letter from Monte Carlo – Alice Clemmison (now Lady Bryne and divorced) going to be married for the 4th time (and older than I am!) and will I go and stay with her and her new husband next winter in Monte Carlo? I will not!

27 June. Almost too exciting a day! I knew there'd be a letter from Harold Blaker because when I woke the first words I thought of were: 'Duchess of Norfolk'. So I knew she and the other two noble parties [9] had signed my deeds of 9 Castle Banks. Then my frock came and then I went out to lunch, always most exhausting.

30 June. Miss Hayward not being here – and somehow the very presence of that girl has a most devastating effect on my mind – did an excellent morning's work.

8 One of AD's disreputable tenants.
9 Marquess of Abergavenny and Earl De La Warr, Lords of the Borough of Lewes.

6 July. Finished *Petty Cash* ready for Miss Hayward to finish typing next week. Very affectionate letter from Philip: sorry I won't go to Trent, insisting that I go to Lympne. Wrote him a nice long letter explaining why I didn't wish to go to either. Wonder if he'll understand. Got some stays from Morrish with an 'underbelt for the full figure'. Getting steadily fatter, but quite determined not to be the usual gross old woman. How horrid to grow shapeless, when I remember my slim body and 20 inch stays!

5 August. Joan arrived looking so nice and really handsome again after years of not-so-handsome! Owing entirely, I think, to her having given up vegetarianism.

17 August. Great fuss with Spangles. Miss Barnes and the man in the basement trying to arrange a marriage, I palpitating on the garden seat! It seemed quite hopeless: the man took the dog off for a little walk, Miss Barnes came out to me and said "they won't tie" (and what she meant, Heaven knows) adding that her dog was getting exhausted and sick of poor Spangles. However back they went into the basement for nearly half an hour and then Miss Barnes triumphantly announced it was all right.

13 September. Travers arrives with his little boy: 9 years old and elaborately polite, poor little kid. Gave them both tea and [jam] puffs as usual for Travers. But he – Travers – refused to eat strawberry jam with them. Never eats anything but *raspberry* jam. I turned on the musical box to amuse the small, speechless boy. Travers found the 3 mathematical books he wanted to borrow and that I couldn't find. Small wonder! He had given me the wrong title.

14 September. Spangles and I on the hills in the morning. Emma is so ill and I know I ought to have her put to sleep, but so shrink from it. And, also, she now and then bucks up and seems quite happy and looks so lovely.

15 September. At 12 Emma came to the drawing room door crying. I let her in and if anything in this world ever pleaded and spoke her lovely eyes did: telling me she *couldn't* bear any more and wouldn't I do *something*.

16 September. Emma put to sleep. Cried myself sick last night, so very little sleep. I wanted to be with her to the last but Tingley said better not. So I kissed the top of her lovely velvet head and let him take her away. And then I quite broke down for a few moments knowing that – as I cried and while I cried – her poor little life was taken. We buried her at the bottom of the garden . . . Spangles crying and looking everywhere for her mother.

18 September. 8 years this very day since Nelson was put to sleep and here we are going through the same torture, and the same ghastly quiet in the house. *Why* do we persist in loving these dogs *so* dearly? I took my precious Spangles on the hills and she was happy there; for a long time Emma hasn't been well enough to go. I bring her home and, instantly, the poor little thing looks round. No mother to be seen, so she relapses into miserable silence.

26 September. David arrived at tea time and the day was lovely and I wore my blue silk frock.

28 September. In the morning we went to the Anne of Cleves' house and I pretty well fainted with weariness. And at night couldn't sleep. Too much talk, too much being told how perfect I am!

29 September. Well – 4.30 – David, bless him, has just gone and I never was more delighted to get my house to myself and to once more lead my solitary, reflective life. And that is what a love affair comes to! What should I have felt 20 years ago when he left me?! What should I have felt 30 years ago at the bare hope of seeing him? In the morning we did go for a lovely walk on the hills. I was happy and rested then. And blissfully slept all the afternoon.

3 October. Wore for the first time my lovely fox fur, and in the evening had the first fire of the season. And *oh* how I miss my sweet dear Emma in her basket by my side! . . . Met Mr Bates – always meeting him! He said: "You amuse me. You blush like a girl." Hastened to assure him that it was merely a bad habit and not turned on especially for him.

19 October. Winnie came up - no puppies, Spangles still screaming . . . but at 10 went down and there she was softly licking one little white puppy. In the

afternoon six little white puppies. And when I went down after tea seven! One, unhappily, with a black patch on his eye – already! Pathetically like my precious Nelson but, all the same, I'm afraid Mrs Barnes will say he's a "dud" (and we know what that means.)

27 October. Met Mrs Jervis [10], just widowed, poor thing, and not quite realising yet what it means.

30 October. In the afternoon went for a walk alone on the hills. Board up: 30 acres in The Coombe to be sold for building! But presently I came across a shepherd with a big flock, a tall crook, a sheep dog and sheep bells: all the usual loveliness which used to be, and which is now being swallowed alive by bricks and mortar.

1 November. Took my fur coat to Mitchell's to be relined and mended. Met Mr Bates on the way and he remarked: "Going to the pop shop?" Mitchell's quite helpless, they no longer repair fur coats. Why not buy, of them, a new one for £20?! Met Mrs Jervis. Says she can't live alone. Tried to comfort her, useless, of course.

6 November. Emily arrived in a fox fur which rather annoyed me, Beast that I am! She won't come for Christmas, felt "out of it" last Christmas. Will come to dinner. Bonfire night and this house a lunatic asylum. Spangles crouching in the corner with *one* poor baby, which had fallen out of bed. All the rest very hungry and screaming blue murder. Brought the whole lot up into the study and sat up with poor panic-stricken Spangles until the last procession, nearly 12.

9 November. Took Spangles for her first real walk on the hills. She enjoyed herself immensely, so much so that she rolled in cow dung and came up to me adorably grinning and plastered from head to heel. Took me about 20 minutes to make her fit to go through the town.

10 Mrs Jervis lived at St Michael's House, High St. She became AD's close friend.

14 November. Started teaching the puppies to lap out of a saucer. Fascinating job but it needs the patience of Job. In the afternoon felt I must cut free of a Dog's Nursery and as Pinker has sold 'Out to Play' for £20 [to *The Windsor*] why not go Out to Play myself and buy a Sunday best hat? So did.

15 November. Miss Barnes arrives: delighted extremely with the puppies and not one a "dud"...

22 November. Infernal noise outside by louts from 7 to 9, some game organised by Percy Arkwell. Shall have to complain to the police . . . Sergeant came up at once, caught the lot and told Percy Arkwell, the ringleader, that he'd be prosecuted (confiding to me – after they'd fled, that he could do nothing: "though nothing would give me greater satisfaction than to punish the young blighters").

27 November. Oh so exhausted with the (yet delightful) job of feeding seven babies and cleaning out the 'nursery'. At 2.30 fell out of the house to buy cakes, met first Lady and then Lord Gage and they both came back to see the puppies.

28 November. Margaret and Mrs Cooke very strident and talking perpetually (in very bad taste as my guests) of being "Catholics" and of "the Protestant Church". I must say it: the mental difference between men and (the majority) of women is surpassing. They (the average woman) have no logic, no sense of conversational proportion. I've got nobody to talk to now. That's where I miss Ernest with his clear, brilliant mind.

30 November. The puppies go this afternoon. Winnie and I *so* sad. At 2.30 Miss Barnes arrived, gave me a cheque and took them away. I could have cried as the car drove off and I saw the last of seven little darling spotted faces.

6 December. Letter from David, letter from Philip. Philip not so lover-like and exuberant now he can't get his own way, regrets that I can't come for Christmas and suggests a night in London, Jan 4th: 'When Louis and I will take you to a theatre'.

1933

11 December. Met Dusart who told me, in strictest confidence, that my 2 cottages in Westgate Street are condemned. I can appeal and if that fails, must pull them down at my own expense and get £25 sale value. They are in perfect condition and cost me £300 only last year.

12 December. Horrible night, waking up often in terror, seeing my Westgate Street cottages a heap of fallen bricks.

31 December. I rather steadied myself before I went to bed by reading in each diary for 23 years what I had done on New Year's Eve. All the dreads, ideals, passions, visions of each year – and all the years – gone. Dead, or surmounted. So why am I so afraid? If I go on living I shall just grin at these now so living terrors. And if I die?! At least, no more terror.

1934

Mrs Brough told me that her grandmother was nervous of travelling in a railway carriage alone with a man. And once just before the train started a man jumped in. She jumped instantly out, at the risk of her life, and into the guard's van. Reproved by the guard, she explained: "But a man got into a compartment." "And there's a man in this one, Madam."

Supposed to be an old country yarn (saw it in *The Observer*). A little boy took a hen's egg from the nest, painted it in brilliant colours and put it back. The rooster came and looked at it, reflected, *then went and killed the peacock*.

3 January. Philip had said: "Do come to tea." What happened? He out, Miss Boyce off to Trent, so tea with the younger secretary! That's the sort of thing, and I'm sick of it. To my room; vast, rich beyond belief and a lovely log fire. Dressed for the evening and at 6 Sir Louis Mallet arrived. "I deputise for Philip". Quite a nice talk with him, then Mrs Gubbay arrived. Then they both went and I was so bored that I went to sleep on my rose damask sofa, till Sir Louis returned and said it was dinner time. At dinner, Mrs Arthur Sassoon, the inevitable Mrs Gubbay, Sir Louis, Philip, me, and the usual rather nice, very shy and quite young flying man. We all went off to see Elisabeth Bergner in *Escape Me Never*. A wonderful actress. In bed by 12 asleep by 3 and woke up, as at Trent, stifling. The central heating is too much and the velvet curtains too much. Over luxury turns everything into a Hell. Philip promised to take me to a matinée and in the morning I went off in the car to see Joan [Fulleylove]. Returned to be told by Miss Boyce that he found he couldn't go!! Would I go with her – or the younger secretary or could I ring up a friend? Said I was tired and would *much* rather go home after lunch. I was furious: poor Miss Boyce was frightened to death: "Sir Philip will be terribly upset if you go home." So to save her getting into a row rang up Joan, who said she'd arrive at 2.15. She did, was kept 10 minutes in the hall and was *furious* (like me) and sick of these everlasting footmen! He didn't – Philip – even send us in a car but I had to pay for a taxi. Play, *Nymph Errant*, not up to much. Taxied back, parting with Joan. Had tea with Philip, he very

gracious, but it no longer cuts any ice with me! Home at 8 (having lost a 10/- note out of my bag) driving rain, no taxi, no outside porter. Straggled and struggled home, breathing deep and silent curses on 25 Park Lane and its luscious inmates. Had a glass of malted milk and went to bed.

6 January. Have quite decided never to go to Philip again, nor to go to Cornwall with Auntie M. I am happier (and far cheaper) at home.

16 January. Posted the proofs of *Portrait of Ellen*[1]. A far better title than mine and told Collins so; Collins having written with many apologies to explain that *Petty Cash* didn't lend itself to a jacket.

19 January. Slum Clearance meeting very boring yet anxious. And I felt awful when, the meeting over, Mr Young and I went to look at the map where the [area was] indicated in red! Thank God not my Mount Cottages, but my two in Westgate Street. Must write them off as a bad debt and (as Mr Monk so sensibly said) "gum the pages of the ledger together".

28 January. After church met 'Uncle Bates' very much on his best behaviour. Probably felt he went a little too far, absurdly holding my hand.

17 January. Muriel Hardy spoke of David as "a neat little old gentleman with silvery hair" I suppose he is but it seems so funny. Poor David! Poor me! Getting so old. Am I "a neat little old lady with silvery hair"?

7 March. Interview in *Sussex Daily News* horribly fulsome and I'm hoping and praying no one in Lewes will see it. I ought to have insisted on a proof.

10 March. *Portrait of Ellen* out. A whole row of her in the bookseller's window.

15 March. Letter from Vere . . . in great distress. Sullivan threatened with paralysis.

1 Published Collins, March 1934.

4 April. Terribly shocked to hear that my dear Mr Wycherley had a stroke and fell dead off his beautiful skewbald mare on Monday. For him the most exquisite death, just falling off the horse he so loved out in the sun.

6 April. Somehow can't work today, although 'Mrs Dudeney's new Sussex novel' is placarded over the town! Went to [Mr Wycherley's] funeral. Felt very sad.

7 April. Saw poor Charles Wycherley . . . he very sad in his father's office, the day after the funeral: "I know I must open his desk and yet I feel I can't." The lovely skewbald horse was in the funeral procession. Wycherley had always said, partly in fun, if anything happens to me, be sure my horse follows me to the cemetery!

9 April. Went into Wycherley's to say there was a window broken in Westgate Street and would they mend it. *So* sad. No dear Wycherley, and Charles Wycherley called me "Mrs Dudeney" and didn't open the door.

18 April. David. The dear thing was so pleased to be here and said the rest did him no end of good. I, too, loved to have him, but only in a way. And not for so long.

19 April. David very much admired my patchwork quilt but thinks it should have a border. So we went to Morrish's and bought pink stuff. By ill luck Auntie M came in! Did not introduce her. She all prickles, like a hedgehog, with curiosity!

21 April. After he'd gone I felt rather dull and stunned: as always, but less so.

22 April. Auntie M as usual and, as usual, Bezique. She never said a word about David. Didn't dare! I've taught her just how far she *may* go!

11 May. To David and Ida. Well, I thought I no longer cared, but – or was it only because the day was May at its most exquisite – I just loved him as I've always loved him, but with a difference. Less tempest, more tenderness. We

went out after dinner as Ida went up to rest, and wandered about in buttercuppey fields and sat on a tree trunk: an old man, an old woman, and yet it seemed 30 years ago come back again.

3 June. Very bad hump in church feeling I was so old and must die soon and I so hate Death and dread it. Comforted myself by thinking I wasn't dead yet and that there was roast chicken and ice cream for dinner.

8 June. Mrs Hyeem: 1.30. Pleasant lunch as usual. Mrs Hyeem said: "You ought to go and stay with Philip as you are one of the few people he is fond of."

9 June. Mrs Jervis looked quite pretty in a thin black frock. The crippled cousin genial, but hideous, with a luxuriant black moustache. Dressed brilliantly and badly, as I maintain all ugly women should dress: a dress, all yellow and red flowers, a blue cloth coat and mustard coloured hat, heaped with artificial flowers; bright but bilious.

11 June. Philip 1.30. In the train going up an old woman with amazingly piercing eyes very close together, one each side of a great nose. Very benign expression but she looked like a vegetarian vulture. Philip quite alone, except for a nice girl, his niece, Lady Cholmondeley's daughter – about 16: knew her as a baby. They drove me to Gorringe's where I bought a nice Milanese silk jumper suit, black, for £2 and a really adorable blue and white crepe de chine for the garden party.

16 June. Margaret in a great state. Had a row with Percy [Arkwell] who, mad drunk last night, threatened to "do her in" and challenged Hill to come down and fight. So Hill has taken out a summons which I think is a mistake. Home again and disgusted with the Germans.

19 June. At dinner time dear Margaret tumbled in, very excited. Gave her some Burgundy. Percy is bound over for 12 months to keep the peace. All the same I sort of feel the Hills will leave the Old Poor House. Hope not.

25 June. And actually before dinner, in the rough I finished *Rings on Her Fingers*[2]. Slept till tea time, then on the hills with Spangles as usual. After supper Hill arrived, looking extra poker-backed and livid. We nervously talked on general topics, each knowing what was in the background. Then he told me that Margaret felt, after the Percy affair, she couldn't stay at the Old Poor House. So they leave at Christmas. I was sorry, very, but not surprised.

27 June. Really, visitors are a nuisance. Winnie comes in to my room and announces that [Ida] can't get up: "so giddy". Elderly women should stay in their own homes. I do. Told Ida she'd better stop in bed all day. Said she would – might she have another pillow? Yes, she might. And got it. Might she have some brandy? Hadn't got it, but went out a bought a half bottle – 8/9d! Which I really grudged, but I suppose it ought to be in the house. Gave her some and she felt better. Chicken, not much, and ice cream for her dinner: complained that the ice cream melted too soon!

28 June. She is up thank goodness, but fussy, as always. An egg "lightly boiled" for breakfast. "You *will* see, won't you, Alice, that she doesn't hard boil it?" Alice (curtly): "She never does."

3 July. Oh the weather is so hot and lovely, and I leading such a quietly lovely life. Cutting roses and jasmine for the pot-pourri every morning after breakfast. Just loafing about the High Street with Spangles for an hour or so in a cotton frock and a big black hat, chatting with this one or that one! Wrote Philip backing out of his party.

7 August. Wycherley came – would I sell the lean-to (for £150, if you please) to Kitty Howard? Or let her rent the garden? Said no to both. Then like a fool – and being the fool that I so often am – went down and tried to make peace. Impossible! Shouted at [by Kitty]! 'I labour for peace but they make them ready for battle.'

---

2 Published Hutchinson 1934. AD comments that everything from 1916 diary put into this novel.

9 August. Vere. At tea time they arrived: Vere, the child, and Sullivan. He looked so appallingly ill that, on impulse, I asked him to come for the 2nd week of Vere's visit. He accepted, obviously very touched. So that's that. But perhaps a mistake as poor Vere says he gets so horribly on her nerves. Still! He is very ill, so I'm glad I did it, and so will she be.

10 August. The child is a darling and *no* trouble.

16 August. Sullivan arrived. He looks *ghastly*. The whole visit went off beautifully. He settled into Ernest's study and Ernest's bedroom and Ernest's lavatory! Came up after supper and talked brilliantly, to my delight. I who never get any clever creature to talk to. But he can hardly walk and to hear him come fumbling up the stairs was so like Ernest, through those last agonising months.

23 August. The parting was really dreadful, poor Vere holding on to me tight as we said goodbye; Sullivan so grateful saying how happy he'd been. And looking *awful*. I feel I shall never see him again: let's hope I'm wrong.

9 October. Took Spangles on the Southover hills. Everything amazingly lovely and clear. You could see not only Seaford Bluff, a sharp patch of darkling chalk, but also the long dim line of the Seven Sisters. I was enchanted and so happy. Spangles found a very nice ball which some child had dropped, so she was happy too.

18 October. Went to Broads, Southover. Sale there today of Miss Gabell Smith's surplus furniture. All rubbish. Seems so ghoulish the way we go to tea with each other while we are alive and go to each other's sales when one of us dies!

2 November. All Souls Day. Took flowers to Ernest's grave, bought all the cakes for the Bezique affair (what a funny sort of mix-up life is.)

5 November. David. He arrived at 12.30, just as I got in from shopping and I found him, when I came down, standing by the study fire, looking curiously attractive (for those with eyes to see) as he always does indoors (out of doors

in London clothes or country he is a failure). I suppose the hat does it. You lose that eloquent pose of the head. Anyhow Winnie went out; the town was full of flares and blares (it being Gunpowder Plot). Spangles was frightened to death, poor beast. David and I by the study fire alone were quietly happy, *very* happy: 2 old things!

6 November. Yesterday he put up the brass blower he has made for the drawing room grate, so it won't smoke like mad any more. The brass is very nice but I'm not sure it doesn't rather overwhelm the mantelpiece. After dinner in a bitter wind and greasy rain we went off to Brighton because I wanted to show him the lovely Regency houses at Kemp Town. Did, but were formal and very cold. That sort of architecture must have sunshine. Tea at Fulgens with crumpets, then we parted. I got home and Mrs Bates looked in before supper. Rather chilled me by saying she didn't like the brass and why didn't I paint it black!

12 November. After dinner took Spangles on the hills. We were so happy and she kept on coming back to say so. Orangey sun and the hills wearing their grey-to-lavender veils. If I could live for ever and walk with a spotted dog on the hills and never feel tired or look old and never leave my lovely house for more than a day at a time – Heaven!

25 November. After church met Uncle Bates, darkly purple about the Rector's Pacifism: "Damned little swine".

9 December. Pacifist meeting [3]. Off we went at 8.15 . . . the whole idea of the thing – as Mr Ensell remarked in loud tones as we came out – *mad*!

24 December. More presents and cards came. Very gay tea at the Bates, concluding with Bates wearing a cap out of a cracker seizing me by the arm when we were all on the point of departure and processing down the High Street as far as Antioch Street.

3 Strong Peace Movement in Lewes led by Reverend Rawlings and opposed by Reverend Ensell. Both had served in WWI. In 1944 an MP asked the Home Secretary to detain Rawlings for subversive activities.

25 December, Christmas Day. Sung Mass at 10.30. Joan came with me. Mabel Smythe had pinched my pew. Very charming gay day, concluding with hot elderberry wine at 11.

28 December. The general effect of every day is too much tobacco smoking on Joan's part and too much card-playing at night. But all very pleasant (for a change *only*). And I *do* wish she would come down to breakfast in good time.

Well: so ends the year and all the emotional conclusions I've written down in earlier diaries seem so foolish and trifling. All the emotions I have now is the wish to be comfortable and keep what I've got, for the little while I've got left. That and the still passionate desire that Margery should flourish and never, never suffer anything.

1935

'There was an old woman called Alice
Who thought that her house was a Palace
The neighbours all laughed and considered her Daft
But Alice knew this was mere Malice.'

Nice clean diary: nice New Year.

1 January. Letter from Philip. [He] has gone to Switzerland for a month. Went in to Thorntons about letting The Old Poor House. The man sat down beside me! They have no manners nowadays. Awful reaction after the Christmas orgy of eating, talking, card-playing and a room always stuffy with tobacco smoke! The only letter was one for Joan which made me senselessly mad!

31 January. Philip 12.45. To Brighton. Sat with Mrs Hyeem and Lady Boyle. Hundreds of people there and Philip made a brilliant speech. Afterward he, I, Mrs Hyeem and Lady Boyle went for a little walk along the front and then he hopped into a taxi for the station. That frigid basilisk look came over his face as he said goodbye: so I'm not – and never shall be – forgiven for refusing the chance so many would jump at, of staying with him. I was very chilled: why can't people be equable? How pleased Philip would be if he knew he could hurt me.

4 February. Mabel Smythe very pleasant and, like all the rest of 'em, urged me to go on the telephone: so when she'd gone nipped round to the Post Office and told them to send a man.

6 February. Mabel Smythe told me that a Miss Harvey Smith, after sending out invitations for her wedding, sent out a later notice: 'Owing to unforeseen circumstances it is now necessary for my marriage to take place a month earlier.'

8 February. Telephone men here. Hope I shall like it and learn to use it. Oh so bitter, bitter, cold. I could eat nothing.

21 February. At night I played with my new toy the telephone . . .

28 February. Met Mrs Hyeem who will see Philip on Monday. I said: "Give him my love". She said: "I shall say I have seen the Queen" (he calls me the Queen of Lewes)!

5 March. Went over to see Emily. She is one of those exasperating die-away-invalids (not necessary, however ill you are). Presented her with a noble bunch of violets: half shut eyes, languid movement of the hand, almost inaudible voice: "Put them on the table". Could have smacked her!

12 March. Got my title: not The Pack Horse but Put up the Shutters.

20 March. Margaret came to say goodbye. Tonight the darling Old Poor House stands empty after nearly seven years of a good and a happy tenancy. Feel exactly as if I had just come home from a funeral.

27 March. It gives 'one' a lovely sense of freedom not having a contract with Collins! But then you say to yourself am I ever going to find a publisher at all?

9 April. I was nearly mad with this and with that. Sent Margery 527 dollars, posted the proofs of *Barbourbrook*,[1] [Put up the Shutters], saw the Bank Manager about repayment of Income Tax. At night, seeing ruin ahead, poured half a bottle of eau-de-cologne in my bath and just lay there, half asleep. So reminiscent of the long ago visits to Lympne and the for-ever gone mood of gaiety and luxury. I enjoyed it then. I shrink from it now. I'm frightened of that and of everything.

23 April. David. Quite nice to see him: but oh how different to what it "used to was"! He keeps up the illusion, perhaps has preserved it. I haven't.

1 Published 1935 by Collins.

29 April. Find that I've sent nearly £450 to USA. Can do no more and I must say so. Worked, but hard to get back into the mood.

1 May. At 5 after I had taken Spangles for a walk, Mr Wigram came and motored me to Southease. I like them both[2]. She said: "Why does Philip like you better than any one else? He constantly says so. Is it because you have always resisted him?" I got driven home after supper. She having put Philip into my head, rang it [him] up. It was lovely and I *saw* 25 Park Lane, the mellifluous voice of the footman: "Yes Madam. I will see if Sir Philip is in, Madam" And then Philip's voice, chaffing as usual. "Have you been to the Gages lately?" "Of course not, they haven't asked me." "Well, naturally, they are diffident"! And then: "What's your number? I'll ring you up every day. But you are the Queen of Lewes. So I shall just say: "'Put me through to the Palace.'"

7 May. More 'suggestions' through Wycherley from Kitty Howard (the Black Mamba). She would like to continue her tenancy: if she might have the garden entirely to herself when 'in residence' and if I would undertake to have the rain water butt emptied at frequent intervals! Told Wycherley she could stay on if she liked but I was not open to any 'suggestions': I should go into the garden whenever I liked and empty the water butt when I thought necessary. Considering the woman is only allowed in the garden by my permission, her impudence is colossal. Winnie went off early to Brighton to see the Jubilee[3] decorations.

8 May. Came home and sat for a long time by the open window. Everything peaceful and exquisite: the lime trees in their new green frocks and one tiny child, with a golden head and a crimson jersey, looking like a little jewel as he flashed about in sunlight. At night I went out and saw the Castle flood-lit, a *wonderful* sight.

17 May. Quite decided that this next novel (probably my last) shall be published by Heinemann, who published my first. Wrote on the subject to

2 Friends of PS, who lived at Southease, nr Lewes.
3 Silver Jubilee of King George V and Queen Mary.

Mrs Belloc Lowndes who is a kindly soul and, also, a regular Nosey Parker with her finger well on the pulse of the literary world. Major Sutton came to see the Old Poor House and told me he recently saw in the photographic section of the National Portrait Gallery a photograph of me (first I've heard of it!) He said, with a candid stare: "of a most attractive looking young woman – *must have been taken a long time ago.*"

24 May. Pinker sent a miserable list of reviews of *Portrait of Ellen*, mostly provincial. Clearly Collins doesn't advertise, so doesn't get reviews. Shall leave them.

25 May. Heinemann will not make a contract; his lists already too full; but if I will let him see the MS will give it sympathetic and careful attention. Don't know what to do.

4 June. There is some mystery about Collins. Pinker quite sympathetic, but very non-commital . . . he also said that Hutchinson wanted me, so I needn't have been nervous about a publisher.

18 June. David arrived with the brass he has made, which is lovely. Said he must go back tomorrow. Then I explained (letting him down as easily as I could) that, old as we were, there had been a certain amount of amused gossip: so, he mustn't stay too long, nor come too often! Not at all sure he wasn't relieved: feeling as I do (although he won't admit it even to his own mind) that it is exhausting to come all the way just to see a white-haired burnt-out Divinity! Perhaps it was a romantic mistake our ever meeting again. And yet I don't know. He is certainly a comfort, but he bores me. He even annoys me (how *incredible* it seems).

21 June. Margaret very pleasant and the ultra modern house is charming inside. Outside, hideous to my thinking. And especially squatting in the middle of an ancient garden[4].

---

4 The Hills moved to The Garden House, Paine's Twitten, built in the original kitchen garden of Caprons, Keere St, once home of Nicholas Yonge the madrigalist.

29 June. Wrote Margery telling her I had no contract, did not propose to write any more novels – and pointing out as plainly and delicately as I could, that I could no longer be relied upon.

3 July. Again our letters cross and he [Philip] begs me once more to come and suggesting I go to Park Lane for 2 nights and then motor down with him to Trent. Impossible to refuse. Also I think I was glad to accept. I've been going through such a rueful time and worse may follow!

11 July. Very slack after gadding up to Philip's, *and* the usual rich food! Sat in the garden most of the day. The roses are heavenly.

4 August. Auntie M. I've always *suspected* her of cheating at cards. Had no *proof*: only unerring intuition. Tonight I caught her out. I drew, she was drawing and it was the ten of hearts – a sequence card – face up, by accident. I stopped her and said: "Oh, but that must go in the middle of the pack". She only laughed and said: "Oh, but it was such a nice card"! Not a bit embarrassed, although she was trying to sneak it! . . . Letter from someone who wants to turn Barbour book into Braille. Consented.

7 August. David and Ida. Quite a nice day . . . Ida very pleasant (I took her one of Wheeler's bouquets) and David, who met me at the 'bus, the usual dear. After lunch she went to rest, which was all to the good, and he and I sat very, very happily in the garden.

17 August. Oh *Lord*! The housekeeping. [Vere and family staying]. Everlasting talk about meals. Ghastly foreshowing of heavy bills. Food disappearing as if we had a cloud of locusts in the house. And the child running up and downstairs and in and out of rooms all day long! A quiet life is my life!

20 August. At last, the one perfect day, which Vere and I will not forget. We, alone, took 'bus to Firle and walked to the top of the Beacon. Exquisite beauty, perfect heavenly peace.

22 August. They went. Vere hugging me so tightly, the child so loving and sweet. Sullivan so grateful, saying he had enjoyed every minute, so of course

they must come again next year (if there is a next year for all of us). Anyhow I blissfully slept all the afternoon ...

3 September. Darling Spangles (one of the lovely scenes to remember) came walking delicately down the stone path between blazing marigolds. All the morning an artist painted the house and when he packed up his traps he looked pleasantly up to me at the drawing room window and called: "I love your beautiful house". . . . I was as pleased as Punch. Always am!

24 September. As I was sitting at dinner an old, tall and remarkably statuesque nun drifted like a shed leaf past the window. I thought – there goes a lucky and a Holy woman. She's not bothered by proofs, terrified at the idea of Slum Clearance, or the roof falling in. And not rent by anxiety (let us trust) about an absent daughter. The effect of her was rather ruined by the quite dapper umbrella she carried!

26 September. Proofs of *Put Up the Shutters*[5] came, so read myself blind doing those. Seems funny to work for a new publisher, after fifteen years of Collins.

2 October. Letter from Margery. Darling Margery says that by common consent the pound I sent for the boys' birthday presents was spent on unbleached calico to make sheets: 'As we have no sheets'. I was horrified, and at once sent her another £1, for pillow cases!

3 October. Pearson offers £10 for the copyright of Ernest's *Modern Puzzles*[6]. Thought it wise to consent as the sales of that book are negligible and Nelson has refused to republish it (even if I could get the rights from Pearson). Also the £10 will just do as a Christmas present for Margery.

5 October. Mabel Smythe such a dear woman. I enjoyed her coming to tea, and she stayed until 6.30!

---

5 Published Hutchinson, set in Lewes. Spangles features as the 'misty-eyed' Dalmatian. AD's last novel.
6 Published C. Arthur Pearson 1926.

12 October. Well! I've always found that if I want a thing enough I get it. Went to Peskett and, at last, after about six years coaxing cajoled him into selling me the turquoise earrings with the tiny gold stars – for 10/-! They belonged to a Countess in mid-Victorian days. Mrs Peskett's aunt was her ladysmaid and the earrings were left to her . . . In the top garden we are going to have roses there instead – General McArthur. So I went to bed very happy and could hardly get to sleep for thinking of red roses and blue ear-rings.

15 October. Went to tea with Mrs Brough yesterday and she, after rather beating about the bush, said she'd been reading my latest novel and was so struck by my "penetration". As Sairey Gamp[7] would say: "*Oh* 'ow kind"!

16 October. Yesterday was a doubly important day for as well as signing my new Will I started on my Memoirs! . . . Have written a Foreword. I think I shall call the book 'Look in thy Heart'.

5 November. Went out and disbursed various sixpences and odd coppers to small kids with "guys". 6d to the wicked little Martin boy: "And I hope you'll behave better in future". Fervent "I will". (he won't!) 6d to Harry Arkwell: "And I hope you'll have a happy day". "I hope you will too". (I certainly shan't – with rousers[8] going off and Spangles stark with terror). The usual penny to the small Percy boy, who hadn't got a guy, poor little waif. Long chat with my dear Mr Spokes who says he is "going downhill" and he looks it.

7 November. David. I do find it so not only boring but exasperating to the point of *screaming* to sit by the fire hours on end, just talking. Also, in ways, he gets on my nerves. And that is what these affairs come to! Which is tragic, if you'd let it be! No, call it funny.

8 November. In the morning the devoted dear thing mended the springs of my bedroom sofa for me. After tea he departed and I had a superlatively

7 Sarah Gamp, character in Charles Dickens' novel *Martin Chuzzlewit*.
8 Alarmingly loud Bonfire rook-scarers. This year the Bonfire Societies burnt an effigy of Mussolini. In 1933 they burnt an effigy of Hitler.

blissful evening alone, speechless. (I think women are beasts. Men are more faithful and simple).

14 November. I gave Emily a whole stack of old clothes, she was glad. We then had tea and Bezique in the study (Winnie being out) and everything went merrily until at supper time I told her that in view of Margery and Christopher being so hard up and 6 of them to keep, I had altered my Will and not left her (Emily) £300 as before. She was "hurt", it was a "great shock" but "I am always being hurt, all the time." I felt very sorry for her but didn't regret telling her. Much worse if she found it out after I was dead.

24 November. The one event of Saturday was a very lovely notice of *Put up the Shutters* in *The Times*. I was so delighted after all the setbacks and bitter disappointments I've lately had. Just walked about the drawing room in fire-light – candlelight – and *joyfully* cried.

6 December. At night pain [in her back] so awful that it was arranged Winnie should put on my shoulder a porous plaster. I was impatient, she poor little soul, was nervous, overheated the plaster, let it curl up, vainly tried to pick it open! It was like a rolled brandy snap! I laughed, flung it across the room and begged her not to give it another thought!

7 December. Secretly bought another Alcock's Porous Plaster and, after my bath, practised before unpacking it and found I could wriggle it on to my tortured self quite nicely. So did. I feel like a hoarding, all plastered up!

8 December. The Alcock's Porous plaster has done the trick!

11 December. I must cultivate the feeling of being glad I have retired, instead of being afraid because the money will no longer roll in by £100s!

31 December. I absolutely started on the 'Memory' [9] book again and was happy and loved it. I shall call it – if ever it gets done (doubtful): Under The Table.

9 AD's Memoirs are given various titles.

1936

I mean to be happy this year: quite likely the last year I've got. It began with the usual dear little adoring note from David, and, also, an especially charming letter from Philip.

1 January. As Winnie was turning out this room and 'won't be druv'[1] (which means she simply *can't* be) I went and had lunch in Brighton . . . then to Emily who was very urbane and looking really nice in a white woollen jumper and the tweed skirt I gave her.

4 January. Lady Shiffner[2]. A nice party: 4 of us. A Lady Someone was there, sounded like Spelmuraline (and wasn't, of course). Parrot-faced woman. I never like a woman who looks like a bird. Poor Miss Wildash is so like one that if she dared wear a tuft of feathers in her hat she'd find herself in a cage.

6 January. Philip's letter unusually charming: the real Philip who is my friend.

8 January. Vet says Spangles, although fat, is in perfect health and "a dear old girl" (seems funny to admit that Spangles is old!) And she's fat because she's got a "happy disposition". On the way down we met a donkey cart. She was enthralled, never having seen a donkey before. I had to drag her along. After tea Wycherley rang up. Pilfold, if he can have a new cooking stove (price £4), is quite willing to pay 1/- a week more rent. Wycherley and I were hoping that he couldn't pay more and would have to go to the Work-us [Workhouse]! Where both he and she ought to be, so that they could be well scrubbed with disinfectant and anti-vermin soap.

16 January. Joan to lunch. I had ordered roast pork and felt some misgiving as to whether an ex-vegetarian would sink to so gross a level. However she

---

1 The traditional saying of stubborn Sussex folk.
2 Magistrate, living at Coombe Place, Hamsey, Nr Lewes.

announced that she loved pork and – in more senses than one – 'hogged it'! Looking quite handsome (would be very if her nose wasn't so big). Hair just washed and and set in little ringlets. She looked like the Duchess of Kent. Very affectionate, very enigmatic, exasperatingly reticent over family affairs.

17 January. Had one of my incredibly tired fits, so stayed in bed till dinner time. Wonder if it's heart, nerves, or eyes . . .

21 January. Great shock. The King is dead. Winnie took Spangles out and I went to the YMCA to hear Mabel Smythe talk about old Lewes to the blind people. A very touching affair. Came home and rang up Mrs Capron. We decided to cancel her party in view of the King's death.

23 January. Went out with Spangles to hear the Proclamation of the new King – Edward VIII. We were all there: Spangles was frightened to death when she heard the bugles. Mrs Lister said she couldn't bring Murray [Dalmatian] because he had brown spots. But Spangles is all right in half mourning. Oh – last night I went to Mrs Jervis's to hear Baldwin on the wireless about the King. But I would far rather have *read* the speech, fresh next morning.

28 January. Requiem for the King: 10.30. Told Winnie she could go to the United Memorial Service at All Saints at 3. First she would and then she wouldn't, the usual fuss! Finally did and couldn't get in. Church crowded to bursting.

29 January. What with a pain in my back and the awful terror that my [new] false teeth might fall out, not much of a [tea] party for me. Also they were in lovely black and I (the King having said we need not wear black after the funeral) mistakenly put on my nice warm (and becoming) geranium red dress. Mrs Jervis laughed afterwards and said: "We thought you'd gone Bolshie".

1 February. Dentist. Lovely teeth . . . met Pa Bates, long talk with him, I can talk now and eat. To the pictures with Mrs Jervis to see the King's Funeral.

11 March. At 2.30, to the tick, she [a Miss Bedford] came. A large redfaced woman talking incessantly in a smooth, slobbery way, just like Tom

[Dudeney]. Showed me photographs of her father: Rector of Denton for 65 years. Started talking about Horology, then about Spiritualism. One night, not feeling very well, she had a glass of wine "by my bedside". Was starting to drink it at midnight when she saw written in flaming characters on the wall: *'Do not drink wine. A green apple is better for you'*. It was signed *Father Brown*. I said: "Did you finish the wine?" She said: 'Oh yes." I thought she was never going. Finally, when I was really beginning to get nervous, she asked me to lend her £10 till Saturday to pay her rates. Finally came down to £5, then to £1. On my refusal went off leaving her umbrella behind, probably as an excuse for coming again

19 April. Gave my seat, where I've sat for years (and gave it not without a pang!), to Mabel Smythe. And sat behind in Ernest's pew which has always squeaked. However, Mabel Smythe has a groggy leg, so mustn't be bothered with a squeaky pew as well.

13 May. Called with Mrs Jervis on the new people at the Red House, Southover [High Street]. A Miss Dicker, over 80, very well bred, very untidy. Same may be said of her nephew 'Tam'[3], an artist: same may be said of the house, crammed with lovely things: furniture that hadn't been polished for years – a blue bloom on it. Delightful couple all the same, as we agreed. But Mrs Jervis said she would like to take 'Tam' and his ancient aunt and boil them in the copper!

15 May. In the afternoon took one of the blue washing basins to the man in Keere Street to be riveted. He, both legs amputated at the trunk (war), so brave and cheerful. A fine man – over 6 foot once! Made one feel that a tummy ache and other tiresome little troubles don't amount to much.

21 May. Very nice party. 'Tam' arrived, exquisitely shaved and cut; the old lady a darling and very elegant in black and with a golden sable tippet (every old woman should wear golden sable if she can get it). Every ancient woman: for me, so far, silver fox is admirable.

3 Nephew of Viscount Lee of Fareham.

30 May. By last post letter from Hove Librarian asking for one of my MSS for exhibiting in the Museum. Managed to dig out *Put up the Shutters*. He also wanted one of Ernest's but I think they were burned. Must look.

9 June. Charming letter from the Hove Librarian. He is enchanted to have Ernest's notebooks which I sent him by request, for inclusion with my *Put up the Shutters* for the collection of MSS they are making at the Museum.[4]

20 June. Got here at 7, found David here. Quite a dear thing. Still very devoted, or thinks he is!

21 June. Such *heavenly* weather. We went to church. I wore my black silk coat and skirt. He says black and ivory is best for me, out of doors. As for the garden: the walls are, as he said, a tapestry of roses. He admitted that he had never, until now, considered this garden, as such. Quite took his breath.

22 June. Well. Quite a perfect weekend: and a weekend is enough of anybody. And never now do I feel that stunned loss and solitude which once I felt when he went. To descend to the distasteful facts of life: Winnie found 6 fleas on Spangles.

30 June. Margery's letter was *real* and broke my heart. Her letters for months have been bluffing and *shadows*. The strain is telling on her, as I knew it must. No good crying, though I *did*. But mopped up. At night wrote her suggesting she should come home alone for a holiday. I must, if she consents, fork out the passage money *somehow*.

3 July. Worked hard and well, in the middle of which the usual flunkey rang up for Philip and then came Philip himself. Would I lunch at The Metropole on Monday? Yes, I would.

4 July. Met Mrs Jackson. She said that Mrs Picton was not married till she was 60 but confessed, with emotion: "I was not a virgin".

4 Neither Hove Museum nor Hove Library can trace these.

6 July. At The Metropole a miserable lunch but Philip was very nice – quite as of old. Mrs Gubbay and Lady Cholmondeley quite affectionate! We all went off in a taxi . . . Dropped me at East Street. Went first to Cresta Silk shop for a knitted suit, then to Hanningtons. Nothing.

10 July. SAS Outing to Bodiam.[5] Not going. Yes I am. Off we went. Got to Bodiam in a thunderstorm, but no rain on us as we walked across sodden meadows to Bodiam Castle; roofless and beautiful, surrounded by a moat covered with water lilies. Then it deluged. Mr Jackson and I, preferring not to stand on wet grass listening to archaeology, climbed to the top of the Castle and kept dry! Lunch at the hotel before which, thanks to him, a cocktail, which warmed and restored me. After lunch to the church then on to Robertsbridge and Salehurst church. Then tea, then home, tired but a nice day. At Bodiam in the hotel garden a lovely Chester rose, quite violet. I cadged some cuttings.

22 July. Lady Cholmondeley 1.15. Both Lady C and the Marquis are the most charming simple people and I enjoyed the lunch and talk with them even more than *Pride and Prejudice* to which she afterwards took me! They, especially he, told me that Philip is becoming quite outrageous in his behaviour to everybody and Lord C can't think why people don't walk out of his house when he is in that mood. Sir Louis told me much the same.

26 July. [Winnie away for 2 weeks] I feel extraordinarily marooned and deserted: the home so big and quiet. Never mind. Soon be over, and I've stuck it! But for Muriel Hardy turning up each morning to paint a picture of the drawing room, should lose the use of my tongue.

2 August. This is David's birthday. He is 74. Sent him a birthday telegram.

28 September. Angmering. Miss Orme met me and we were taken by the now owner, a nice man Gerald Molson by name, over my dear Pigeon House now quite 'restored' and a very lovely 14th century house.

---

5 Bodiam Castle, East Sussex. Ruined medieval castle now belonging to the National Trust.

4 October. Again poor Auntie M entirely alienated me by her unquenchable vulgarity. Was talking of Dusart the hairdresser getting married again and thought Mrs George Holman would do. I said she was far too good, socially. "Oh", screams and trumpets Auntie M: "You want him yourself."!

13 October. 10 a.m. The most curious thing happened just now. I had brought up the typewriter, was feeling very well (and looking nice!) The fire burned; there was a jug of flowers and Philip's green tray on the table and I thought as I cleaned the keys of the typewriter and as I looked round – and also considered my adorable gilded clock on the landing – "*How lovely everything is*". And I heard Ernest's voice distinctly and felt him quite near me: "*Everything is lovely, my darling.*"

29 October. I made myself a slogan: '*Stormy and Sour*' (which lately I have been): '*Sweet and Serene*' (which I propose to be). On the hills as usual, but I wish Spangles was not always so ready to turn back and come home! How well I know that dreadful sign of impending old age. Nelson, Emma, and now Spangles.

3 November. After dinner made a bonfire of old MSS, proofs (of *Put up the Shutters*) and all Ernest's diaries, not a single interesting one. He always said so: "Don't think that, after I'm gone, you'll find any revelations". Mine are *all* revelation. His are: 'Went to London. Went to Brighton. Mass at St Michael's with Alice. Cheque from Nelsons.' Well! They are all curling up nicely at the bottom of the garden, under a heap of pear leaves.

10 November. Mrs Dunstan's [6] usual squash! About 15 of us. Mrs Miller, regular old garbage-er, talking hard about the King and Mrs Simpson!

2 December. Awful Crisis over the King and the Simpson woman. He wants to marry her. Why not be content? He's got her as his mistress.

---

6 Dr Dunstan (the Medical Officer of Health) and Mrs Dunstan lived at 1, De Warenne Road.

4 December. Mrs Dunstan and I nearly came to blows. She saying she was very sorry for him. I said that if he broke up the Bezique Club that would be the greatest calamity of all. Old Peskett the watchmaker's father said of the affair: "When a man gets to be forty, he's either a Fool or a Philosopher, and he's a Fool".

5 December. We talk, up and down the High Street, in and out of houses, of nothing but the King. Some say he has made over the Duchy of Cornwall to that Simpson fiend. Others say he can't. Some say she is a spy from Russia.

6 December. Auntie M and I, of course, talking of nothing but the King and Mrs Simpson. To play Bezique was almost impossible. Garvin's article in *The Observer* much too sentimental and flowery.

7 December. Bitterly, bitterly cold but, would you believe it, quite heavenly on the Southover hills. And I tried to forget all this squalid affair about the King and Mrs Simpson. He doesn't matter over much, and she less than nothing. What does matter beyond everything, is the stability of the Empire.

8 December. I pulled myself together, finished and packed up my Memory book and sent it off to Pinker: *Look in Thy Heart*. For the rest: nothing but rain, solitude, silence and "worreting" about the King.

9 December. Everybody – everywhere – talking about the King and feeling against him very strong.

10 December. Feel perfectly awful just as we did in the war. He will certainly abdicate and there are all sorts of rumours. Mrs Langhorne, the Rector of St John's wife, who is deaf, was talking in the shop to Mrs Peskett the watch-maker's wife, and she said: "That Mrs Simpson is pretending to the King that she is going to have a baby". Didn't hear the shop door open, turned round – saw a man: just shrieked and fled!

11 December. King Edward abdicates. So utterly done for with so much excitement that I stayed in bed till dinner time and slept most of the morning.

At 10 went by invitation to Mrs Jervis and listened in to the ex-King's broadcast. Not touched in the least. Much more artistic if he had just faded out and said nothing.

12 December. Muriel Hardy 4.30. She recovering from 'flu and "wetchedly depwessed." The room so lovely: pale green walls, green and gilt Rockingham tea service, on a white cloth. She said that when she came down for the first time her sister had got it arranged on a checked cloth, and the effect was so bad that it very nearly sent her back to bed again. . . . The broadcast moved me not at all. But I see that when he got on board the ship, he remained for a long time on deck until the lights of England faded out. That melted me. Also, he has taken his little dog.

19 December. Yesterday's party was delicious. A Christmas party. We all pulled crackers and wore caps at tea time and were like a lot of schoolgirls: and everybody over 60. When you are young you think old people are dull and wretched. Not so.

24 December. A letter from Margery giving all the figures for her trip over and saying she must, if she came in May, have the money in hand so as to book a passage when she got the chance as ships are crowded owing to the Coronation.

28 December. Great blow, yet I don't seem to mind! I dread misfortune until it comes. When it does, I stand up to it! The Poor House tenants have given notice, so I shan't be able to pay Margery's fare over.

So ends 1936. My Memory book in the balance, Margery not coming home. The Poor House tenants leaving. Not over cheerful. Muriel Hardy said that one of her mother's uncles was dissipated. His father sent for him: "Son – I understand you keep a mistress?" "I do, Sir". "Very well then, but keep her out of sight." (Why didn't the ex-King keep Mrs Simpson out of sight?)

1937

20 January. Margery so plainly disappointed at not coming: so I wrote 'come'. And then I was most terribly excited for the rest of the day.

25 January. I do somehow fill up the mornings, it is 12 now. I have made a rabbit stew and put on some pears in a casserole and filled up this and done a little mending but it's all so barren. I'm quite lost without the imaginative side to life and I just can't do as David says he always would – and must do – work, even if there were no chance of selling.

26 January. Mrs Arkwell turned up in tears. He dying of consumption and the awful Baker woman at number 5 mocking his cough. Said I could do nothing. However I did. Went to Mrs Pilfold, protesting first and then pleading with her to be kind to Mrs Arkwell whose husband was very ill: "Suppose it were your husband". But she only met me with her silly giggle and malevolent stare. Then went to Arkwell, having previously cheered her up with tea in the kitchen and a present of eggs. He a shocking sight, fighting for breath, but managed to gasp out that "a little brandy, Mrs Dudeney" would relieve him. Said I had none and then, after hesitation, that I could spare a little whiskey. She came at once and fetched it.

2 February. In the afternoon it rained – of course! Spangles stood at the front door, deliberating, in a quite human way: Shall I? Shan't I? The no-es had it! She returned to her basket and I went off in the rain alone.

11 February. Sent through Barclays £50 – or the equivalent in dollars – to Margery for her voyage home.

16 February. Off to tea with Tam and Miss Dicker. Queer little stump of a manservant opened the door, very dignified and funny. The drawing room straight at last and looking perfectly adorable. A lovely room with just a few

exquisite things in it. After tea Tam took me down the garden and then into the cellar to see stones from the Priory [1] let into the wall.

17 February. Letter from Lord Abergavenny's agent: would I buy the Brack Mount [2]? Saw Mr Spokes about it. Saw Godfrey. Both of them amazed, anxious. It might as at Bramber Castle [3], be turned into a Pleasure garden with roundabouts! But Godfrey says the Sussex Archaeological Society would move heaven and earth to save it from that.

21 February. Winnie came rushing out, Sir Philip Sassoon had rung up. Poor Philip! In bed with chicken pox! We had the usual little bantering talk. He begged me to write and I said so I would, tomorrow.

24 February. Letter from Eridge. They ask £75 for the Mount. Accepted. So excited that I thought I *must* have a stroke, and in the end no doubt I shall!

25 February. I thought very little of the Mount: except to prowl about - outside and in - wondering if and where a door could be knocked through. One thing is *certain, if* I buy it then I must go on writing to pay for it. And for Margery's sake, I dare not neglect to buy it, for it would raise the value of this house. So, at night, alone – Winnie out and Spangles took herself off at 6.30 – scratched my head as usual and got a plot for a novel. "Married Couples Only". Rather trivial. Shall think of something better – did: "Shell of a Lady" [4].

1 After the dissolution of the monasteries, the stones of the Cluniac Priory in Lewes were looted by townsfolk for their properties.
2 Second motte of Lewes Castle standing up against CPH which probably had a shell keep like its twin. It was used as an Observer Post from 1925, later moved to the Castle Keep.
3 Destroyed in Civil War, now owned by National Trust and cared for by English Heritage.
4 Turned into short story.

14 April. Seldom have I lived through such a day. Letter from H Blaker – would I go at 10.30. He had the Contract for the Brack Mount. Went. Paid the deposit: £7.10. Returned, found Emily patiently waiting and full of a new flat she's taken and would I draft a letter for her to the landlord? Did. At 2.30 cometh Harold Blaker with the Contract properly ingrossed and ready for signature. We then went on the Brack Mount and discovered, to begin with, a hole in my roof on the north side. He now thinks I am quite wise to sell to the SAS (was against it to begin with) but suggests I keep about a foot round my house: in case I, or future tenants, wish to throw out a window. He went. Had a fair night but woke at 4.30, clammy with terror – suppose the Brack Mount wall fell down before I sold it to the SAS?!

19 April. Terrible letter from Vere. Sullivan's case quite hopeless. Took me all the morning writing to her, Sullivan and packing up and posting the whacking Bagatelle Board [for their son Navin].

22 April. Mr Bentham Stevens had rung up – might he call and see me at seven? Did. A nice man, rather reminding me of Sir Louis Mallet. Not only will the Society buy the Mount but he, and all of them, are "very grateful to me". And I may make a door! And he will see Harold Blaker tomorrow.

30 April. Not only has the SAS bought the Mount of me but all the members think it *"exceedingly kind of Mrs Dudeney"*. So excited that, of course, I hardly slept.

2 May. Auntie M, Bezique. Told her I had bought the Brack Mount, she thought I meant the public house! So indicative of her mind.

7 May. In the morning I went to Woolworth for Coronation decorations which Olive put up. And Spangles is sporting a bow on her collar.

9 May. We've got all the Coronation decorations up and flags flying from the attic windows, east and west. Went in to see Mr Spokes after church. Auntie M as usual.

12 May. Coronation of George VI. It was a dull, cold, wettish day. Most unfortunate. I took Spangles out for a little toddle between the showers but before that I romped off in the most rapt and easy way with the sudden idea of a short story to fill up the short story book if Hutchinson insists (which means if it is in the Agreement). If not, then I'll see him damned first.

19 May. Worked like the dickens at that story and got it done – 11,000 words, rough copy and clean – in 5 days. Quite done for, but triumphant.

25 May. Wycherley came along wth a Mr and Mrs Amos, very nice people and they will take the house [OPH] if I put in an Ideal Boiler. Said I would, but it means more money out of pocket. Gone are those halcyon six years and more when the Hills paid me £65 a year without an Ideal Boiler.

27 May. Dear Mr Spokes arrived and we went together through my door, up the Mount.

2 June. Letter from Margery dreading leaving her family: quite maternal but neither cheering nor complimentary to me!

7 June. In such a frantic state of excitement that I can't keep still. Now – 9.30 – shall go to bed, wishing that the night was over. Wire from the Cunard people. The *Aquitania* gets to Southampton at one o'clock tomorrow. Dear Mrs Jervis has just rung up, wishing me God speed.

8 June. Auntie M yesterday with her detestable vulgarity asks: "What class is Margery coming?" I said: "Second". "Oh then she'll have to wait — a long time – while the *first* class passengers come off. I travelled first, of course, when I went to America and also had the best cabin on the ship." Why hadn't I the wit to say that Margery was travelling steerage? Met Margery on the *Aquitania*.

9 June. Mrs Godfrey: 4 pm. Very stiff party at Mrs Godfrey's. Lots of cakes and no conversation. Margery wore the fashionable Halo hat, which I think hideous. The rest of her clothes I like very much.

11 June. All this coming and going is very enticing without doubt, also exhausting – beyond *question!*

12 June. Emily very pleasant and loving. Greatly improved in Margery's opinion.

24 June. At Mrs Brough's[5] party Margery looked quite adorable, in a simple but very smart cotton frock, shortwaisted, full-skirted. I was complimented on my "charming" daughter, with the doubtful additional compliment: "Does she take after her father?"

25 June. Another delightful day. Dear David met the bus. Margery jumped out, hugged him and complimented him on his straight back. Ida was especially affectionate.

30 June. Angmering. So lovely to go about together like this, but, always, with salt welled up behind my eyeballs. Terribly reminiscent and romantic the visit to the Pigeon House. Tea there with Gerald Molson and then Margery and I walked up Highdown. She turned round suddenly laughing and said: "Well, you *are* a sport, clambering about all over the place." Adding that Keturah [relation] in her letter said that I was 'very frail' and that really was what decided Margery to come over! And she finds me, so she says, looking better *and* younger than when I went to America seven years ago.

7 July. Margery sails. Less said about this day the better. At 7 we went down to the station together. Oh, I shan't write anything at all about it.

18 July. Before church met Mrs Bates and she told me dear Zeb had been put to sleep. Auntie M very subdued and giving you that impression of deafness and pathos which makes you forgive her. Moreover she said, with obvious sincerity, of Margery: "How pretty she is". So as a reward took her up the Mount!

---

5 Mrs Brough lived at 'Bogle Tye', Brighton Road.

23 July. Most exciting post. Formal letter from the SAS giving me access to the Mount. Formal letter from Bentham Stevens telling me the SAS had elected me a Vice President. I went to the hospital and saw Muriel Hardy with her broken leg.

10 August. All day long I did nothing much but write letters and sit about in the garden, because I thought it was good for me! But the midges bite me and make bumps. And the garden is full of Ghosts. I can't sit there alone.

11 August. Went off to the police station and lodged a complaint about the odious Martin boy with his impudence and his toy pistol. Mrs Pinyoun says that the Arkwell girl, Emmy, only 16, has gone away to have a baby. I remember what Winnie said she overheard some louts say of Emmy Arkwell: "She'll get what she's asking for one of these days." Evidently she did!

12 August. Letter from Vere – Sullivan unconscious and dying. Sent her a wire. Not at all a happy day, Vere's news apart, which would have saddened me anyhow. The beastly children letting off pistols and shrieking [on Castle Banks].

26 August. Every day after dinner I go up on the Mount, which is my delight.

1 September. Every day I think will be Dull but something happens! Today it was my new tenant at the Old Poor House, Mr Amos, calling at supper time half drunk. I'm so unused to this and so impressionable that before we'd been talking five minutes I was as vague as he was! In fact: I was – psycholligaly – half drunk: and he may have thought so.

9 September. Winnie asks: "Do you wish me to change into a black frock on my afternoon out?" I said she always had so why not? Oh well, other servants etc. I rapped out that what other servants did and other mistresses allowed was nothing to do with me. Walked off and when next we met she was in her black frock.

10 September. Mr Spokes – met him in the High Street – told me the saddest thing. Old Mr and Mrs Fuller at the White Lion (wickedly condemned under the infamous Slum Clearance [6]) this morning got their final notice to quit and were found gassed. Both dead.

13 September. Yesterday down Rotten Row met Mr Bates who always waylays me, for the sake of stroking Spangles now that he has lost Zeb. And darling Spangles showed off beautifully, wriggling and grinning just like her half brother!

27 September. Pleasant party but poor Mrs Hyeem plainly disappointed over the Brack Mount: "Second Keep of Lewes Castle". She had expected to *see* a Castle.

29 October. Pinker returns the Memory book. The publishers say "charmingly written, but would not make a large appeal".

9 November. I worked a bit at 'Shell of a Lady' but not with much heart. I admire David who goes on joyfully painting water colours with no chance of worldly success. I am more gross and must see money at the end. In the afternoon took Spangles a lovely walk on the Southover hills . . .

11 November. Cheque – £38 7s – for the Westgate Street cottages: all I shall get (less income tax) for houses which cost £240. Less said the better, anyhow. I don't at the moment owe a penny in the world and I've got a balance of £220.

12 November. Mrs Brough's party. Seventeen of us, the biggest gathering known, Very nice one indeed and Auntie M in her new green dress and hat looked really nice. Mrs Jervis, commenting on this rare achievement, said: "If she would only powder her nose!" But I don't think powder would stay put on that nose.

---

6 The 'slum' cottages and pub were replaced by a car park, the only redeeming feature of which is the fine inn sign of the White Lion mounted on the town wall.

26 November. But, sad reflection, I am getting a little weary of Bezique every week. (Is there *anything* left that I don't lose the savour of, or lose altogether?!)

12 December. 21 years since I met Philip. Wrote and sent him biscuits as a birthday present: our 21st birthday!

23 December. Dorothy Dusart rang up: Auntie M still in bed and quite unable to come for Christmas.

25 December. This goes down on record as the most desolate Christmas I have ever spent. Never before have I been alone. Never again will I rely on Auntie M. Second Christmas she's let me down, but when she was ill here I had Joan. Everything went wrong. Nobody came to see me on Christmas Eve, usually someone does. Mary Carr sent me a silver grey scarf, never wear that sort of thing, gave it to Winnie . . . Mr Whyle instead of sending shortbread (which he has done for 15 years) sent a box of chocolate, cost I should imagine a bob at the outside. Margery sent a belt, and I never wear belts. Mrs Bates a small pot of preserved ginger, and it was beastly. The only person who *did* come up to the scratch was Philip with a divine green velvet coatee. For all that it was a nice Christmas! I made my communion at 8. After dinner Winnie went off and Spangles and I dug into the warm study, gay with Xmas cards and flowers, a bit of mistletoe over Ernest's photograph.

31 December. And so ends 1937. Everything as satisfactory as any old woman has the right to expect (and many don't get their 'rights'!)

'But since there is more evil in Fear than in the Thing itself which is Feared' (Cicero) I cease to indulge in it.

1938

1 January. Nice New Year's day for me! Giving out "Happy New Years" to my friends and neighbours, who grinned back. But in the afternoon went to see the Smythes taking an offering of peppermint creams. There they sat, easy chairs each side the fire. One hopelessly paralaysed, the other – upon whom everything has depended – suddenly laid low by heart trouble and will probably in the grim way of affairs, die first. (And did.)

8 January. Both Bertie and Mabel Smythe in bed, and little or no money. I said we must all get together and do something. But I shall point out later on that I can't nowadays afford to do much.

15 January. . . . went to see the Smythes: both in bed, one with a heart, one paralysed. Took a custard and promised Mabel a shawl, she wearing over her nightdress a hideous and grubby brown scarf. After supper worked like mad at the shawl, which is only 3 parts done. Meant it for Ida but it will be of more value to Mabel Smythe.

17 January. Took it round to Mabel Smythe. She overwhelmed: so all my three chain, one treble was worthwhile.

21 January. Very nice party and I won a prize, a Woolworth willow pattern jug (no prize must cost more than 6d!) Winnie said: "It's willow pattern, how nice it will look on the dresser with the other blue china"! My lovely Spode! Asked to keep company with a Woolworth jug.

2 February. Quite blind, through (usual fool!) reading Aldous Huxley's *Eyeless in Gaza*. A wicked book and all the more devil-born because so clever.

11 February. I got a Valentine. Heaven knows who sent it. Very pink and flowery with the legend 'I love you'.

21 February. Miss Boyce, Bedford Hotel. Mrs Hyeem also came to tea at the Bedford and I rather like Miss Boyce after disliking her and sort of patronising her in those far-off days at Trent or in London when Philip was making such a fuss of me.

1 March. Now all day long I was entirely happy: thanks, in a large measure, to the Mount. Never, since 1100 or so when it was thrown up and the wooden keep built, has anyone loved it more . . . The view up there is divine. You are on top of the world.

2 March. Margaret came to tell me that Bertie Smythe died last night. I met Mr Jackson and he said: "Good morning, Valentine!" So it was he who sent it.

10 March. Asked Godfrey why, as the SAS is going to Angmering, not visit the Pigeon House?

2 April. Alice Bryne rang up from Brighton staying at the Metropole, might she come over? Did to tea. Very smart: 75 and looking old. But the auburn wig was a little obvious. Quite sure she's mad. Says that the 4th husband Colonel Sharp was like the 3rd one – Sir William Bryne – a sexual pervert, and is now living "in sin" with an Algerian man. That all her 4 husbands have been mad and, finally, that her daughter has seized her flat and its furniture and all her securities! "I am homeless, penniless, living in one room: that is, I have a sitting room, a bedroom and a bathroom at the Metropole"! I was done for after 2 solid hours of her.

8 May. Auntie M, after an interval of 5 weeks, most spiteful and snobbish. My sister had so aged that AM hardly knew her! And I looked very ill and was I *sure* my back wasn't something "really serious"? And her nieces had been out to dinner and there met two bank clerks and found them "a scream. They had never met young men of that class before". She is a little hornet in a beer bottle, going round and round stinging everything.

11 May. Auntie M's room quite charming. So was she, in place of the little hornet she has been lately. I suggested one or two alterations in the placing of the furniture, which pleased her.

21 May. Met Mrs Breach crippled with lumbago. I suggested an Alcock's Porous Plaster. She said: 'But they cost 1/3 M'm, and I've only got 9/6d a week to live on after I've paid the rent." Mrs Breach being no cadger presented her with the 1/3d. She overwhelmingly grateful.

23 May. Spangles is 9 years old today. Sent back *Who's Who*. Took Spangles out in the afternoon but I was so tired. Nowadays I am content to go up on the Mount and look at the hills where so often, in such joy, for many years I have walked.

24 May. Godfrey rang up: the Pigeon House is to be included in the Angmering outing. Rang up Mrs Brough, would she be my guest? Yes, gladly. Dear David turned up: very thin and old, terribly worried over work and money. He left at 4.

25 May. It turned into a wet afternoon, so Olive and Winnie 'did' my bed: always a very solemn part of the spring clean and which "we must *do together*." Makes me feel as if my bed were the Augean Stable [1].

15 June. Angmering. One of the most triumphant days of my life! . . . Commander Molson so charming and so generous. Saying, as he took all the Sussex Archaeological members over the Pigeon House, that the real credit was Mrs Dudeney's for she discovered and partially restored it. Then we went up to Ecclesden and then home. *Very* tired, but more jubilant.

23 June. I happened to say to Emily that Kitty wanted to buy the Town Wall cottage and garden and I wondered whether I would. Emily quite passionate: "Give me the first chance". She is haunted by the idea of having "nowhere to go in my old age" (being now 68 and having the lease of a flat for 5 years!). So I said I'd give it her for her life (after my death). She was immensely touched and grateful. . . . I also handed over a perfectly new 'corset and brassière' (the corset having a busk, which I can't 'stomach'!) Also the figured crepe de chine dress I've had for 2 years, but quite good.

1 One of the Labours of Hercules was to clean out the Augean stables containing 3,000 cattle.

25 June. I walked back with Mrs Bates and went in for a chat. She left me in the drawing room a moment and Bates came in – gave me a steady look. "Nice to see you here." I put out my hand, which he took: "Nice to be here". So now that difficulty is over!

26 June. It was rather nice when, after church, I took Spangles down Rotten Row to see Mr Bates 'as usual' waiting about for me, after an interval of 8 or more weeks. My little rap over the knuckles has done him good and now we can go on being very good friends. And it seems that, even if you are 70, there is no end to this 'man and woman' business.

2 July. Signed the Codicil to my Will giving Emily the lean-to and garden for life after my death. Ida begs me as 'their oldest friend' to go to their Golden Wedding party! Very piquant!!

11 July. Mrs Blaker asked me to tea (tennis if fine!) for Thursday. Mildly gratifying to decline because "I am going to the Garden Party at Hampton Court Palace"!

14 July. Off we went in Mrs Jervis's car and got to Hampton Court in elegance and comfort. Philip very much engrossed with Queen Mary. He received her. We thought she looked cross and common! The Duchess of Kent[2] very smart. Two-thirds of the peerage there but, of all the notables, we only recognised the Aga Khan and Lady Oxford, who looked as always evil and hideous. Mrs Gubbay there, very much made up – all pink and white (the present fashion for paint pots!). But it didn't conceal her obvious Indian blood.

28 July. The Golden Wedding. Funny affair. A bridesmaid there. A Miss Shinner – 80 – a confirmed invalid and brought in a car by her nurse. Handsome old thing. Stone deaf, and flirting heavily with David!

5 August. I must write to David, but what a burden a dead and gone love affair becomes!

2 Princess Marina of Greece. PS lent Trent Park to the Duke and Duchess for their honeymoon.

8 August. Went to Miss Cheale for black sealing wax since for 35 years David and I have sealed our letters, just for fun. (35 years, but with 17 years utter silence so its only 18 years). All dear Miss Cheale's sticks of wax hopelessly broken but together we picked out sixpennorth of fair length.

15 August. David. He arrived, looking as he always does in the summer very nice, with his good figure, wonderful in a man of 76. Before that I looked in to see Mabel Smythe who now seems to have lost all power in her legs.

16 August. At night we talked and talked, he telling me all his troubles. No work, or very little. Small prospect of more and practically nothing in the Bank. Result I never slept till 4. Nor, in comparing notes at breakfast, did he. I said, as Winnie brought in the bacon: "David, we are two wretched old creatures!" Winnie very much amused. Each evening I wore my yellow frock with the black Maltese lace cape and got complimented on my appearance.

17 August. We went down the High Street and he carried the books, 5 of my novels, which I am presenting to the Public Library. Met every one. After tea he departed and (I know it sounds devilish) I was so happy to have my pretty house to myself.

31 August. Major and Mrs Stanley 5.30. They [admirers] arrived: he a typical English soldier, well bred, conventional. She, impossible to describe, except by speech. *Vast* – bust and belly! Practically naked. Her great breasts like bladders of lard naked to the nipple (they *just didn't show*). On one a great yellow bruise. A skimpy dress above immense legs and with just a shoulder strap. Enormous bare arms. Not a *trace* of self consciousness. Very pleasant and cultured: obviously admiring me enormously (my books). How well I know that adoring look from worshipful women . . . When they had gone Esther Meynell [3] said: "When she came into the room I thought she was something that had escaped from a madhouse and left half its clothes behind"!

3 Member of SAS and writer of *Sussex*, from the County Book Series published by Robert Hale.

2 September. Pinker writes that the *London Mercury* has accepted Shell of a Lady. I'm so pleased . . .

3 September. Mr Spokes told me that Dr Doyle [4] was Gideon Mantell's [5] assistant at one time – about 90 years ago! GM bought a horse, sent Dr Doyle out on it to see what it was like. At the bottom of the High Street near the bridge, 2 boys shouted: "*Up King George*". The horse instantly stands on its hind legs. It was a *Circus* horse. Dr Doyle returns. GM asks about his horse. "Oh – an excellent animal, *but a little fresh*. You'd better try it."

8 September. At Southease, after looking at the frescoes and while we were having tea the Rector told us that Haile Selassie [6] (a name so suggestive of Harry Lauder's song 'Here's a Lassie') had been to his church. He – the Rector – peaceful in his study, presumably chewing the cud of a sermon, when in rushed an agitated lady parishioner : "Come at once. The Abyssian Emperor is here". The Rector in agitation asks: "How am I to behave?" "You are to make a *very deep* bow and *frequently* say 'Your Majesty'". This was done.

13 September. Sent Pinker 'Shell of a Lady' for America.

19 September. We all talk of nothing but the Crisis, and of Chamberlain's wonderful gesture. Some wish (me too!) that Hitler might be struck by lightning, or anything. Others say that Germany has been badly treated and that Hitler means to push out to the Black Sea, and why not? Tam says he doesn't care who governs him, so long as he is left in peace. The Rector wouldn't lift a finger even if his wife was murdered.

20 September. I took Spangles down Rotten Row and coming out of the Cemetery were two people – a man and a woman – so emaciated, so yellow-

4 Father of the Misses Doyle.
5 Surgeon and distinguished geologist, finder of dinosaurs and fossils, author of *Thoughts on a Pebble*. Lived at Castle Place which bears pilasters decorated with ammonites by Amon Wilds.
6 'The Lion of Judah', Emperor of Abyssinia (now Ethiopia) from 1930–74.

white and frail, so uncertain with their limbs, so vague in their looks, that I strongly suspected them of being ghosts broken loose from the graves.

21 September. I wake every morning to the joyous sense of a peaceful and a pretty day: almost nothing to do with human society! Just Winnie, arranging about the everlasting grub. Just Spangles (not human, canine and much better!). Going up the Mount with her and picking marigolds, pottering about the garden, picking asters and windflowers, arranging same in bowls and jugs all over the pretty house. Then I have moments of mental agility. Shall I write a book: 'Philip Sassoon: as I knew him', leaving it behind to be published after my death and his?! Or shall I ask the Sussex Archaeological Society if they would like my diaries, not to be opened until – say – 20 years after my death? Rather ghoulish this craving for post mortem reputation!

23 September. I am very much up in the air! The London Mercury editor writes expressing his 'great pleasure at publishing so distinguished a story as Shell of a Lady.' So nothing matters to me just now but writing (not even the Crisis!).

30 September. Thank God . . . the Crisis is over. The Prime Minister has seen Hitler and Mussolini (two wretches who ought to be strangled) so peace, for the present.[7] "A Lady" had been [while AD away] to ask how many rooms there were in the house. We are to have one "refugee" – child or adult – for every habitable room in the house. If they had included my attics and basement I would have had 12! Thank God it now won't be. But, a shock. And lots of us never slept properly for nights. Mr Jackson said that a Goverment that could pass such a measure would do "anything". We should have had the East-End, verminous and perhaps diseased, let loose on us!

2 October. The Rector couldn't let us enjoy ourselves even today. Said that in the midst of thanksgiving we ought to be penitent for the abominable way we had treated the Germans. I went to see Mabel Smythe who is cheek by jowl with him. Told her to tell him from me that if I broke into his house, looted it

7 The Munich Agreement to cede the German-speaking part of Czechoslovakia to Hitler in exchange for a promise of 'peace for our time'.

and ill treated his wife and child, I wouldn't expect people when I came out of prison to say: "Poor dear Mrs Dudeney, it wasn't her fault but ours. We have misjudged her and must make amends"!

6 October. The children are very disappointed. They were looking forward to this wholesale exodus into the country. One little boy when told that now they would not go said: "I suppose that bloke Hitler has let us down"! I am so diverted when I get a letter from David at tearing it up very small: so that all the exotic 'dearest dears' and 'darling loves' are destroyed before they go into the waste paper basket (and really rather wonderful – at 72 – to get such flaming love letters from a man of 76 with a record of 40 years unchanged devotion). Mrs Hyeem 1.30. A niece of Mrs Hyeem's there, fingernails and mouth blood red. These rich Jewesses who move in exalted circles (she is an intimate of Princess Arthur of Connaught's [8]) are odd. She opened a very 'spensive bag with an inner contraption to hold cigarettes, lipstick, nail varnish, powder and so on. Quite filthy. Smears of cream, dusts of powder, and the glass all greasy finger marks. She said, by the way, that Prince Arthur of Connaught (lately deceased) had been in love for years with a Russian lady who lived in the house with him and the Princess.

11 October. Margaret came in after tea full of gloom: "In two years Hitler will be marching in triumph through London!" This so upset me that after supper I couldn't sit idle by the fire and dream as usual, but started fiercely making French Knots in my new tablecloth . . . Got fitted for my gas mask and sent a short story 'Round the Table' to Pinker.

13 October. I bought myself a 6d Penguin book to read. Evelyn Waugh's Vile Bodies. Filthy and blasphemous. Shall burn it (but finish reading it first!)

17 October. The Crisis! Mrs Miller said Miss Harvey Smith told her of a man who was told by a soothsayer that before a month was out, he would travel by train with a dead man, also that before Christmas, Hitler would be dead. Sure enough, he was in a compartment alone, the guard came in – a man had

8 Daughter-in-law of Queen Victoria.

just died in the next carriage, which was full, would he mind giving hospitality to the corpse until the next station? "Not at all". So this was done but we are still waiting for Hitler to die! Met Mr Spokes. He thinks that if we can only keep the peace till March, there will be no war. We shall be fully armed and even Hitler will think twice (but I'm always hoping he'll be assassinated. I'm trying to will it!) Dr Dunstan – our Medical Officer of Health – said compulsory [evacuation] would be very hard on the children and that he had written to the Minister about it. I said: "Good Heavens! How about us?" He saw that point too and asked me to strengthen his hand by writing myself to the Minister, putting the elderly householder's point of view. So I did and got a formal answer from the Home Office. My letter was 'receiving attention'. Couldn't get any one else to write, everyone so apathetic.

22 October. Met . . . Lord Gage, very pleasant: "When are you coming to see us again?" "Delighted – when asked! But please not to lunch, tea time is my time." I don't suppose Lady Gage will write, and I hope not. It means a car each way. Funny – Mrs Gubbay, Philip's cousin, says: "You've been to the Gages. What an honour! And they've been to you." Neither Philip nor she have ever been asked[9]. I suppose, however rich you are, that being a Jew goes 'agin'. And probably Philip feels it, and that is the secret of his occasional insolence – to others, not to me! His beastly bouts towards me have a more sensitive source.

25 October. David wrote: 'A woman came, said I was to have 8 Eastenders and provide them with coal to cook in my kitchen. Simply showed her the door, wouldn't discuss it. She was very rude – *and I've heard no more.*' Poor darling! of course he didn't. The Crisis was over.

30 October. Mabel Smythe has been presented, by Norah Harvey Smith, with a bath chair – so was at church in my pew! Met Mr Holland who is certain that there won't be a war, but is equally certain that we shall have to give Germany back all her Colonies.

9 Lady Gage had met AD at Lympne.

4 November. *Margery* urging me to sell up everything and settle with them in America – quite *certain* there will be a war. Went to Mrs Amos at the Old Poor House. For the first time since I bought it (ten years ago) it is properly furnished and properly kept. I was delighted, and amply said so.

12 November. Made her [Emily] give me – with a view to Christmas – her exact diet. And wrote on a large card and presented it to Winnie: 'What Miss Whiffin *Can* eat', 'What Miss Whiffin *Can't*'! She may not touch bacon or tongue but can eat Sausages, "The *best* Sausages", says her lady doctor. I don't believe in her, or any of them. It is immodest to talk about your body to a woman.

13 November. Spangles seemed restless and odd, which terrifies me – I now love her as much as I loved Nelson. And the Rector preached what I consider a 'treasonable' sermon; I don't see why the congregation of St Michael's should 'sit under' such a man.

25 November. At the [A.]R.P. meeting we had a lecture about Bombs and their baleful effects. Also permanent concrete shelters are to be dug out under the Downs. "Burrowing like rats" as the Rector of St Michael's very properly says.

3 December. Went to the Peace Meeting with Mrs Brough to hear a woman Pacifist – Mary Gamble by name – and a more Tom Fool speech I never heard.

17 December. Quite a shock. Met Miss Bond (Dr Spokes' housekeeper) who told me he was very seriously ill with pneumonia. 2 nurses, an oxygen tent and all the rest of it. Took him some anemones with the message that he must get well, for Christmas and his 87th birthday on Boxing Day.

19 December. The usual frozen misery. Bath water hasn't run away. Lavatories not frozen – yet! Forgot to say that on Saturday Philip sent me a sumptuous green velvet cape, twin sister to the coat he sent last year, both from the Royal School of Needlework.

20 December. Frightful blizzard and in Germany coldest weather for 83 years (if it would freeze Hitler & Co we should all be easier in our minds). Put in a whole morning packing up little presents and addressing and stamping 45 Christmas cards. The older I grow the more friends and acquaintances I seem to get, which is all to the good.

23 December. A great blow! There is no end to the horrors of this Christmas. Just seen in the paper that my dear friend Sydney Spokes died on Sunday.

25 December, Christmas Day. Snow and frost and cold. A taxi to church and back with Emily who, used to the baldness of chapel, found the Sung Mass and full ceremonial confusing: "I don't want to be irreverent but they seemed to me" (the priest and servers) "like so many children at play". Also she seemed just amused by the Crib.

And so ends 1938. A nice year. I am happier than I ever was in my life. I am at peace. I live in freedom. I hope I may live to be – say – 81. And die in this dear house. 9.30 pm New Year's Eve.

1939

Mrs Jervis in her letter said that there was a very old lady and nearly 90 staying in the hotel, half blind, half deaf. And she said with glee: "My dear, isn't it beautiful to be living in such stirring times"! Bloodthirsty old wretch!

Ist January. I don't think I ever started the year in a more peaceful – even succulent! – mood.

3 January. I read all through Virginia Woolf's *Three Guineas*. An over-rated woman, I think, and a sort of nagging tone which makes you feel sorry for Mr Woolf. These feminist women with their shrieking and clamour. An intelligent woman (with certain other qualities thrown in!) can get what she wants without making such an ugly fuss.

19 January. Yesterday in bed and sent for Dr Irvine to thoroughly overhaul my back. He says a slight curvature and some muscular damage due to that awful fall at Brighton years ago. Nothing could have been done then, nor anything done now. Must be careful not to overstrain, shall always be liable to attacks. So now I know just where I am and need say no more. He thought me very healthy and my heart good "for my age". I said I didn't mind Death but what I dreaded was some "loathsome or lingering disease". He didn't think I should ever have either. I told him how terrified I was at the idea of a war, which meant East End urchins billeted on me. "You'll never have them. *Leave that to me.*"

30 January. After tea a drive with Mrs Jervis and then back to tea. Mrs Vallance there. She says that Mrs Simpson (the Duchess of Windsor, so called) was Von Rippentrop's mistress while she was, also, King Edward's!

2 February. Mrs Whittington called with the Billeting paper. How many refugees could I take in case of a war? I behaved urbanely, as Dr Irvine advised. I made great play with my age and the pain in my back. Said I could not undertake to look after children, but would take 2 teachers if necessary (there will not be a war, nor do I mean to take anybody).

23 February. Feeling somehow that my precious grandsons were so lost to me, now they are grown up, I sent Julian [Barney] Galloway Porter's list of scientific books (which still comes for Ernest) and said if there was any book he wanted, I was good up to 10/6d: and that the same offer applied to Jamie for any hobby he had.

1 March. Macey (Tam's servant) called. Miss Dicker died last night. Tam in a terrible state, his relations come and gone! Macey very anxious, thinks he ought not to be left alone. Said that, in emergency, he might ring me up, though what I could do is not quite clear!

4 March. At the funeral [Miss Dicker's] found that all the others . . . had sent a wreath and I not. Tore down to Southover after dinner with the carnations Mrs Bateman sent me and put them on the grave.

8 March. After dinner I went to the film *Sixty Glorious Years*. Came away feeling . . . what a pity (although quite seemly and necessary) to have to show the old Queen in her horrid widow's black after the adorable early dresses, all colour and frivolity. And the fat old face, sandy in the film. But David, who saw her in extreme old age, said her face was violently purplish-red, like a port-wine mark.

9 March. Margery's birthday. She is 49. So! 49 years ago there was I, very young, very black-and-white (dark hair and pallid face) tucked up in a Southampton Row house (now part of the Waverley Hotel) with a fat old 'Gamp' [midwife] in attendance. It was Sunday morning and birds were singing in the gardens of Russell Square.

15 March. A very nice tea party. Young Spokes in many ways like his delightful father . . . The rumour now is that Hitler is either dead or disposed of but has half a dozen doubles, and that Goebbels is the real villain of the piece. Mr Spokes said he couldn't understand why our Secret Service hadn't "got rid" of Hitler long ago: "It is always done". People said the same of Mrs Simpson, now the (so-called) Duchess of Windsor: "Why don't they bump her off?"

22 March. Went to Miss Durrant's sale at The Gables, Southover, and got for £1 5s a very pretty mahogany table as I want an extra one for my Bezique party . . .

23 March. Mrs Jervis came after tea in a state of alarm. Miss Gill had told her that Miss Durrant had died of cancer. Thought I ought to be warned. But as the said table was in the drawing room, is highly polished and arrived drenched, rain pouring all over its top and down its legs, I feel no fear. But promised Mrs Jervis I would have it polished with beeswax and turpentine.

25 March. Talked to Mr Bates, Mr Morris and Dr Wells: everybody blaming Roumania for letting Germany have her oil and corn. Hitler is nothing but a mad dog, and the mad dog gets shot in the end, but not until he has bitten a few people (or swallowed a few small nations). Went after tea to see Muriel Hardy. The room so lovely – in particular a jug of pale petunias – that the thought instantly came how *horrible* the possibility of a war, which would destroy such pretty peace in thousands of homes. Poor Muriel Hardy – another operation to her broken leg, which won't grow bone.

30 March. At 7.30 a knock at the door and there was Tam. He stayed till 9.30 and he told me his secret: he wishes, he means, to take Holy Orders. Has lunched with the Bishop [1], who talked of nothing but Art and Literature! He – the Bishop – will probably think him too old, he is 42. Tam said, in that case, he would try in another diocese. He is still broken-hearted over the loss of his aunt (she was 85 and did he suppose her to be immortal?!) Says he can read nothing but Proust. But I considered a really 'citing detective story would be better, and sent him off with *Trent's Last Case*.[2]

1 April. . . . my bedroom, with the small electric lamp burning, looked so spacious, *safe* and luxurious; my clothes in a heap on the chair, a tumble, half

---

1 Bishop Bell of Chichester.
2 By EC Bentley.

pink, half white, the fat bed with it twisted posts and flowered eiderdown, the Regency sofa – all of it. And I thought how horrible it was to know that all over Europe thanks to that mad dog Hitler rooms as lovely and more lovely had been wrecked by bombs, and our turn may come.

20 April. Miss Harvey Smith, The Shelleys. Such a nice party . . . we had great fun pretending it was for Hitler's birthday and drank to his destruction.

24 April. Mrs Bates said – as many others have said – that I was "the dearest, most sympathetic friend" and so on. I don't think I am. I think I'm cold-hearted, but with a sense of drama, and a sort of trick of expression which gives the illusion of sympathy!

30 April. What a tiresome thing the material mind is. I've had such joy curling up my hair in papers off oranges from Palestine. But Auntie M says: "Think of the dirty Jews who have *sat* on them"!

7 May. After being exasperated by the crudities of Auntie M for 18 years, I am now so dreadfully sorry for her and quite fond. She is, clearly, so ill and so brave about it. I look ahead – in my Tom-fool way – and I shrink from the Sundays that may be without her, without Spangles.

10 May. Mrs Lister 4.30. Major Lister very affable, but not an attractive object with that great wen on his head and a wall eye. I can't think how she could have accepted that wen! Perhaps he proposed with his hat on.

12 May. Mrs Hyeem, Lady Boyle 11 am. Lady Boyle had been in bed 10 days with sciatica but was now reclining in her boudoir, very elegant in pink quilted satin, with a broad hair ribbon to match. She told me that Philip was very very ill: high temperature and emphysema of the lungs. Had influenza, got rather better, then against his doctors' orders went first to stay at Windsor Castle, then flew to Paris "at his own risk".

17 May. Mrs Milne, 4.15. . . . and me, in my new mulberry-to-brown frock. A hat with a wreath of blue and wine coloured tiny flowers and Philip's

'celestial' earrings of blue enamel, spangled with gold stars. Poor Philip! Lying very near to death in that vast Park Lane house, "Parkers" as we always call it.

18 May. David. And I do wish to goodness that David would cut his hair. And be better groomed and not wear that odious overcoat! What is the thing which we call Love?! Between a man and a woman I believe it is just physical attraction and nothing more, unless it is ripened and sanctified by married life. Here is a man for whom 30 years ago I nearly (not quite, thank God) threw over everything. For 17 years of silence I loved him, or believed that I did. And now! I am bored by him, a little embarrassed, even ashamed.

20 May. . . . went off with both [David and Spangles] on a lovely walk down by the Croquet Ground [Southover] and beyond. Buttercups and cows and Kingcups and lots of baby swifts and a blue, blue sky. The old magic nearly came back and might have done *quite* if he hadn't worn that horrid coat and if he hadn't kept on calling me "my dear". As if I were his wife which I, now, never wish to be and am thankful I never was. After tea he went, very worried, no work to speak of. Overdraft at the Bank £800!

27 May. Miss Boyce writes that Philip is 'very, very ill – no change in his condition'. But the bulletin in *The Daily Telegraph* today says 'a little progress'.

31 May. Nice fat cheque from Nelsons – dear Ernest's Royalty for the half year. I get no Royalties, my novels are as dead as mutton. I feel very proud and sad when I get his. He was an abiding genius and I just a brilliant novelist.

2 June. No bulletin in *The Daily Telegraph* and nothing from Miss Boyce, so I am hoping that Philip is better. The day went as usual, peaceful in heavenly weather. But at night I couldn't sleep. I reviewed all the happy play-time and times at Lympne each summer. And the things he'd said and the first funny laughing kiss he gave me soon after I was a widow. And then, half asleep, I not only saw but seemed to be in that Park Lane bedroom where I knew he was lying and I saw the nurse moving about in her capable, starched silence.

3 June. In Mrs Jervis's car we all went off to the Sheffield Park Gardens . . . back about 6.30. Got out of the car, saw the Hills in theirs. Margaret then prepared me for a shock: "*Sir Philip Sassoon died early this morning.*" I was stunned. He died, then, in the night as I lay awake[3]. It seemed impossible to go back to an empty house so I went off to Mrs Jervis and told her. She was very kind. After supper I put on his little velvet wrap – the Christmas present and his last – fastened it with his jade and fire opal brooch, and got out his letters. Whole stacks, from 1916 till now and I'm thankful I kept them. I went to bed late and could not sleep for hours.

6 June. I still feel a little lost and stunned, far more than I ever thought I should.

8 June. All the morning I wrote (typed) voluminously to Margery about Philip's death and David's awful financial state. Three men have influenced my life: Ernest, David, Philip. The first and third are dead. The second is stony broke!

17 June. Margaret came in. She saw in a Sunday paper that Philip was cremated at Golders Green and his ashes taken by aeroplane and scattered over Trent. Quite lovely. And, somehow, he doesn't seem so lost.

21 June. Whenever on the Mount or in the garden I see and hear an aeroplane fly over, there comes the poignant sense of Philip's ashes being flown to Trent to be scattered over the flying field. And then I remember those happy summer days at Lympne and the day when I went up for my first (and last) flight.

24 June. Philip, who left two million, might – after expressing a peculiar devotion for 22 years – have left me a small annuity: £200 a year[4]. I should have given £100 to Margery and played with the other £100. Mrs Bates said as well he didn't, as Lewes would have thought the worst and that (for some

3 PS had always had a premonition of his early death.
4 He left Trent Park and Port Lympne to Hannah Gubbay, and a year's salary to more than 100 servants.

obscure reason, which she didn't give) an annuity was worse than a capital sum. I said: " But I'm old enough to be his mother." "That", said the worldly Mrs Bates, "would have made no difference to the Lewes gossips."

17 July. And at night who should arrive but Jean Garlick [5] and her new husband, a nice much-travelled man called Massey. He says that Hitler was bluffing at the Munich time.

19 July. I packed up the 1912, 1913, 1918, 1922 diaries, all being small so altogether, and put a fat black seal on the paper cover. Very thrilling and quite unbelievable, of course, that I shall be dead when those seals are broken! But, whoever breaks them, Beware! A very much amused ghost may be peeping over your shoulder!

29 July. Vere. It was so lovely to see her beautifully dressed and with her good looks got back, now that the terrible strain of Sullivan's illness and death is a thing of the past.

1 August. Lady Cholmondeley wrote to me. She said: 'Philip was so very fond of you and he knew whole passages from your novels by heart.'

16 August. Went off to Emily . . . sat in her funny little garden in Springfield Road. She again ghoulishly remarking that, although she didn't want to "lose" me, she did very often think of what she would do to the 7 Castle Banks and its tiny town wall garden when she came into this inheritance. Rather acidly reminded her that I was not dead yet!

17 August. Mr Travers 11. He arrived and I found the hall filled with him and his family, a plump, very pretty wife and four – out of his seven – children. They went off, he was taken to the study where he now is. Later on, he chose a few mathematical books which he wished to buy and I consented. Said he wasn't a rich man, so gave me ten shillings and a ticket for the Irish Sweepstake . . .

5 Contemporary of Margery, friend of AD's since she lived in Surrey. Involved in secret service work, her new husband worked in the Admiralty.

20 August. Exquisite weather, so one must [be] happy. But all the signs are of gloom. Auntie M very so-so. Doomed, I think. Spangles with a bad leg and that blasted Hitler keeping us all on the hop.

22 August. Fearful blow, or it seems so to me: Ribbentrop flying to Moscow to conclude a non-aggression pact between Germany and Russia. I've felt all through that the treacherous Soviet with its many delays was only playing for time. I looked at young Palmer the gardener yesterday, so handsome and clean and altogether good. And the thought of slaughter, the destruction or the maiming of tens of thousands of such beautiful lives – of any nationality – drives me desperate.

25 August. Everybody down the High Street in deepest gloom. Harry Morris saying Lloyd George had been perfectly right when he said that to promise to help Poland *before* we had a pact with Russia was lunacy. Mr Holland says that France is the stumbling block and that the Italians have a case. They were promised Tunis and it has not been given them. The one optimist was an old man at Browne and Crosskeys [6] where I went to enquire the price of dark green blinds: "We ain't goin' to have a war".

29 August. I was feeling rather optimistic until I met Mrs Holman down the High Street! She said that soldiers with fixed bayonets stood all along the cliffs from Seaford to Newhaven.

26 August. Mrs Bates, 11.27 to Victoria. A very enjoyable day – if it wasn't for Hitler! But we forgot for a little while and we enjoyed the revival of Oscar Wilde's *Importance of Being Ernest*. I thought of 1895 when it came out and Ernest and I saw it. He extra handsome, as he always was in evening clothes. And the very pale-faced, black-haired young woman in the funny aesthetic frock was Me!

30 August. Thank God Dr Irvine rang up to say he was giving me a medical certificate saying my health makes it impossible for me to billet children.

6 Lewes drapers, outfitters and furnishers frequented by shepherds buying smocks on Sheep Fair Day.

31 August. Emily turned up. She is to have in her tiny flat (if war comes) a "worker". Was told that if she refused to take this woman she would have a soldier billeted on her. Which frightened poor Emily: "Soldiers come in drunk". I said drunk or sober I'd rather deal with a man than a woman. While we were playing Bezique after tea a loud speaker van came along: 400,000 children being evacuated from London and other danger zones tomorrow.[7]

1 September. So down and out – war now seeming inevitable – that I foolishly went and sat on a pile of logs on the beloved Mount and just cried. The world is so beautiful, the thought of slaughter so frightful. Went into Wycherley's office and was told to my sorrow and dismay that he died last night, after a week's illness: double pneumonia.

3 September.[8] As we came out of church there was Dusart, an ARP man, waving and shouting "Bombers overhead. Get under cover at once!" So we all helter-skeltered towards home and when the 'All Clear' signal came, I took Spangles up on the Mount.

5 September. Policeman came and frightened Winnie to death. Some one had 'reported' us for showing lights and if it occurred again we should be fined. This house stands so high you can see it all over the town.

7 September. Not a bit of black stuff to be had and 21 windows to be darkened. Fell back on brown paper and my delicious sunny house is a tomb. How different this war is from the last, for me. Then I was all fire and storm. Margery married and gone to Canada, David (as I then thought) vanished into a for-ever silence. There was the re-adjustment of my married life with Ernest – a pretty tough job! And one consolation that I then had, the fever and delight of my writing. I was doing *The Secret Son* 25 years ago and going up to the attic at 138 High Street each morning, typing like mad, forgetting everything and everybody while the mood lasted. And now! Old, not wanting to write, no more to say. Ernest dead. David a bore! Now, as then,

7 14,000 evacuees came into the area, 6,500 for Lewes, the rest for rural areas.
8 War declared against Germany.

there is a spotted dog. And now, as then, I feel somewhere deep down if I could only touch some spring and release it – invincible gaiety. Perhaps that is one of the first secrets of the life to come. We shall be so heavenly merry. And everything that we see will be pretty. And there will be no more terror.

12 September. Went to Charles Wycherley's funeral. His death a shock and a great loss. He was my man of business.

[Extracts from typed copy of letter sent to Margery at this time and loose in diary] 'My sister . . . is to have a woman billeted on her. The woman must have a room (which you are not allowed to enter) facilities for cooking: water and so on. Emily to be paid by the Government five shillings a week. So she is to have the sitting room and poor Emily will camp out in her bedroom and kitchen. . . . I had a brain wave. One of Mount Cottages became empty only last week. Why not put in some odds and ends of furniture and let the Government have it – on condition that I kept this house to myself? They [Town Hall] thought it was very 'public spirited' of me. They would provide bedding . . . Got Wycherley to send a man round with a handcart and sent him down with two tables, two chairs, some bits of china, some coal, fender and fireirons, washing up bowl, kettle and cooking pots . . . An East End woman with two children was taken to the cottage. Wouldn't look at it!! About noon I saw approach a woman with a badge on her arm and another woman carrying a bundle . . . a 'helper' was left upon my hands. She is a sort of drudge for the teachers: Mrs Gambel by name, from Croydon . . . The government will pay me a guinea a week for her keep. A nice simple woman of the artisan class. After a couple of weeks her husband came down: she said quite pleasantly that she must have "hubby" here for the weekends. I said that it was out of the question . . . so she went to a place which suits her better. Going down the High Street for the first two or three weeks was AWFUL. All of us complete with gas masks swung from our shoulders, there is a fine if you venture forth without one! The street crowded with the most fearsome women you ever saw, and more fearsome infants – either sucking ice cream cones or squarking on being smacked – and sometimes sworn at! Then we had expectant mothers, but they seem to have vanished. Mrs Bates said: "Dick will make such ribald remarks. He sees all these expectant ladies and comes home saying: 'Somebody's been busy'". Did I tell you that on the Saturday when the evacuated children came I escaped up onto the Mount and sat there, in high serenity – of landscape, but not of soul! – and watched what seemed an endless procession of children all with gas masks and with their small belongings, sometimes in pillow cases or sacks, on their little backs. All being shepherded by voluntary helpers with white armlets. In the case of RC children by nuns. These children were shot in at the particular houses which had been allotted to them, but the householders nearest on the route had the pick. And I was told that one poor boy – big for his age and about fourteen – was left until the last. I suppose they thought he would eat too much. Any parent in a danger area can send off any children. One woman had ten and sent the lot! And the Government (which is Me) pays for the lot. But there is some talk of making the parent contribute – when they can. An easy way of getting rid of your responsibilities.'

15 September. I met all sorts of people . . . and (of sole import!) the Rector of St Michael's. I said that, although I should hate to do it, if he preached any more Pro-German sermons saying we were responsible for the war I should walk out of the church. He said had I read Muriel Leicester's book, adding that she was "a very great woman". I said, be that as it may, I had never heard of her. In it she alleges that in 1918–1919, for a year after the Armistice, we continued to blockade Germany so that women fell dead in the streets from starvation and eighty per cent of the babies died for want of milk. I said I flatly declined to believe it.

19 September. 500 more children come to the town and Mrs Taylor tells me that lots of the officials haven't anyone billeted on them. After tea went to see Winifred and Muriel Hardy. Winifred terribly up against it. 2 boys billeted on them tomorrow. Muriel a cripple so able to do nothing, rather cynically indifferent. If the Government thinks people will stand this obnoxious intrusion into the home for 3 or 4 years it will find out its mistake.

20 September. Paid the coal bill. Find I can have as much as I like until rationing begins on October 1st . . .

23 September. The Rector of St Michael's wrote a 4-page letter, insisting as before that our Blockade continued for 12 months after the Armistice and that as a result thousands of Germans were starved. Also he said that there was 'a growing opinion in England that we were just as responsible for the 1914 war as Germany'. Also that 'but for our cruelty and injustice to the German people, there would be no war now'. I wrote to George Gordon, Billy Massey, Admiral Beamish and Commander Molson, 4 naval men, determined to find out the truth about the Blockade.

25 September. Went for a walk, returned and found Gerald Molson's letter. The Blockade did continue for a few months after the Armistice, but only to prevent the entry of munitions of war. Food was allowed to enter Germany and we also sent shiploads free. George Gordon wrote that he had asked an Admiral who said that the Blockade was called off directly the Armistice was signed.

28 September. Income Tax up to 7/6d in the £. I felt crushed . . . Dear Winnie and dear Olive having heard about the rise on the wireless come along this morning, offering to take less wages. Isn't it lovely of them, and quite out of the question.

29 September. Letter from Admiral Beamish, regular old sea-dog! violently denying the Rector's Pacifist utterances and asking to see his letter.

30 September I decided to send Admiral Beamish extracts from the Rector's letter and send the Rector extracts from A.B.s. And to say to the Rector that 'in view of these irrefutable facts from such a source' it was clear that he had been misinformed about the Blockade and might therefore welcome the opportunity of gaining further information from Admiral Beamish!

18 October. I said to Mrs Pinyoun at 10 Castle Banks that either she or Mrs Richardson at 9 showed a light in the kitchen window. Mrs Pinyoun said: "Not me, M'm. I'm so nervous that I even take my false teeth out in the dark".

23 October. Took Philip's lovely green velvet coat to be cleaned. The equally lovely green cape, his last present, I simply haven't the heart to wear. Met

Mrs Brough and she said that going to the hairdresser's with all these verminous evacuees about was highly dangerous. So when I got to Dusarts I was quite frank about it and bought a comb and a net for my own use.

3 November. Sent for young Wycherley, only 18, poor boy, and with all this responsibility on his shoulders. Told him firmly but kindly that unless he could make a very substantial reduction, I should not let them do any more repairs: deeply as I should regret the step after 25 years of pleasant business relations with his father and his grandfather.

10 November. Dear Winnie . . . she is so intelligent and yet so irrelevant. When I told her that the Dutch were flooding their country in case of a German invasion, she said: "Why, and just think of the lot of rain we've had here"! Lots of people wearing red poppies and some white – as Pacifists. Silly Miss Dowdall wearing red and white "for I am a Pacifist – in a way"! I said: "Then why not a white *feather*?"

18 November. David writes that he has got the Royal Academy pension £50. That with his Civil List pension of £80 gives him £130 a year without lifting a finger! I wrote rather cynically, saying that I was 'delighted beyond measure if it gave him ease of mind'. Otherwise I didn't see how it would help! These thriftless people always fall on their feet. Dear Ernest only left £5,500 after years, a lifetime, of scraping and slaving.

2 December. Now who was it said that the greatest happiness in life is the departure of a guest?! I was very glad to have dear Mary [Carr], yet when she'd gone – handsome as ever (with her hat on!), I sat by the fire and purred and washed my whiskers.

4 December. I was very happy at church this morning and when I came home and passed through the drawing room all starred with winter jasmine and rosy pink with the cyclamen Winnie gave me for my birthday I couldn't somehow be happy *enough*. I wanted to *see* God and fall at His feet with gratitude.

6 December. I actually went out in a 'blackout' and, with an electric torch, it is not too bad. We [Mrs Jervis] saw the film *Confessions of a Nazi Spy*. A lot of German brag and ridiculous goose-stepping. What children they are! And yet very terrifying. I hope I shall live long enough to see them utterly beaten.

11 December. See in the *West Sussex Gazette* that Commander Molson, who bought my Pigeon House at Angmering, went down in the *Rawalpindi*.[9] Very sad. Such a charming man.

18 December. Cecil Roth, the author of *The Magnificent Rothschilds* to whom I wrote, saying I hoped we were to have a book on the Sassoons, very flattered (or so he tactfully says) at having a letter of appreciation from 'Mrs Henry Dudeney'. There is to be a Sassoon book, but somebody else is writing it and it will soon appear.

19 December. Told Cecil Roth that I had all Philip's letters from 1917 till his death last June and that I thought the early ones, written from France, when he was Private Secretary to Haig in the last war should be of interest. But I assumed it was now too late – as the book is probably set up.

25 December, Christmas Day. Auntie M's 11th Christmas here! She beats the record. Couldn't go to early communion, roads like ice. But at the midday Mass St Michael's looked exquisite. The crib and two big Christmas trees , lighted with coloured electricity each side the altar. But our Christmas dinner was awful. Beautifully cooked. Chicken and so on. But poor Auntie M insisting on carving as usual but in the kitchen this time made a frightful job of it, her poor paralysed hands unequal to the job. So when at last we sat down it was stone cold and she kept dropping her food about.

31 December. And so ends 1939: which started – for me – so happily. And now Philip is dead and also Wycherley, both only 50 and both meaning a lot

9 Two German warships, en route to divert attention from their battleship *Admiral Graf Spee*, sank this armed merchant cruiser patrolling the Faeroes and Iceland.

to my life. Philip to my heart – Wycherley, my business agent, to my pocket and consequently to my peace of mind. And dear Christopher writes that he may lose his job (and I haven't now a penny to help them with if he does). And he says Margery is not well but I am not to mention it as she hates sympathy. So I am like an old hen who has hatched ducklings! I go vainly squarking round the pond, and the Atlantic is such a great big pond! However! I've got my delicious house and my door on to the Brack Mount. And got Winnie and got, so far, Spangles.

I shall tie up [this Diary] with the 1916 one. 1916 was the middle of a war, this is the beginning of another. But in 1916 we were fighting Germany and that was that. In 1939 the whole world is in a ferment. There seems no end in sight. Meanwhile this study is so gloriously warm and pretty. And through the door, leading to the kitchen, comes a slight bouquet of onion. Hot-pot for dinner!

1940

4 January. Letter from Robert Hale, the publisher. He would like to see my Memory book which I now call: *Record of A Victorian Lady*. It is still so slippery outside that I am afraid to go out.

5 January. Found Mrs Bates looking terribly ill and thin: a bad nervous break-down. Mr Bates warned me not to stay more than ten minutes. I then went on to see Mabel Smythe. The billeting officer had actually tried to billet 4 secondary school boys on her. So she got a medical certificate and now says merrily: "I've got paralysis-agitans" [1].

9 January. Letter from David: 'One dull day succeeds another'. My dear, although we are old and I care nothing for you now, I do note that it is 35 years ago today since you and Ida and your little son, now a Colonel serving in France, came to stay with us at Littlewick. And after dinner, all the evening – while your wife and my husband (never liking each other) chatted by the fire – I was supposed to be teaching you Bezique. And we so desperately in love that we hardly knew hearts from spades.

16 January. It looks as if the Germans mean to overrun the Low Countries. I begin to feel that I shall not live to see the end of this war. Robert Hale rejects *Record of a Victorian Lady*. He finds it as all the publishers find it: 'Charming, but not of sufficient popular interest.' I am glad to have it rejected as each time I am glad because I think these intimate revelations vulgar. Yet the other side of me can't quite swallow the snub of 'Mrs Henry Dudeney' being rejected.

17 January. Nelsons accept Ernest's book[2]! That's £30 advance royalty, out of which I've arranged to pay Travers £10 for editing. My book rejected yesterday and yours accepted today! Well, my dear, I am glad and proud.

1 Parkinson's Disease.
2 *A Puzzle Mine.*

18 January. The government has evidently commandeered the Malt House. Tons of bacon going in and the young man told Winnie it is being done in case London is Bombed!

7 February. Meat rationing is to start on March 11th. Each person may spend 1/10! I don't know how we are going to manage for Spangles, whose life habit it is to have quarter pound of minced shin of beef daily.

10 February. Decided to pretend we were rationed so had marrow pudding. 2 lovely bones Appleby sent. I clapped them together, built a suet crust round them and then found it too big for the biggest pot we'd got . . . In 1885, a little bride of 18, I made the first pudding – a steak and kidney one – of my life and *that* wouldn't go into the pot. Fat and filthy Mrs Pursell, our Gray's Inn laundress, volunteered to borrow a pot off 'Mrs Slater' at 4 South Square for whom she also worked. And did. Ernest much amused when he got home, but warned me not to get friendly with Mrs Slater who was a 'Kept' woman. He then had to explain to me what a 'Kept' woman was!

14 February. A delicious affair, the Valentine – all Lace and Love! 'To one I love: It happened here Down in my Heart – A feeling warm all through – And I knew right from the start – It came from Loving you.' How he [Mr Jackson] must have enjoyed buying it.

24 February. The Archdeacon wishes Tam to be ordained, but the Bishop is 'adamant' Tam is too old and not virile enough. The Bishop wants a muscular type who will 'appeal to men'. He'd like Tam to remain a Lay Reader, which is like his Episcopal cheek! Mrs Rogers[3] rang up, would I go at once, Auntie M "sinking". Went, but she didn't know me.

25 February. Spangles vainly waiting at the gate for an 'Auntie' who perhaps will never come again. I just howled! She is the last one left of what Ernest called the 'old gang'. Five of us at tea every Sunday: Agnes Doyle, Mr Gale, Mrs Miller, me and Ernest - *and* my adored Nelson.

3 Mrs Rogers ran a small nursing home at Ashdown House, St Anne's Hill.

2 March. The sheets came . . . Mrs Milne told me the other day that her husband's grandparents had sheets specially woven for them: half cotton, half linen, for their double bed. He couldn't sleep in cotton, she couldn't in linen.

4 March. Auntie M is in the most amazing state: the doctors can make nothing of her. She had a good breakfast, egg, toast, coffee, marmalade: for dinner chicken and Queen's pudding, a second helping of pudding, for which she asked. And then, at 5 o'clock, becomes unconscious and seems to everyone's belief, to be dying. Why don't they give the poor thing (just what I know she would wish) an extra and a fatal dose of heroin?

6 March. Poor Auntie M. She has had a stroke, has long wished to die and is now apparently getting better, doomed most likely to years of invalidism. Meanwhile, every night she has been on the point of death and instead of letting her go – which is Nature's merciful idea – they call the Matron and then inject some stuff with a long name which stimulates the heart's action.

9 April. After dinner, in poisonous north wind, took Spangles down by the Dripping Pan.[4] Saw on the placards that the Germans have invaded Denmark.

12 April. The war looks rather hopeful on the sea side anyhow. But I dread their attack on the Maginot Line.[5] Meanwhile, every German sings a little song: "We are sailing for England." Some of them will, as prisoners of war.

15 April. David – just as he did in 1904 and so onwards – sticks a tiny bunch of spring flowers through a slit in the letter. Men are so sentimental. The Navy is doing wonders. As I went to church a whole covey of RC nuns, billeted at the Hubert Powell's old house[6], came down the High Street, voluminous with

---

4 Rectangular earthwork in Southover. Thought to be a former Tudor enclosure for aristocratic recreation.
5 Fortification built to protect the Eastern frontier of France.
6 118 High St.

flowing habits and extra large umbrellas! By two by two like the animals out of the Ark and behind each nun a small girl carrying a minute suitcase.

24 April. Tea with Mrs Jervis. I said of the Rector of St Michael's and his Pacifism and the 'Peace' leaflets which are dropped through people's letter boxes, that somebody ought to drop through *his* the phrase from the Litany: 'From all sedition, privy conspiracy and rebellion, Good Lord deliver us'!

25 April. I've been feeling tonight as if it were October 1914 all over again when, night after night, I threw on the wood fire in the panelled room of 138 High Street packets and wads of David's letters – one daily from 1911 till Sept 1914 – burnt until the spinster chest was empty. And the coast clear for Ernest's arrival and our fresh start. Tonight I've turned out and read over, some only, of Margery's letters also since October 1914 when she went away. All of them, helter-skelter, stuffing the drawers of the little bureau in the ante-room. Philip's letters are mixed up also, all of them from Dec 1916 till April last year, two months before he died. Tomorrow I shall start burning the lot.

26 April. So I did start burning directly after breakfast some of Margery's and some early ones of Philip's when he was with Haig at the Front. And I'm hanged if in the evening I didn't get a letter from Dr Roth saying that he after all was doing a book for Robert Hale, *The Magnificent Sassoons*, with 'a special mention of Philip Sassoon.' He would be 'grateful for my assistance' and may he come down and see me after May 21st?

1 May. Mrs Clarke at Swanborough 2.30 'bus. The Clarke's house is delightful. . . . Mr Clarke said his uncle was born in 1808 and clearly remembered the coach coming through the village after Waterloo and all the passengers standing up and waving and shouting "*Boney's taken.*" If only a Southdown 'bus could rush down the High Street now with everybody yelling "*Hitler's Murdered*".

4 May. At 4 I went and had tea with Auntie M. And we went for a little walk afterwards. She is curiously, quite – *gone*. Her brain. Not idiotic, not mad. But just not *there*. And her little brown eyes, never expressive, are just points of dulled glass, with nothing at all behind them.

7 May. The men – Wycherley's – were splendid and finished the drawing room. It looks so elegant: dead white walls and sea-green paint. Though as the carpenter said, when he hung up the looking glasses and the gilt candelabra, wouldn't look up to much if Hitler got it with a bomb.

8 May. Winnie said that the milkman said German planes went over the town at 6 o'clock this morning. I then went to Reeves the photographer, whose son (a consequential young fool) is an ARP warden and said they must warn the cottagers on Castle Banks not to show lights, which they do every evening.

11 May. Holland and Belgium invaded. Four bombs dropped on Canterbury: it is *crushing*.

13 May. The Masseuse [for AD's back pain] lives near CockFosters and she told me that Trent Park was now a Concentration Camp for German prisoners and is floodlit every night. Why, nobody seems to know, Princess Juliana of Holland after making the heroic utterance: "After 500 years, people should realise that the House of Orange never deserts" is now in England with her infants and her German husband! Also Queen Wilhelmina.[7] I go down the High Street, foaming at the mouth and saying: "How about Queen Boadicea?"! And am told (with perfect truth) by some persons like Dr Wells that time have changed since Queen Boadicea's time. Also I want to know why, when we are already rationed and when in the end decision of victory may rest on whether we are starved or not, are 2,000 Dutch refugees allowed to come here?

16 May. Mrs Holman said that 12 young women at Barcombe were in the family way by soldiers. The battalion was assembled – and all the girls pointed to one man! What a valiant!

---

7 Unlike Leopold of the Belgians whose surrender (see 28 May) opened a gap in the front through which Geman troops poured, Queen Wilhelmina ordered the Dutch fleet and her gold and diamond reserves to be placed at the disposal of the British to continue the fight against Germany.

17 May. Well, it shall be my last tea party until the war is over and the cakes cost 5/3d! The school-marm Miss Parker said some girl she knew was in a train and opposite her 2 nuns reading their Brevaries. One dropped hers, stooped to pick it up, her habit fell back disclosing a thick hairy man's arm. The girl told the police and the man was arrested! "All nuns" concluded Miss Parker "should not be allowed to wear their habits in wartime. They should wear football shorts and sweaters"!

20 May. Winnie spring-cleaned the bathroom (Hitler may as well find it clean).

22 May. The Germans are getting the Channel ports: the pain in my back is agonising. Patching who cut my hair said this war would probably mean the end, not of the British Empire but of England, and that the Royal Family and the Government would go to Canada and we should be left to the mercy of the Germans. Mr Ensell, not so dramatic, but equally depressing said the French had let us down : "They always do", and we shall be bombed out of existence.

23 May. I went down Keere Street to buy a Daren loaf and had a long talk with Pinyoun the baker. He said that in the last war when we were all told in case of invasion to assemble at the north-east corner of the prison, that he and other tradesmen had orders to put as much food out of the shop as possible, pile it on a hand barrow, take it with them and then before leaving *poison the rest of the stock! The Germans are at Boulogne.* Dr Irvine thinks it will not be an out and out victory for us: "We shall have to give up something. Probably the former German colonies."

28 May. Gardener came at 3 . . . he brought the perfectly awful news (from the 1 o'clock wireless) that the King of the Belgians had turned *Traitor*: capitulated to the Germans and that our army in Belgium was surrounded. I didn't sleep all night.

29 May. The Darkest Hour, the Blackest Time! [8] Dear Tam came at 4 . . . full of his Ordination plans. He says give the Germans back their colonies, or even Australia thrown in! Anything to put an end to the carnage. But it wouldn't end it. It is like the man who threw his children, one by one, out of the sleigh to a pack of wolves. Miss Harvey Smith's chauffeur – Welfare – said of the King of the Belgians: "Give me five minutes of 'im down a dark lane, and with my bare 'ands"!

1 June. When I retrieved an earring from Peskett the Jeweller in Market Street (no good trying to be haughty with Peskett!) he produced a *Daily Mirror* which avers that the real King of the Belgians was killed in the motor smash when his Queen was killed in 1935 and that this man is a Nazi German posing as King!

5 June. Mrs Dunstan rang up. Dr Dunstan had just been told by Walton at the White Hart that my dear Mr Jackson [9] shot himself on the Downs last Friday 31st, the very day he wrote to me. So that when I tapped out a long letter on Saturday, trying to cheer him up, he was already dead. My dear 'Valentine' Jackson!

7 June. And at 1.30, if you please, an Air Raid warning. Then Winnie came pattering in: "Are you all right, M'm"? Told her not to be afraid, but just go back to bed. But no sleep for me.

11 June. *Italy is in the war now.* I don't see how we can win.

14 June. *The Germans are in Paris.* Dr Irvine came . . . very gloomy about the war, thinks there was treachery in the French Army. Hitler certainly seems as Margery says 'invincible'. He said he would be in Paris by the 15th. He now says he will be in Eastbourne by August! Met old Dusart as I came home from Mrs Jervis and he says the Germans could easily land by parachute 100 men and if here blow the High Street to pieces.

8 On 30 May began the evacuation of British troops from Dunkirk.
9 A report stated he was depressed by the possibility of a German invasion.

18 June. Such a queer world! Sometimes I feel I shall wake up some morning and find I've just been having a doubly bad nightmare . . . No sign posts, no milestones, no church bells, except as a warning that we are invaded. My chief terror is being compulsorily evacuated. Mrs Jervis and I have in that case to go to Cornwall with Winnie . . .

20 June. Air Raid warning just before midnight and the All Clear signal (so I'm told) at 4.30. I got out, drew my heavy curtains over the window near my bed in case of broken glass and went to sleep again.

26 June. Some young woman called with a disc, a scheme got up by Turnbull the Vet for Spangles to wear on her collar so that, if caught in an Air Raid, she would get 'first aid'. Cost a 1/-, made of cardboard and she'll have it off her collar in less than a week!

2 July. Roumania has come in now with the Germans. When and how can this war end?

3 July. The great sensation of this day is that Kitty Howard, after 10 more or less turbulent years, is giving up the lean-to in September. Why was I such a fool as to refuse her offer of £250 for Emily's sake? Emily, who since I generously by a codicil left it her in my will has done nothing but (by implication) wished me dead. I have written and told her that in view of the war if I don't let it I shall have to sell it.

6 July. Great excitment: just when Winnie was giving the order to the grocer's young man, three of our Spitfires flew over, very low, chasing a German bomber. They all looked up and ran out (although we've been warned not to), Winnie, the grocer's boy and the young men from the Malt House. After tea I went to see Mrs Brough and listened to the 6 o'clock wireless. Two German machines have been brought down, perhaps ours was one. I feel more angry with the French than with the Germans! The Germans openly fight us, the French have stabbed us in the back.

16 July. Dr Roth finds it impossible (owing to the war) to come down – wonder if he's an alien and his movements restricted? Will I send him any letters of Philip's and any personal notes that may help him in writing his book *The Magnificent Sassoons*?

22 July. Mrs Hyeem and Lady Boyle. Park Lane, they tell me, is empty and for sale [10.] Trent and Lympne taken over by the government. Mrs Gubbay has left Hertford Street and has been living in Brighton. Never came to see me! Sent to Dr Roth for his book all Philip's letters and 2 photographs.

31 July. Dr Roth, when I had expected a learned – possibly bearded – and certainly elderly 'don', proved to be a handsome dark young man, quite obviously a Jew, in an immaculate pale grey suit.

6 August. Meanwhile the report is that Hitler will 'invade' on the 8th or the 10th.

7 August. Felt I must see and talk to someone who really mattered to my heart. Margery out of the question and also Vere. So wrote to David who really does love me, or insists that he still does . . . the papers say that invasion may happen at any moment and it is useless to say I am not afraid. I am.

8 August. This morning about 10 an Air Raid warning with the usual results: Spangles wild with terror, Winnie white as a sheet . . . sudden appearance of Air Raid Wardens, speedy descent of pedestrians into the Air Raid shelter on the Bowling Green. The All Clear didn't sound for more than hour and there was the constant drone of planes overhead. Evidently a big affair on somewhere.

9 August. It was a big affair, the biggest yet [11] so the paper says . 53 German machines brought down.

10 It later became the Playboy Club.
11 The Luftwaffe switched its attacks to targets in Southern England. The Battle of Britain began in earnest on 18th August, more than 1,000 German planes being sent over daily. 2 days later Winston Churchill paid tribute in Parliament to the pilots: 'Never in the field of human conflict was so much owed by so many to so few.'

16 August. The usual twice a day Air Raid Warning. One on now 6.30. It started at 5. Dear Winnie came up 10 minutes ago looking frightened. The windows were rattling. Did I hear the guns? I did and she stayed a little while. Rather disturbing, the constant noise of planes overhead. Anyhow, we brought down 144 German planes yesterday. And very likely even more today.

21 August. I took Spangles on the hills towards Kingston. On the way home, just as we got to the Grange, another warning! So sprinted up Keere Street and took shelter at the Hardy's. Now – 8.30 – Spangles has gone to bed, guns are going and the windows rattle. On Monday night, that is 2 am, a terrific explosion woke me. Everyone heard it and Muriel Hardy has been told that it was a bomb dropped at Ovingdean. I know that somewhere, at the back-of-beyond-of-me, I'm frightened to death all the time. But what's the good?

23 August. Planes were overhead all night and I never slept until 3.30 and then only till 6.

26 August. 4 Air Raid warnings – after an awful air raid last night. Brighton has been knocked about they say: Tamplin's Brewery, a timber yard and the York Road school. . . . What with unexploded mines about and people being machine-gunned as they pick blackberries on the Downs – Life is not dull!

27 August. David for the day. I wish it was over. Well, it is over! And not so bad. But a dead love affair is very fatiguing and he instantly wanted to kiss me, which I bluntly said was absurd. Now and then some turn of his really fine head or a pose of that still youthful figure vaguely recalls the past. He announced that he must catch the 5.20 bus . . . so after tea I walked through the Castle [Precincts] with him and he was so frightened that he'd miss that bus. His blue eyes quite alarmed, as if he were a boy late for school. And that brought back the past! Afraid of his wife – always! Anyhow the day, his day, is over.

30 August. I was to have my hair washed and set but just as I was starting at 11.30 an Air Raid warning and Winnie said Dusarts would certainly be shut. So brought in Mrs Taylor with her dog Angus – no dogs allowed in shelters. And the All Clear sounded at 1 o'clock. Dinner time. So thoughtful of Hitler.

31 August. After tea who should arrive but poor widowed Mrs Jackson. Air Raids in London quite intolerable. No sleep. So down here at the White Hart for the weekend. She was very moved talking of her husband's suicide and I gave her that last letter he wrote me the day he shot himself. She was very glad to have it.

9 September. No newspapers yesterday nor today until noon. Terrific damage in London, they say. We are not told much. Meanwhile we carry on . . . I did go to see Auntie M, very weak. She just whispered: "I'm sinking". But she loved the roses and said: "Beautiful – your garden", with a faint, reminiscent look in her eyes.

12 September. Turned into an emotionally strenuous day! First Winnie announces that Eastbourne is being evacuated, people must leave this week or be sent to some place in Gloucestershire next week. Later on Winnie Hardy came in and also Mrs Jervis – the evacuation is purely voluntary: old people, invalids and those with children are advised to go this week, if they decide to go at all. As, in the event of invasion, transport would be impossible.

13 September. Auntie M died this morning. I'm not surprised . . . she was practically dead when I saw her yesterday. So there goes a tradition of 20 years! . . . Her relatives have said they are not coming to the funeral and there is to be no car! But Harold Blaker is furious and says to Mrs Rogers: "I won't have it". And says that there shall be one and that he, Mrs Rogers and I are to ride in it! Very grisly! The relations are a callous lot.

16 September. Lovely warm, wet, misty day. I went at 11.15 to Ashdown House and directly inside the front door was confronted by her coffin and the undertaker's men. This for a second nearly broke me down. . . . Back from the cemetery to Ashdown House where we had a little consultation. I agreed to store Auntie M's furniture – there is very little – until the nieces decide what to do with it.

18 September. Winnie has been here 16 years today and it is 15 years since Nelson died. It comes back: Auntie M so kind. Ernest fetched in from the Bowling Green and kneeling by the dear beast's basket: "You are going a long journey, dear old chap." Never was a dog loved more, never was a dog's master more exquisitely tender.

26 September. See that Cockrom & Holder, the funny little shop down School Hill has a notice in the window: 'Retiring from Business'. Another bit of old Lewes gone. All cheap and fearsome underclothing and equally fearsome texts. *'Fleecy-lined knickers at 1/11'* and just below an illuminated text: *'Prepare to Meet thy God'*!

29 September. At tea time the most frightful bang, rattling the windows, shaking the house. I rushed out but the darling old thing stood unscathed, serene, as it has done since 1814. "The colour of a nectarine", as Philip once said.

5 October. The Nazis have at last found Lewes. 9 [10] bombs this morning. One in Southover churchyard demolished Mrs Jones's memorial to her husband; one behind Martin's garage blew up a car; one, a time bomb, in a house on Chapel Hill, so all the dwellers on Chapel Hill are, for the time being, evacuated.

8 October. I had a talk with him [Mr Godfrey]. 'Thebes', to which he has migrated because soldiers are in Lewes House, quite charming. A flat made out of some of the vast stabling of Lewes House by the late E P Warren. He retired there whenever he found the domestic affairs of Lewes House ('adopted' children[12] and all the rest!) too much for him. And his butler put his 'grub' on an arrangement – ledge etc. – just inside the front door.

12 Osbert Burdett maintained in his joint biography with EH Goddard, *Edward Perry Warren: The Biography of a Connoisseur*, that EW paid for expenses of several Lewes boys. EW adopted a son, Travis, in 1911. Thebes was saved from demolition by Walter Godfrey, who lived there from 1936–45.

11 October. Called on the Byng-Stampers who have bought the house[13] opposite the Hubert Powells. It was a tobacconist and barber's shop, but they have restored it and made it beautiful.

14 October. Frightful bang last night at 11.30. I got out of bed, took my torch and climbed up the attic stairs. My one thought an incendiary bomb. But – not so! Now I hear that it was lovely Ashcombe House[14]. Very badly damaged and one woman killed. Her throat cut by falling glass. Mr Tracey, the old clergyman who is another boarder there, sat reading: the whole room fell on top and around him, but he was dug out unhurt.

25 October. Spangles and I went shopping as usual and (as usual) a toddle down Church Lane for her private benefit. Soldiers were being drilled in the garden of School Hill House and seemed so sad and grotesquely unsuitable: clatter of feet, raucous roar of the Sergeant where there ought to be (and for generations has been) a lady picking the last autumn roses.

29 October. At the Hardy's Mrs Byng-Stamper and her sister. I like them very much. I even like their make-up. It is so obvious and daring. Such bright red sealing wax mouths! Muriel Hardy showed me an advertisement of Cecil Roth's forthcoming 'Sassoon' book. Wonder if he'll send me an autographed copy. He ought to.

15 November. Mrs Holman once said of me (when my wits, such as they are, were at their brightest!): "Mrs Dudeney is not *dull*".

1 December. I always put a jug of flowers on the tea table opposite where Auntie M always sat. I think she'd like that, perhaps she *does*.

13 Miller's, 134 High St. Frances Byng-Stamper and her sister Caroline Lucas, 'The Ladies of Miller's', were influential patrons of the arts and put on exhibitions, recitals and lectures throughout the war.
14 Ashcombe Farmhouse, just outside Lewes.

2 December. Hear that Hanningtons[15] has been bombed. The High Street is quite changed and most dispiriting. Half the shops to let and those that are not with very little for sale. . . . The town is full of horrible evacuees – young women with prams and sham leopard skin coats. I'm always hungry and as weak as a rat. Got yesterday by luck a bit of cheese (sounds like a mouse!). Also the nice 'bacon' man at the Malt House said he had told my maid that he could let us have half a dozen eggs a week.

4 December . . . the Germans are trying, as in 1917, to starve us: 19 [9?] ships sunk this week. And the silly old Pope [16] is pleading for an Armistice over Xmas.

19 December. Sent Christmas cards to all the people who sent cards to me. Really grisly and a bit of a mockery, the world being in the state it is.

28 December. Went to Applebys. To my horror no meat. One bloody sheep's head on the counter! I said I must have a rabbit, but they were all 'bespoke'. Besought Appleby to find me something. By rummaging he produced a tiny bit of rump steak – less than half a pound – and then, by another hunt, a fragment of pig's liver. I turn out, in the evening, very often my electric lamp and see such amazing pictures in the fire. They constantly change. Lovers on a seat merge and become one stout lady sitting in the stalls of a theatre! A horse lengthens his face until he is an elephant with a strongly marked trunk, and so on and so on! I can't think why people want wireless so long as there is a fire, constantly changing.

31 December. So ends the year. . . . I said to Winnie, and I say it every day, we are like the dog: think and speak of nothing but Food! How to get it? How to pay for it? Prices go up and up: supplies go down and down. Goodbye 1940. Good riddance.

15 The former Brighton department store.
16 Pius XII.

1941

9 January. Meat ration now cut to ½d each and may be only 1/-. We are told this is to save shipping, but at 'Janets' where I had some cocoa the manageress had heard that enormous stores of food had been destroyed in the German Air Raids and that when the war started there was enough meat in cold storage to feed us for 5 years.

15 January. Dr Holman came in after tea last night. He had been told by a woman – Barber her married name – whose people once kept the Lewes Arms that there was an underground passage leading out from their cellars and running under the Brack Mount. Afraid to explore it they sent their dog who ran down it and never came back (in such cases there is usually a dog who never comes back). Dr Holman said did I know anything about this passage[1] the legend being that there was a 90 feet well somewhere near. I said it must mean the well beneath my harness room which one of Batup's men fell down when Batup rented the stable. Oh ye Gods! More snow!

21 January. [Yesterday] I looked in on Mabel Smythe and stayed to hear Roosevelt on the wireless. Very declamatory and formless. Today is a lovely day; warm, dim and very wet.

22 January. A paper came of voluminous questions. Had I a stirrup pump or a shelter? Was I or any member of my household capable of putting out a Bomb? Which side of the house and on what floor did we, individually and collectively, all sleep?

29 January. . . . Mrs Brough has lost her parrot Sennacherib, a cherished pet for 23 years. And she cried all day. Flora Blaker said that the Miss Shiffners once lost their parrot for weeks, gave him up as a bad – and a sad – job. But

---

1 A blocked passage has since been discovered in the cellar of CPH. It possibly once led to the castle

one evening they heard a voice in the garden: *"I'm feeling damned queer"*. This, constantly repeated, led them at last into the garden and there was the truant parrot *"feeling damned queer"*. (A very good parrot story with the advantage of being true). The Misses Shiffner, although delighted to get him back, couldn't think *where* he had "learnt such language"!

30 January. . . . Mrs Bates, with the news that Mrs Brough had found her parrot roosting in the garden next door.

6 February. Jean [Massey] came in with a good story. Count Ciano, who married Mussolini's daughter Edda, came to Mussolini in great distress saying: *"Edda's in bed with peritonitis"*. Mussolini: *"Those damned Greeks are everywhere."*

7 February. I went to the Animals Supply Depot, stood in a row with some rather defiant looking ladies from Bermondsey and bought one pound of cow beef and half of liver for Spangles.

1 March. There was a sheep's head for dinner and it came to table with no brains! Winnie rang up Appleby and was told by Mrs Appleby: *"We had to take them out"*. God knows what that implied! So no dinner for me. And no sheep's head any more (war or no) grins up at me from a dish.

18 March. The last link with my writing life gone! Ralph Pinker, the Literary Agents, gone bankrupt. Got a formidable official notice this morning. First Meeting of Creditors on March 25th. Fortunately he doesn't owe me money, though I've dropped £6 13s on having *Sidelights on a Victorian Lady* retyped at his suggestion. And I expect he just pocketed the money and never had it retyped at all!

19 March. Dr Dunstan said that the new Sanitary Inspector (and new to Lewes) was at Rodmell near the 'pub' when he saw the most shabby, miserable-looking man and woman slouching along. He was so moved that he went into the inn and asked the landlord if he thought these poor wretches,

clearly 'evacuees', would be offended if he asked them in to have a cup of tea at his expense. The landlord, very tickled, advised him to make no such offer, adding: "That's Virginia Woolf and her husband[2]".

20 March. Miss Withers the chiropodist, who is most embarrassingly religious, said that Mrs Engell's mother (killed by a bomb and blown up onto the roof of her house) would *"only know she was in the arms of her Saviour"*. I at once became voluble about the painful corn on my little toe.

23 March. Day of United prayer for Peace and Victory. Went to St Michael's as usual and the Rector preached a Pacifist sermon, saying if we were victorious he hoped we would remember our own sins as a nation. Refrained (with difficulty) from throwing a hymn book at him!

27 March. Pinker says the bankruptcy is his personal affair and nothing to do with the firm (which I don't believe). Thinks, but not sure, that my luckless MS was burned at Hutchinsons in the Air Raid on London: December 29th. Mrs Jervis came in after tea, very jubilant (so am I!). Jugoslavia has *not* given in to the Germans.

29 March. After several days of 'shall I, shan't I' decided to have a shot at a Civil List pension. As Marion Cran[3] (herself on the List) said a Lord, if I knew one, would help, wrote to the 'nobility' (Lady Cholmondeley, Lord Hugh Cecil and Maurice Baring) and shall keep Lord Gage up my sleeve for extra use if necessary!

2 April. Dr Roth's book *The Sassoon Dynasty* came with elaborate thanks in the preface to 'Mrs Alice Dudeney' and copious extracts from Philip's letters to me. Not quite comfortable. I hate any personal limelight[4]. Pinker sent back the *rough* copy of my Memory book.

2 Leonard and Virginia Woolf lived at Monks House, Rodmell.
3 A writer friend.
4 On p 264 Cecil Roth says: 'A house where Balfour, Boussus, Hewlett, Alice Dudeney, Shaw, Sargent and T E Lawrence (not to mention Charlie Chaplin) were among the visitors could not be commonplace; and the host whose invitations they accepted must have had far more to commend him than his wealth.

4 April. At Mrs Jervis's . . . Mrs Ranson opened fire on Socialism: the same old *clichés* . . . that the working classes never "had a chance". And when you return that they've had free education for more than 70 years the same old answer: "But not the *right* education". See that Virginia Woolf has drowned herself[5] so perhaps Mrs Pember was right when she said VW was "mental". I took it as an excellent joke of the (to quote Thoreau) 'whole witted against the one and a half witted which the whole witted think half witted'.

5 April. Mrs Ranson charmingly left a bunch of daffodils with a note: "Forgive me". Rang her up, said: *"Talk about coals of fire!"* So she asked me to go to tea, but I said "after tea". And did. Her cottage at Kingston once the shepherd's and now 'Little Orchards'[6], charming and perfect if you like that sort of thing. I did, and now don't. Feel that the rustic people and the rustic life is lost, owing to these moneyed people transforming the labourer's 'hovel'. For 'Little Orchards' started as nothing better. She has bought a field adjoining, so as not to be "built on". Also a cottage, and does not allow washing to be hung out in view of her house. All of it very funny, for a red-hot socialist.

10 April. Ernest's birthday. He would be 84. Also Emily's. She's 71. Emily never wrote, nor did I. No heart for anything, nor I suppose has she. And then Churchill talks glibly about 1942! And Mrs Churchill like a fool says she sympathises with the girls "in the forces" who can't get cosmetics. "Neither can she." Have these women nothing to think of but the paint pot?!

15 April. Went and stood in a queue outside the Pet Shop to get meat for Spangles. They have now dyed it a verdigris green! So that people shouldn't buy it and eat it. Too loathsome! Thought I should be sick as I stood there.

20 April. Very depressed. I shall give up *The Observer*. Garvin is too old. He heads his article 'Britain at Bay' and then says that if we, with America, pull ourselves together at once, we may yet win the war. But if not, we shall lose it.

5 She weighted her pocket with a stone and walked into the River Ouse on 28 March.
6 Now the Juggs Inn.

23 April. Same old agony of back, as this time last year.

25 April. To tea at Mrs Jervis's to meet these artists[7] who have taken the shop next to Briggs the tailor . . . Nice people, these Adamses. They so hoped I would "come and see them". So I will directly my back no longer feels like snapping in halves.

3 May. The 'dog' affair goes from bad to worse . . . Met Clark the jeweller almost in tears. A lovely bull-terrier, Sally, and nothing to eat! I said why not get together, make a combine, and take it in turns to go to Ringmer and fetch the meat? He seemed impressed, said he'd make enquiries.

5 May. Met Fr Flannagan, also almost in tears about his dog. I like the Byng-Stampers. They now call their house in the High Street 'Miller's'. A little too elegant and super-cultured for me. . . . Bank Manager says that when the 10/- Income Tax is taken off I will have £250. *Froze me.* And then to think of those days when I took £650 as a matter of course.

7 May. Mrs Bates motored me over to the man – Muggeridge by name – at Ringmer. He has kennels and sends in horse flesh by bus if you order it. A charming man, also his wife. I pitched a pathetic yarn about my Dalmatian, 12 years old, and that I had kept Dalmatians for nearly 30 years. We parted on terms of warm friendship and he is to send in (when he's got it!) 21 lbs of meat by bus every Saturday and the account to me once a month. I hope it isn't too good to be true.

8 May. Long Q outside Pryor's for sausage meat. But no more Q's for me. Met Father Flannagan dancing along with a bundle under his arm. Another rabbit for his St Bernard, four this week at 2/3 each! Meanwhile, there is a great run at Coppard and Likeman's on cods' heads, mostly for confounded cats.

13 May. I felt "all of a *sudding*" as dear Father Wood[8] used to say, so ill when I got up that I realised if anything had got to be done, let it be done now. So

7 The Adams lived at 90 High St, later rented AD's 'lean-to' as a studio.
8 London priest (referred to in 1910–13 diaries)

I fired off and sent by registered post my application for a *Civil List Pension*. With an imposing row of 'backers': Marquis and Marchioness of Cholmondeley, Viscount Quickswood, Viscount and Viscountess Gage, Lady Desborough, Professor Hardy, Professor Cecil Roth, Wilfrid Meynell.

23 May. Frightful shock: as if I were not crushed enough already. Christopher [Fulleylove] has lost his job, no fault of his. But it's heartrending. So clever, such a 'might have been' and such a failure. Meanwhile my precious brave Margery is working herself to death over her weaving. Full of courage, full of hope, or else for my sake splendidly pretending at both.

25 May. The battleship *Hood* has been sunk[9]. The Germans are landing Airborne troops on Crete. I read *The Observer* and *The Sunday Times* till I was quite desperate and the first chill admission of a possible defeat froze my heart.

27 May. . . . went to Brighton armed with a basket on the chance of Food - but Hurdsons had no pies, no tinned fruit. Sat on the front near the West Pier[10] and staring through hoops and arcades of tangled barbed wire at an incomparably lovely and innocent sea. Saw, with joy, on the placards that we have sunk the Bismarck.

28 May. Great joy over sinking the German battleship[11]. On the other hand, things in Crete look bad . . . met Dr Nicholl. I said: "What would you do to the Germans after the war?" He laughed, blushed and said: "Can't tell you. It wouldn't be nice." We knew what he meant – emasculate the lot. But it is impossible, from every Christian and civilised ethic.

29 May. Met Mrs Byng-Stamper who impressively told me that the friend she was bringing on Saturday was "*the* Miss Elsie Cohen". I said: "How very delightful" with not the least idea of how this Miss Cohen was distinguished from the vast host of other Cohens.

9 By the Bismarck with the loss of 1,400 lives.
10 One of Brighton's two piers, now derelict.
11 Claimed to be unsinkable.

31 May. The Miss Cohen proved to be a delightful person, interested in films. A charming trio - Mrs Byng-Stamper, her sister and Miss Cohen - cultured and easy, the sort of thing you don't find in the Lewes natives. In the afternoon to the film *Escape* with Mrs Phelps and Mrs Jervis. Pleasant women, and perhaps more worthy and with more staying power than the morning three. But what a different (and more dull) proposition.

1 June. Clothes rationed now, you have to give coupons. Everything rationed, registered and so on. I said to Winnie that in the end we should want coupons for a coffin and register with an undertaker! Winnie, as always (with no cynicism and little humour) faintly troubled by such remarks. Seems to think they are either impious or mad! You buy by Coupon - cut out of the ration book. 66 a year! I worked it all out as well as I could and think I can manage. But the restriction, on top of so many restrictions, is quite hateful.

2 June. A cold, sunless venomous day. And we've had to get out of Crete. *Crushing!*

5 June. Letter from Lady Cholmondeley, very 'cordial'. Signing 'Yours affectionately' with a PS: 'Do call me Sybil'. So I'm very relieved, all embarrassment about the Sassoon book over [12].

6 June. Lady C gratefully accepts my offer to send her, give her, all those letters of Philip's which escaped my impulsive bonfire on the night of his death.

13 June. Read *Flush* by Virginia Woolf, all about Mrs Browning's dog. So exquisitely perfect that I never wish to read any other book of VW's.

15 June. I stand on the wooden platform just outside my door that leads to the Mount every day after dinner and wait for Spangles – beloved dog – coming along in her leisurely way and never treading on bluebells. Coming slowly because she is 12 and gracefully because, always, she is lovely.

12 Letters were quoted from PS to AD revealing his unhappiness and emotional sensitivity.

16 June. My heart beat fit to split as I tore open that envelope marked 'Prime Minister'. But it was only to say that my 'application for a Civil List Pension would be considered in the early months of next year'. So I assume they haven't turned the said application down? And will now put the affair out of mind and hope for the best.

28 June. These exquisite, peerless June nights (summer at last with a vengeance). I sit by the window and watch the swifts with their long, strong wings, and then comes the roar of aeroplanes and there they go south, high up in the cloudless sky. It is, with the extra daylight saving hour, daylight till nearly 11. I got out the hat – immortal – which went as a 'model' hat to Lympne nearly 20 years ago. And, as I do every summer twisted a new ribbon round it . . . such a brilliant gipsy ribbon, green, red and yellow flowers woven on a black ground. How David would love it and love me in it, or say so of long habit. Don't suppose I shall ever see him again.

29 June. I'm getting so alarmingly thin. Everybody notices it. They say: "Nothing of you". Sometimes I wonder if it is just owing to the war and short commons. Or whether I'm just painlessly and insidiously being eaten away by some unknown, unseen mischief.

5 July. Thank God Christopher is back at his job. But then my own precious child says: 'I am getting leaner and greyer'. However she will always be lovely. And it is such a lovely day and the roses both in this garden and the Town Wall garden are magnificent. In the Town Wall garden the valiant Paul's Scarlet Climber has, the trellis having fallen down, run right up the old apple tree.

21 July. The pictures [13] at Miller's lovely but Mrs Jervis has a provoking way of leaving you if she sees a man she'd rather talk to . . . Mrs Byng-Stamper asked me to become a member, annual subscription one shilling. So am. The

---

13 First exhibition of English and French Paintings under the CEMA 'Arts for the People' scheme. Included paintings by Cezanne, Pissarro, Matthew Smith, Sickert, Roualt. Opened on 12 July by Walter Godfrey in place of Sir Kenneth Clark.

pictures by famous men, Augustus John, Matisse and others. Dr Holman says: "*Not one he would have in his house*"!

23 July. Margaret Hill said that all the Lewes girls were having babies by the French-Canadian soldiers in the town. She cynically added that if they must "sin" they might just as well have babies, as we should want as many as we could get after the war and these soldiers are "good stock".

28 July. David [writes] that someday I shall find him 'on my doorstep'. I devoutly hope – *not*!

8 August. Last night it rather comforted me to see the Land Girls come trooping home from their work on the land. Such a fine set of young women and looking delightful in their uniform, grey corduroy knickers, Lincoln Green sweaters and broad brimmed hats. You think of Robin Hood, the Forest of Arden and all sorts of delightful things.

11 August. The War Damage Bill [£15 18 6d a year compulsory insurance] goes on for 5 years. However I assure myself that I shall get [a] Civil List Pension. The Land Girls living in Castle Place (dear Dr Spokes's house) have put up net curtains and one of them was sitting at the open window of the drawing room upstairs knitting. Nice Palmer, the gardener, put up all the blackout curtains I've been slaving at.

14 August. At 3 went to Mrs Jervis to listen in to Attlee's speech, some disclosure of importance he was to make. . . . Thought perhaps that Churchill was ill or dead! But only that he and Roosevelt had met for conference somewhere in Mid-Atlantic[14].

22 August. The aimless pleasant days go on, stretch into weeks – months! And it is five years since I published a novel, three since I wrote my last short story, that triumphant 'Shell of a Lady'. Yet how *dull*, how elderly, how starved of all reality this aimless life is. And sometimes I would give a great deal for the fever and the thrill and the exhaustion of the past.

14 The Atlantic Charter – a declaration of war and peace aims of both nations.

27 August. Went down to Mitchell's and spent the last 4 coupons in my ration book for 2 pairs of Lisle stockings – supposed to wear much better than silk but I shall hate the feel of them after years of silk . . . And got to register for Onions now! 2 lbs a head to last through the winter. Seventeen million eggs gone bad in 8 weeks since they were controlled! We get one a week. I had mine for supper on Sunday, or rather Spangles had it as it was next door to rotten.

28 August. Parson Newbury and his wife from Barcombe at Mrs Jervis's. Such dear people. Mrs Newbury voluble about the immorality at Barcombe, as everywhere. Girls and married women "expectant mothers" by soldiers. She also said that a German plane came down at Barcombe. A dead German in it. "We hoped to just pop him quietly into a corner of the churchyard but, would you believe it, when the Rector arrived to read the funeral service there were 300 bicycles outside the church and the place packed with people!"

1 September. This is the day Hitler is supposed to invade us.

18 September. The Adams's came about 6 . . . they are keen on my idea of turning the Lean-to into a studio.

23 September. We all thought the 'Thousand Years of Lewes' show[15] at Miller's a very poor affair. But it was fun meeeting everyone and talking. Miss Foster, extremely smart and handsome, arrived with Tam if you please! The best thing about the Miller's show is that they've managed to get the sign of the White Lion on loan from George Beard and don't mean to let it out of Lewes again – to his Tally-ho pub on the Landport [housing] 'estate'.[16]

29 September. I let the Lean-to to the Adams (a studio for him) for £26 a year. So thankful that Kitty Howard couldn't get permission to build on to it. I was a Fool to say I'd sell.

15 CEMA exhibition, the idea of Walter Godfrey. Several drawings lent by Councilllor Tam Dicker.
16 The sign was erected by The Friends of Lewes on the original town wall site in 1954.

6 October. Tam and Mr Adams between them ate up all the 'rich' plum cake I'd been meaning to hoard for myself. Tam had just seen the Borough Surveyor. They are thinking of taking our iron railings for munitions, unless we appeal . . . we agreed to appeal and pointed out to said pundit – the Town Clerk - that as this house was one of the most characteristic Regency houses left in Lewes I wished it to remain unchanged.

2 November. On All Souls' Day I put on Ernest's grave a little bunch of the last roses in the garden and some rosemary. If he knows, he'll like that better than bought chrysanthemums which every grave blazes.

15 November. People are steadily losing weight, not because they don't get enough to eat but because all the food is adulterated and filthy. And we get no fruit except a very few apples and about every 6 weeks a quarter lb of prunes.

30 December. Sharp attack of bronchitis, which unless I am careful will get worse. Dr Irvine, looking round my dear, pale drawing room: "I should like to see your bed down here". I: "So many things you'd like to see that you never will!"

31 December. Muggeridge can send no more meat (at present) for Spangles. Rang up Turnbull. He has none either. General shortage, he hopes only temporary. Several dogs - paying guests - who came to him for Christmas have had nothing but soaked biscuit and gravy. This struck me as being very funny. The poor beasts coming to a 'luxury hotel' for Christmas, and then sopped biscuit only! Managed to get a rabbit, also a sheep's head from Appleby.

Goodbye 1941.

1942

5 January. Fearful shock. Letter from Ida. David died last Friday. Funeral today. I'm just *stunned*. Whatever the immediate past has been: a tradition arid, outworn – there remains the glowing tradition of our long rich passion. The only *romance* of my life: 45 years all told, in all the aspects. And we gave each other something which the others never had. I shall, for the rest of life, reproach myself for not breaking the long silence. I might have known he was ill and as Ida said 'so tired'. Wrote to Ida.

6 January. Today my head bursts – probably because, when safe from Winnie's gimlet glances and the risk of more visitors, I cried mysef blind.

7 January. . . . I sat, stunned, in the 'once blue' chair, until bed time. Oh, David, my dear. I can hear you say it and see you as you say it: *"The legend of that chair is blue"*. And, not yet, do I realise that you are dead.

10 January. If I had saved but one letter of David's. Instead of tearing them up and throwing them – latterly rather contemptuously – on the fire, feeling them too exotic from an old man to an old woman.

15 January. Last night, with no feeling (seems I've got precious little emotion left!) I began to tear up my 'Memory' book, as Winnie is short of paper for the fires. . . . So goodbye to it, the last flicker of my creative life. Yet I still can't help thinking that, as intimate record from the late 1860's beginning with the recollections of a child of only three years old, it had its value.

21 January. We are now reduced to half a pint of milk a day for the 2 of us. Add to that it is the most bitter winter since 1916 – that we have 1/- worth of meat each a week and 2 oz of butter. I can't think why we are alive or what there is to live for. No letters: everybody dead – or on the other side of the Atlantic.

28 January. I drew up the blind this morning on the most lovely sight: a tiny girl – Emmy Arkwell's poor little bastard, dressed in a medley of entrancing primary colours – biting cerise, bright scarlet, dark blue socks, a sugar almond pink hood and dancing under the bare lime trees hugging a pale blue dolly . Over her head a great white gull wheeling and circling. This made me very happy. Also not a trace of snow. . . . Oh I wish I could tell David – or even write and tell him – about the little girl and the gull. That was the way – the best way – in which we met. '*Conceal it not. He was the love of my heart – if I loved every other.*'

7 February. Mrs Jervis said there was a perfect *famine* in elastic and that I had better go to Mitchell's – the only shop that had any – early on Monday. Newspaper says that the Japanese are now scattering plague germs and dropping infected rats. Talk about Hell! We are living in it!

8 February. The Rector preached a Lenten sermon. Said there was no need to tell us to fast as, owing to the war, we already did. He added – with Pacifist gloating – that we should all probably know for the first time in our lives what it was to be *"really hungry"* before very long!

9 February. *Soap rationed now!* And Winnie looking as black as thunder!

17 February. Most heartrending letter from Ida. Everything sold to pay David's debts I assume. And she in two rooms . . . Asks me to go over, which of course I shall. And I feel such a *Pig* for having unkind thoughts about her.

26 February. About the bitterest day of the year, a frightful north-east wind. But off I went . . . no dear, still-youthful figure to meet the bus. Ida had left her two rooms and was at the Hotel opposite her old house which is already let and full of painters, whitewashers and so on. I then said that I had been . . . very unhappy at David's long silence and that I bitterly reproached myself for not breaking it . . . She said he had been "going downhill" for months. That his sight was going, also his memory and his mind. So that when he once asked if I'd got the letter he wrote "about 2 weeks ago" (not having written for eleven weeks) he probably believed that he had. And every day up to the last he constantly said: "*I must write to Alice*". But he never went

near his desk. He just shut himself in his studio and painted. On December 22nd he returned to the house for lunch and fainted, a dead faint. She got him round, put him to bed and sent for the doctor. But he never rallied and died on January 2nd. She's been compelled to sell all the furniture and had practically nothing to live on. We then went to the Studio, and people kept coming and going – some were dealers. The pictures were selling well, the unfinished one still on his easel. I knew no one, obviously, and (as obviously) was not introduced. Naturally Ida was much in request. I felt forlorn and rather ridiculous! I don't know why she made such a point of my coming on that particular day when I was clearly *de trop*. Perhaps she shrank from prolonged talk and intimacy. Our relationship for so many years has been so forced. I did say to her, when for a minute or two we were alone: "What queer cards life turns up! Did we 45 years ago when we were young and carefree foresee this day?" She said: "My dear, I suppose this is the pattern we made." We felt fond of each other then, but only for a moment. At last, feeling I could bear no more, I slipped out and walked to the church and, later to the churchyard I asked a man who was weeding the path which was [David's] grave. He pointed to it and I stood there looking blindly down at the grey turves that were patted over it.

4 March. So that is the end of the story. So ends it! The one man I ever was 'in love' with. Affection and tradition and having a husband (as he had a wife) – that's a different affair. I see it all so clearly now, after many variations. He is dead. I stood by his grave and it is over. 'Heigh-ho! Said Anthony Rowley.'

11 March. Mrs Brough after tea very keyed up over the war, and we agreed within the sanctity of my four walls that our people – that is, the working classes – are not worth fighting for and don't deserve to win. Spoonfed and pampered ever since the last war. And, now not pulling their weight. Nothing but wage increases, bonuses, dog-racing, strikes, going to the pictures – lots do 4 times a week.

16 March. Mrs Bates was to have taken me for a little 'convalescent's' drive, but just as we were starting the Air Raid warning went and 'Dick' would not allow her to be out at such a time. Moreover, she must get home to 'superintend' (with 3 maids, a husband, a chauffeur and a gardener) the closing of all

the shutters in St Anne's House! So I just took Spangles for a walk. Nobody takes much notice of an Air Raid now.

23 March. *Black Black Day*. Got a shabby looking letter in a redirected envelope with a rubber stamp: 'Downing Street'. 'The Prime Minister has not felt able to recommend your name to the King for a Civil List Pension.' So that's that!! And – one consolation, I shan't appear to my neighbours as a polite Pauper. Cecil Roth was right. Unless you are – as it were – living in a bedsitting room with a gas ring the Government does not consider you 'necessitous'. I feel defiant and depressed: furious, yet downtrodden.

28 March. The show at Miller's[1] was amusing and Jean came with me. We got more fun out of the people than the pictures. Professor Keynes opened the show. His wife, the Russian dancer[2], was with him.

8 April. Margery's letter dated February 10th! She tells me that Christopher has lost his job, was out of one for 6 weeks and now has another. And that, worse, her tweed-designing job has gone thanks to this Blasted war.

10 April. Yesterday Tam turned up and stayed to tea. He is going to a curacy in Leicester in the autumn. Unfortunately, poor wretch, through an 'orgy' of Devotions has developed Housemaid's Knee.

11 April. Shelley's 4.45. Such a delightful party, old Mrs Hyeem, Lady Boyle and a very charming friend Miss Blanche Fair (lovely name). Old Mrs Hyeem gave me a lovely Indian scarf, stroking my hands and saying: *"Philip was so fond of you"*. I came home, very cock-a-whoop – to find Mrs Brough immensely perverse and tragic. Had been talking to Mr Bedford who was *"broken-hearted"*. We are to have an Invasion Rehearsal on the Downs, with Tanks. "And", says broken-hearted Bedford: *"the Downs will be gone"*. This prospect kept me wake half the night.

---

1 '12 Painters' including Duncan Grant, Matthew Smith, Vanessa Bell, Frances Hodgkins, Ivon Hitchens and Caroline Lucas. Exhibits selected by the artists.
2 Lydia Lopokova, wife of Maynard Keynes, the economist.

1942

23 April. One shock after another! Not only have the military taken over the South Downs but the village of Stanmer[3] is evacuated: the church dismantled and the inhabitants, some of whom were not only born there but their parents and grandparents before them, turned adrift. I hope that we shall bomb Germany to bits!

1 May. There is no doubt that the affair between me and David really died 10 years ago. On that marvellous morning when, first, at Freeland and Geerings we bought for 25/- the little glass in the gilt frame and then walked up Chapel Hill with the dear dogs – Emma and Spangles – and on towards Glynde. Suddenly I stopped and quickly kissed his cheek: "David. I'm so happy." "Darling Alice – yes, we are happy, after sixteen years." The dogs were racing and playing . . . The day was perfect, the great hills were all round us. That was the last occasion of perfect romance. We kept up the illusion for years but love was withered. It was wasted away by his debts and many anxieties, by my many other interests (including Philip Sassoon). And he's dead too. And Ernest is so long dead that he's sort of gone away. And I am a very old woman alone. But in my house and with the Mount for romance, blessed by God. And with Spangles, though I can't hope to keep her much longer.

2 May. Mrs Jervis told me that Mr Matthews, the Rector of Southover, had seen his Bank Manager in London and that this man, a Home Guard, told him that the Germans in their 'E boats'[4] made 'Commando' raids: landing in little creeks and quiet places, principally on the East coast and *that they kidnapped people*. Our Government hushes it up. Mrs Topham told me that this was common news, had been given out on the wireless and that these Germans, speaking perfect English, go and drink in the pubs and pick up news.

3 In Stanmer Park on outskirts of Brighton. Taken over as "Town Fighting Area". Released in dilapidated state in 1946.
4 Torpedo-carrying ships.

259

10 May. Hear that the Rector of St Michael's had a Pacifist meeting with 'coloured person' to speak, that they both attacked the British Empire, and that the new minister of the Unitarian Chapel across the way[5] so opposed them and kicked up such a row that the meeting closed.

11 May. Jean lent me DH Lawrence's letters. Very interesting – a lot of them are written to that American Witter Bynner[6], one of my 'admirers' 38 years ago. We corresponded for a long time and he sent me his poems *An Ode to Harvard*.

13 May. I'm so wretched about Spangles. She has suddenly thrown up the sponge. Lies in her basket all the time. Gets out for her dinner and eats nothing but a very little meat. Goes down the garden when necessary but never on the Mount with 'mother' after dinner. Very weak on her legs, always asleep but apparently no pain. So I went off to Margaret and said would she come to tea and play Polish Bezique afterwards. She did and that helped a little.

17 May. I was utterly miserable. Spangles constantly sick and in the intervals sitting up in her basket and looking at me so beseechingly.

18 May. Turnbull came. He examined her, said she had kidney trouble, but no reason why she couldn't be given "another chance". Will send some medicine . . . Been reading the letters of DH Lawrence and also the life of Edward Perry Warren by Osbert Burdett[7] (very interesting as I knew both men). But Lewes House seems to have been an odd enough ménage, or menagerie! I like *balanced* people.

19 May. Rang up Turnbull, said would he take Spangles as a patient for a week to give it every chance? Yes he would. I feel I ought to have her put to sleep but haven't the courage.

5 Westgate Chapel. In 1913 John Every, the Ironfounder, converted this meeting house for dissenters into a chapel.
6 Wealthy homosexual American poet. Visited Mexico with the Lawrences.
7 He lived in the 1920s close to AD in Bartholomew House, Castle Precincts.

25 May. We rang up Turnbull the vet. I shan't forget Winnie's pathetic little voice on the 'phone: "Is there any hope, sir?" "Yes, always hope."

2 June. Turnbull said Spangles was just fading out, old age, no pain. She no longer barks, nor moves except to take a little food. I'd better not see her, might distress her. He said he'd give her an injection, quite swift and painless. I don't know how I got home without crying. Locked myself into the house, tore off my hat and coat and skirt, flung myself on to the bed and cried as I haven't cried for many years, and for hours . . .

3 June. Such a perfect perfect day, and the blackbird fluting, that sweet, heart-rending song. I told Winnie, I left a note on the kitchen table asking her not to enquire about Spangles when she called me. We just cried together, broken hearted. Oh, these dogs! Why does one love them so wildly? I went up on to the Mount, my unfailing consolation, and there stayed till dinner time. Then back again till tea time. After tea Mrs Jervis came. Very kind, but I don't want to see anybody.

9 June. I met everybody down the High Street, all very sympathetic and all with the same advice: "Get another dog", anything with 4 legs that barks! That may do for some people, not for me with a record of 3 pure-bred, lovely Dalmatians.

11 June. The house is so silent. I went out and desperately gardened all the afternoon when Winnie was out. At 6, by mercy, the nice Adams's arrived, so friendly and understanding, such dog lovers. After they'd gone, I framed the photograph of Nelson and hung it in the study. So now, in that intimate, haunted room I can look at everything that stands for love: Ernest, Margery and the two baby boys – and the dogs, Nelson, Emma, Spangles.

17 June. The garden is so lovely, and so lonely, the house also. Yet I think, paradoxically, that I am sad not because I am alone but because my setting is so satisfying and, to me, so lovely and without flaw, that I dread losing it: and I know that I must die and leave it (perhaps I shan't leave it?)

19 June. War news not too good. Rommel 20 miles from Egypt, the British Is-raelites prophesy that we shall lose Egypt[8]! The Germans nearing Sebastapol, and many, far too many, of our ships being sunk.

20 June. Went to Mrs Jervis's after tea by invitation and listened to the news – as bad as can be. Met Mrs Adams who had borrowed my mower for the Town Wall garden. We went down there with her as Mrs Jervis had not seen it. They have made it charming. How lucky I am to have such tenants.

23 June. Gunfire. Winnie's day out. I dreaded it. The house so silent, so empty. And when I came back from my dinner at the Tatler, no dear, spotted figure and eager face (for dinner!) behind the front door. To make matters worse, Margery's letter very controlled and stoical, but I read between the lines. Christopher 2 months out of a job and the two boys earning big money. Only youth is wanted. Christopher, with his gifts, tramping New York for work. He should never have left England but for that old mollusc, his mother.

14 July. I was in Kenwards the fruiterers when a regiment of women with a band came marching down the street. A magnificent lot, carrying themselves beautifully. ATS women: the Captain a really lovely girl, but the Drum Major thrilled me most.

20 July. Mr Godfrey, to whom I wrote about railings, has resigned from the whole affair. I understand that they – the Sub-Committee – are taking Tam's from The Red House, Southover, and also from outside St Michael's. Also from round the vaults in the old churchyards, the very thing I suggested in a letter to *The Daily Telegraph* months back, and they never put the letter in.

29 July. Letter from Margery. She said: '*What's the matter with the British? One defeat after the other.*' I wrote back: 'I am very angry with you. The matter with the British is that they saved the world in 1940, fighting alone while America was sitting back and licking her chops!'

8 On 21st June the 8th Army lost Tobruk.

9 August. At 11.30 . . . awful bangs and flashes of light – I thought it was the beginnings of a thunderstorm and went to sleep again.

10 August. Winnie said she nearly came to me, did get as far as my door and then was afraid to come in. Thought I might want "company"! Got some herself by putting her head out of her bedroom widow and talking to 'Bert' at the Malt House, he being on night watch there! Palmer the gardener said 2 houses down at Newhaven, a boarding school at Seaford and tremendous damage at Portslade.

12 August. We are all tired today. Raid in the night, great damage done at Eastbourne. Lots of people got up and dressed and looked out of the window. Said it was a grand sight, like a firework display at the Crystal Palace! I stayed in bed as usual: my proud boast – so far – that never have I got up. As I tell Winnie, if we are to be killed, just as well in our nightgowns as our combinations.

15 August. One irritant after another. Policemen coming now to see if we have cleared out our attics. Winnie and I have been hauling down cardboard boxes. Mr Holland says he's got enough to fill a furniture van in *his* attic. Dear old Holland – 89. They give him 2 weeks to do it. Ida Blaker in despair over their attic, over a wardrobe which she doesn't believe can ever be got out! As I sat in the garden this morning none too cheerful, a baby robin sat on the rounded top of the wall dividing the upper from the lower garden. Quite fearless, very uncertain on his pins and more experimental on his fluffy wings. It so delighted and calmed me and I felt that if in the other world there are robins, roses and all the things that delight me, then the sooner I got there, the better I'd be pleased. For this world now holds nothing but terror and bereavement.

17 August. Last night I dreamt of David as he used to be in the young, magic days. I flung myself into his arms and said: "Lovely to see you, darling". Winnie was standing by, but I didn't care whether she heard or not. A *respectable*, elderly widow would dream of her husband!

19 August. Emily says there is now to be no evacuation at Brighton and no military to be sent there. To her great relief, and mine. There was really no fun in the visit to Falmer . . . every road and lane was an inferno of tanks and Army lorries. Useless to try and get on the Downs.

20 August. Awful night. Planes going over. Sirens going . . . Heaps of Scottish soldiers marching down the High Street playing bagpipes.

22 August. Yesterday Olive and Winnie under my direction cleared out both attics and distributed the contents mostly in the basement. So now the policemen may turn up to inspect whenever they choose. Could one have dreamt, even 10 years ago, of all this local and governmental nagging. Again – gas masks! First, you were ordered always to carry them (which I never did). Now you are forbidden to!

26 August. Mrs Jackson said she met one of these modern girls who said she meant to have 3 babies before the war was over. I said: "Do ask her to hurry up and make it triplets."

5 September. . . . when I was in my bath and Winnie in her bed 2 policemen arrived and said the bathroom light was showing and must go out at once or they would report me. Winnie, at the bathroom door, very voluble and would have burst in if I hadn't hastily burst *out* of the bath and locked the door. So out went the light and I had to dry myself, get into some garments and fumble upstairs in total darkness. Reminded me of the lovely story: Policeman to lady of the house: "You've a chink showing upstairs." Lady: "Why he told *me* he was the Japanese Ambassador"!

11 September. So lovely, so extra lovely, to get out at Horsham station and see Vere waiting for me as I got out of the bus. We did the same as last year, had a good lunch, ambled up to the church, sat about on Altar tombs, the day being hot and perfect, talked incessantly diving into the never forgotten past, had our tea and soon afterwards came the really agonised parting.

24 September. A bad raid at Eastbourne on Wednesday. Woman in a grocer's shop was pushed by the proprietor under the counter for safety. A woman in a *butcher's* shop, half cripped by rheumatism, was put by the butcher for safety into the *refrigerator*! So even Air Raids have their lighter side.

26 September. Mrs Bates 1.15. A really decent, pre-war meal. Exquisite young chicken with peas and potatoes and the most lovely savoury rice. Apple tart and *cream* to follow. The Bates get these luxuries from their son-in-law Demetriardi who farms at Plumpton.

1 October. Awful thing has happened. A school at Petworth has been bombed and about 30 small boys and the headmaster killed.

3 October. See that all the 29 little boys with their Headmaster are to be buried in one grave at Petworth today. The first Air Raid Petworth has had and most cruel.

12 October. The German prisoners have been manacled. A great mistake. The Germans will only treat our prisoners with more brutality. Not only that, it is so degrading to try and beat them at their own beastly game.

17 October. As I went down Rotten Row this morning in mist and the flame of blowing leaves a woman came out of the cottage near Antioch House and shook a mat. Reminded me so vividly of that morning 30 years ago when I rode up Long Furling from Angmering to meet David . . . Mist then and pearly sheep and a dusty woman at a cottage door bashing a dusty mat. Struck me as so odd that she should be doing that while I in a mood of glory rode away singing as I rode.

20 October. At 3 when I was resting bells were ringing. I thought if that's an invasion goodbye to my tea party. It was the prison bell. Canadian prisoners got loose, climbed the roof and rang the bell in protest saying they ought to be let out to join the Army. Heavy rain storm soaked them to the skin. Finally the fire engine was brought and – drenched – they capitulated!

21 October. Such a *happy* birthday. Winnie gave me a cyclamen, Mrs Jervis chrysanthemums, Mrs Bates half a barrow load of roses, rosemary, verbena and the rest. The house looked perfectly lovely and the sun was shining all day long. And Mrs Phelps gave me a pot of very special Apricot jam . . . I don't know when I had such a pretty birthday, and it may well be my last! What with German bombings and the fact that I am 78, a doleful fact which I never can believe or feel like.

11 November. The railings went and the gate. Two dogs at once rushed in assuming it to be a public lavatory!

17 November. Asked him [Dr Irvine] to give me an order for a hot water bottle - only to be had, according to Wyborn [9] on a doctor's order. He rang up and was told the order had been cancelled, no hot water bottle (rubber) now obtainable. He tried to persuade me to buy an electric pad, cost £7 7s. Refused with firmness. So at 4 o'clock that heavenly man returned with a hot water bottle (rubber) cost 10/9d. Wouldn't say where, or how, he got it. Bound me to secrecy.

19 November. I was very annoyed because Tam's railings at the Red House, Southover, had been taken and hers [Mrs Arthur Jones] not: as she had pointed out to the authorities that 'The Croft' [10] was an *'historic house'*. Such nonsense! It is an old house of no especial interest. Lewes is full of such.

21 November. Met Mr Ensell *furious* at his railings being taken and those at the Shelleys left. Yet feeling as I do that he would be uncomfortable if his gate was left and poorer people's taken.

27 November. . . . had to ring up Dr Irvine who said I was to go to bed at once. So did. He came at 11, prodded my 'tummy' which I could hardly bear him to touch. Said a little internal inflammation and I was to stay in bed, perhaps for a week. I was full of the most horrible dreads . . .

9 Wyborn the chemists, still in Lewes.
10 The Croft, Southover High Street, built c 1825. A Quaker centre in 17th century.

2 December. We are all very excited – and alarmed – at the Beveridge Report[11]. But Mrs Brough, with an optimism for which I can find no warrant, says: "Nothing to worry about. The Government wishes to make things as easy as possible for us old people." I said that the Government had so far shown no sign of it, with their 10/- in the £ Income Tax. While we were at tea, Dr Irvine came, so she had to go. He again, as every day, prodded my stomach and didn't hurt me a bit. So I may get up and come down for a little time tomorrow.

3 December. Resigned from membership of Miller's, rather glad of the excuse. They are all too 'precious' and artificial for me. Said I hadn't been well and was not proposing to come out after lunch during the winter. Feel very shakey and depressed. But Winnie is wonderful (though a touch too talkative, but will fall into line once I am back to normal). And they are all so kind. And Dr Irvine says no need to worry.

7 December. Mrs Lomas[12] came to iron the pull-over she had knitted for a Prisoner of War. While she was at it a plane flew over very low, almost on the roof and she saw the German markings. We heard later on in the day that it was brought down at Eastbourne. Well! She went on ironing and we both went on chatting. Odd how immune from terror you get. That thing might very well have crashed into this roof or dropped a bomb. Then goodbye to the pull-over for a Prisoner of War!

16 December. Ida's letter with a sketch of the proposed tombstone for David upset me very much. She has got permission from the Rector . . . to put the little anvil David used as a footstone to the Memorial. Would I suggest an inscription? '*Do*' adds Ida. But I couldn't, and can't. Like the December thrush's song the whole subject – for me – '*lies too near the heart to touch the brain.*'

11 Sir William Beveridge's proposals for a Welfare State.
12 Former owner of Southover Grange, staying at Shelley's Hotel.

18 December. After tea Jean came in. She has got the Beveridge Report. There is to be no pension for anyone over 50 unless, of course, they have a stamped card like servants have. So all my fiendishly joyful plans of going to the P.O. and digging £1 a week out of the Government perish forthwith.

19 December. Rottingdean [13] village street, so the paper says, 'demolished' in an Air Raid. How much of our exquisite England, what with German bombs and 'slum' clearing fanatics, will be left for future generations?

31 December. Rang up Hanningtons. Had they any Shetland dressing gowns? They had! £1 8s and 8 coupons. Tore off by the 10.30 bus and got one, pale pink. To sleep in over my nightgown . . . Heavenly night, swathed in the softest wool. A luxurious end to 1942.

---

13 Village near Brighton with many artistic and literary connections.

1943

6 January. The 4th winter of war, and everybody fed up, with not being fed at all! It is all very cleverly managed, but we are being kept just above starvation level. And I, who have never cared much for food, in fact bored by it, feel I can no longer stand these make-shift meals, these horrible messes and mouldy bread that tastes like chaff.

20 January. *The Big Raid on Lewes*. At 12 when I was peaceful in bed [with flu], the most terrific bangs. The bed and the house shook. I was stunned and so defenceless undressed. Winnie came rushing up with some loving incoherence about "dying together"! A plane rushed past the window, flying very low. The black shadow of it shut out the light. I shall always think of the Angel of Death and the 'beating of its wings'. I shall never see a blackbird fly past my window without remembering. Three more followed, very close and low, they seemed to be at the window pane. More bangs, rushings, vibrations. I expected the house to go. Then silence. We learned later that 2 people were killed and many injured . . . We, and the Lucas's, have escaped with broken windows. Winnie came up with my supper at 9 and the news that they "couldn't dig out poor old Mrs Digweed". (They did in the end.)

21 January. People were so kind . . . all called to see if I was all right. I insisted to Dr Irvine that I must dress and come down, that to lie up there and be buried alive was *too* ghastly a thought. So I am down here, feeling an awful rag.

22 January. The most awful devastation in the town, especially in North Street, New Street and New Road. The 'Stag' Hotel[1] burnt to the ground and Stevensons the Corn Chandler has lost his windows with almost the last lovely fanlights left in Lewes. All the people have got to clear out of St Martin's Lane, which also was hit. I sat in my chair all day, half asleep, but jumping like a shot rabbit if even a cinder dropped out of the fire.

1 On the corner of East Street and North Street, now a car park.

24 January. Caroline Byng Lucas. Might she come and paint this room tomorrow? Rang up – delighted; yes, of course.

25 January. What very nice women she and her sister, Mrs Byng-Stamper are. She sat and painted till lunch time and I stayed in my bedroom by the electric fire. She, like all people of imagination, in *Despair* about everything. No Freedom left, nor any chance of it, war or no war. All elegance and charm, the things that we value, to be ruthlessly crushed out. They, she and her sister, had difficulty in finding the money to buy the Newington's house in the High Street[2]. But did and let the two first floors to the Red Cross and planned to start a School of Painting on the top floor. Suddenly their telephone rings, they are told that the whole house has been taken over by the East Sussex County Council and that it is useless to protest and to point out that the house belongs to them. *"You have no appeal."* She now proposes to start her School in the stable[3] at the bottom of the garden, but begs me not to say a word, because if they got wind of it they'd take that too! What nonsense to say we are fighting for Freedom. German rule could not be worse than this.

26 January. Went and slept on the spare room bed after dinner and would gladly have stayed there but Mrs Brough had proposed herself to tea. She says that when the bombs fell last week, Margaret Hill's parrot lay flat on its back at the bottom of the cage and *Swore*!

28 January. Mrs Lomas came to iron yet another pull-over she's made for a Prisoner of War. Tells me that 40 houses in Lewes must be demolished as they are not safe to live in. She wants some new corsets but hasn't enough coupons. Told her I could, if necessary, spare one or two . . .

29 January. Everybody all around mended up, and we are left! Rang up Wycherley who said our case has been reported as 'Urgent' and the repairs would be done tomorrow morning.

---

2 No. 208.
3 Now The Studio, East Street. Vanessa Bell, Duncan Grant and Caroline Lucas were teachers.

31 January. . . . the kitchen window not mended. Struggled downstairs and helped Winnie rig up some of dear Spangles' blankets to help keep out the draught. . . . 70 miles an hour gale which very soon disposed of Spangles' blanket. At 7.30 there was a terrific explosion somewhere. Milkman told Winnie next morning it was mines blown up at Hove and windows shattered all along the sea front.

1 February. At 2 o'clock man outside making copious notes came to the tradesman's door. Said he'd been sent by the Borough Surveyor to Castle – *Prisons*, or Castle *Plimsy* House to mend the property of "an old lady close on eighty" (what blows my pride is getting . . .) "Dunno now" said he, rapidly giving me the once over, "if I'm in the right house or not. Are you the old lady?" Admitted that I was and also enlightened him as to the meaning of *Precincts*! By tea time the window, thank God, was in. Thick glass, not giving so much light, but *Glass*!

11 February. Mrs Brough proposed herself to tea and why she did very soon became clear. Awful storm in a tea cup at Westgate Street Chapel, the congregation objecting to their new minister – Revd Harry Maguire – being so friendly with our pacifist Rector at St Michael's, Revd Kenneth Rawlings. "We won't have it" stormed Mrs Brough. I said: "But his personal affairs have nothing to do with you." "But they have. We (the congregation) chose him and pay him." In brief, would I allow her to bring Mr Maguire and Miss Cobbe here and let them read the letters for and against Pacifism which passed between me, Mr Rawlings, Admiral Beamish and Commander Molson? I said (privately rather horrified) quite impossible. They were confidential and I should feel like stabbing Rawlings in the back. But didn't I see that Maguire must be enlightened as to the very black sheep Rawlings was? However I stood firm and we parted good friends. My letter about George Elphick[4] in the local paper. Of course he ought to go to prison and all the other 'conscientious' cranks with him. Weak, conceited lot and all of them influenced by Rawlings.

4 A pacifist who refused to firewatch.

15 February. Yesterday was St Valentine's day! 38 years ago since I rode up Bisley Lane and found David waiting for me on the thrown tree near the church. What a magic time! And now! Old, the war half killing me, alone! Still, there are still moments!

18 February. Winnie's afternoon out and I was thankful. She has been 'nerves' all the week and in this mood you can do nothing with her. Poor little thing. I'm glad I'm leaving her a little money so that she won't have to stay in a situation where she is unhappy. And few mistresses would have the patience to get through this black temper and realise the bright sunshine that lies behind and is her *real* self.

19 February. See this morning that they are taking [the railings] in Priory Crescent, Southover. With the exception of the two middle houses, Jean's and Mrs McLeod's, as they have drawing room windows reaching to the floor. Still. So long as the railings at The Croft, that 'historic house' remain, what else matters! I do seem to have my knife into Mrs Arthur Jones over that! Wonder if they'll take the balconies along Grand Parade, Brighton? However. Regency Brighton is doomed anyway, and nobody cares a hoot.

21 February. We are all very anxious about Winston Churchill who has inflammation of the lungs. Also the American forces have fallen back in Tunisia and had to be 'stiffened' by our Guards! That perhaps will 'larn' them not to brag so much!

23 February. Very excited; no, not excited but horribly afraid, because *The Daily Telegraph* quotes a report (from Sweden) that we are invading Europe quite soon on the north west coast of Europe. I wish to Heaven we could do it through Greece or Italy! Here on the South Coast we've already stood so much.

26 February. Practically all night long planes going over – ours, thank God. And now, nearly all day long, the High Street an Inferno of tanks and motor-cycles.

5 March. After tea Mrs Arthur Jones came. Had heard that I wasn't well [back pain]. So kind of her and I won't grudge her her railings nor sneer at her 'historic house' any more.

24 March. See that Lady Cholmondeley's appeal has failed and Hannah Gubbay gets her £11,000 a year which, if she goes on living, will swallow up all Philip's fortune, leaving nothing for Sybil. The whole affair mysterious to me, who knew them all so well. Was Hannah G his mistress (never saw a sign of it) or had she a more subtle, perhaps mesmeric, hold on him?[5]

5 April. Yesterday and today the weather and the look of the world is so exquisite. I *don't* want to die and leave it. Yet – as things are – constant pain, no fun to be alive. So often I think of that phrase: *'The kind warm earth was all he knew.'* It is all I know, and when I die I don't want human companionship for 1,000's of years, if ever! I want to have – what so often I've had – the top of the Downs, say, between Black Cap and Ditchling Beacon, a perfect day, a cushion of little flowers, a dog's warm velvet neck to fling my arm round. Three Dalmatians – Nelson, Emma, Spangles!

13 April. Pilfold, our prize Pauper, has just lurched by, quite spring-like in a pale blue sweater. 22/6 a week out of the ratepayers' pockets, that gentleman, who boasts that he's *"never done no bloody work"* in his life. Nor does he mean to. No doubt when the mad Beveridge scheme is launched, he and his like will get even more.

15 April. We met Dr Nicholl all agog because the *Evening News* puts a series of questions to its readers and one was: *'How do you pronounce the name of Mrs Henry Dudeney the novelist?'* I was quite naively pleased, feeling that I wasn't such a spent squib after all. So absurd of me!

20 April. Mrs Jervis came in after tea. She told me that Dr Irvine, in conversation with her, said I was *"the most charming woman in Lewes"*. This ought to "cheer up me". But nothing does.

---

5 Hannah Gubbay, PS's cousin, had acted for years as his hostess.

1 May. SS Philip and James. In 1905 on this Festival I rode in warm wind and spraying rain from Cheltenham to Prestbury for early Mass. All day that has been in my mind and while I was resting this afternoon Ernest suddenly seemed so more than near: but I couldn't hold the line, one never can. Yet these moments, so rare, so more than real, do strengthen my belief in a Future Life. So often Faith wavers.

8 May. A frightful day, raving wind, water spouts of rain, tiles falling, the poor garden gone mad. We have taken Tunis and Bizerta. So this horrible war begins to get a move on.

10 May. The ink was hardly dry in my discarded pen when the siren sounded and the Pip, Pip from Every's iron works[6], meaning that enemy craft was overhead. And then frightful bangs. Winnie in her devoted dramatic way came tearing into the drawing room, one shoe on and one in her hand – she was dressing to go shopping. I was just up from my knees having said, as I always do when there is a raid on, the prayer from Compline. However nothing happened to us. Sounded as if the Wallands got it.

12 May. [Springcleaning at CPH] The extraordinary courage or fatalism which at such a hellish time of danger induces the British housewife to have the usual spring clean is a source of wonder to me!

13 May. Marjorie Cooke told me that Geering, the antique dealer at Cliffe Corner is a splendid craftsman and for sentimental reasons connected with his early married life made for his wife a very exquisite bureau of walnut and cherry wood (they had a romantic memory of a particular cherry tree). He also made for each of his 4 daughters on their 21st birthdays very lovely little jewel cases. When, some years back, Queen Mary[7] visited his shop she asked to go over his house, where he has beautiful furniture throughout. Wanted to buy the bureau. *"I'm afraid, Madam, that I cannot sell. It was made for my wife."* The Queen took an even greater fancy to the jewel case, belonging

6 The Ironworks' steam hooter.
7 The acquisitive Queen Mary expected to be given anything she admired in people's houses.

to the one unmarried daughter. *"Mr Geering, I really must have this."* *"I'm afraid, Madam, that I cannot sell. It was made for my daughter."* Nevertheless, the Queen carried it all over the house, only putting it down under protest when she got to the shop door. And left without buying a thing! Well! What would one expect of a woman who is seven eighths a German?

14 May. Winnie and Olive have worked like bricks at the spring clean, and we have driven the Germans out of Africa and captured Von-Arnim.

25 May. The letter I wrote to Margery has been returned by the Censor as I told her about the Air Raid here. I suppose I'm lucky not to be fined. A lengthy paper enclosed saying things you may not say in a letter. Quite right and necessary and wise: but a prison existence we are leading with the additional inconvenience that you don't even know the length of your sentence! . . . Very bad raid at Brighton and quite near Emily. . . . I wonder if the beastly German women are spring-cleaning! Somehow, although Heaven knows no pro-German nor pacifist, I feel worse that we are so mercilessly bombing them than when they were, in 1941, with equal savagery bombing us. There is a certain heroism to suffering pain, but none to inflicting it. However this is a dangerous train of thought. They richly deserve the thrashing they are getting and the harder we whack them the sooner they'll howl and the war will be over.

2 June. Emily told me about the raid at Brighton, the worst they've had. A big bit of the railway viaduct broke, so no trains through London Road Station. In Springfield Road many houses with broken windows, damaged roofs, ceilings down and so on. Her house escaped. People machine gunned in the streets. The official list of killed 24 and injured 51 . . . one woman stuck her head out of her window – her head instantly blown off! Brighton full of Germans, especially women married to Englishmen. People are saying that – by the Morse Code – they tell the Germans when the weather and other factors are suitable for raids. Altogether there are too many aliens in this country. Poles, trying to widen the breach between Poland and Russia. And Jews with their Black Markets and dog racing! Eden himself admitted that it would not be wise to admit more Jews as there is, already, a strong anti-Semitic feeling.

16 June. We talked of the rift between De Gaulle and Giraud - really these French people make you sick. They are, and always have been, our natural enemies, repeatedly have let us down and yet we must be, geographically, bound to them. Hear that the King is in Africa.

3 July. Quite a a nice party at 'Little Orchards' as garden parties go. Semi-public affair . . . Mrs Ranson very kind and wearing a very smart hat. I complimented her on it. She returned that it *cost a lot of money*". The party was really for the District Nursing Fund and the Women's Institute. The whole garden buzzed with about 40 to 50 of those capable, self-important women who fill you with terror. There was a great deal of talk about jam-making and evacuees and ambulances and bandages . . . But Mrs Jervis said we needn't get an "inferiority complex" as all these women were enjoying themselves like mad and, although they wouldn't admit it, will be sorry when the war is over and they relapse into their native obscurity!

8 July. Marjorie Cooke told me that Dorothy Rawlings had left her husband solely because of Rowena Bingham[8]. That the town is full of the most awful gossip: that she is so afraid the Bishop will come down on Rawlings for immorality (if immoral he is). Anything like a scandal at St Michael's so much to be deplored, especially in a Protestant town like Lewes with its knife in the Anglo-Catholics.

22 July. Marjorie Cooke said that the gossip about the Rector of St Michael's increases. And Lionel Cooke saw the girl Rowena Bingham go into the Rectory with Rawlings – carrying a suit case!!

28 July. The great news is the fall of Mussolini.

29 July. In the night a very bad Air Raid. Heavy gun fire, bombs falling, shrapnel flying. I was in abject terror . . . Seemed worse as I was alone.

---

8 Rowena Bingham was an actress at the Lewes Little Theatre, recently founded by the Rev Rawlings.

30 July. George Beard told me that we brought down 2 enemy aircraft near Newhaven. What an odd creature I am. Down like a stick. Up like a rocket! Yesterday I wished to die, and the sooner the better! Today I am full of life and joy. If *only* this blazing hot weather would last for weeks.

15 August. Bad air raid in the night: 25 Germans over and we brought 6 down. I was so tired that I slept through the Alert and was awakened by a Phantom Presence and Voice! Winnie. In pure anxiety and affection she had broken the bond we made, that I would never lock my door, on the condition that she would never come stealing in during a raid.

28 August. In the night for nearly 1½ hrs planes going over in a regular Armada. So no sleep till past midnight.

2 September. Mrs Jervis told me a lot more scandal – well authenticated – about the Rector of St Michael's and Rowena Bingham. If true he ought to be unfrocked. But Dr Belcher was no better. Probably worse!! See that the Pope is appealing for Peace and urging *"the strong to be generous"*. The old Fox, did-n't bother about that when London was being bombed. Now the boot is on the other leg.

4 September We have invaded Italy. Though why in the extreme toe at a mountainous place like Calabria[9] goodness knows.

5 September. The Rector has a big poster outside St Michael's, advertising his war sermon "How can we help to end war?". A wag wrote underneath '*Fight!*'

7 September. I do like those nice Newberry's. Mrs N said that not long ago she, in the middle of the night, heard what sounded like the scraping of chains on the roof. *And it was a runaway German plane.* The pilot had been chucked out and killed. The thing was full of bombs and had it come down in the village, goodbye to Barcombe[10].

9 Reggio de Calabria was a vital centre.
10 On 30.5.43 a Junkers 88 crashed at Longford Farm with an intact bomb load.

8 September. *Italy has surrendered*. How long before Germany follows suit?

12 September. At 2.30 Miss Stevenson and her mother came; the 'admirers' who turned up 6 years ago and who live at 'Peter Pan' cottage behind the Metropole, Brighton. Had a Polish Pilot outside. Might he see the house and Me?! Had read some of my books, he can read English, but speaks very little. Had tried to get *Brighton Beach* and couldn't. Very artistic and interested in lovely settings. So he was brought in and taken everywhere, including the Mount and the Town Wall garden. I noticed that he admired most the more ornate furniture – my work table and the walnut and ormulu cabinet. Had been two years a prisoner abroad somewhere. It seemed so odd to have one's hand kissed. I gave him some roses and rosemary. He asked for my autograph. So I gave him a copy of *Brighton Beach*. He took from under the lapel of his tunic a little silver eagle and presented it in return. Quite an excitement. We went from the study through the kitchen to the back staircase and the Mount. So Winnie was introduced. She is quite thrilled.

15 September. The war is enough to break your heart! Just as we thought the corner was turned, another setback. The Germans have liberated Mussolini, not that he matters, and one report is that he's been shot. We are being driven back to the beaches at Salferno. It is the old story, the English tradition '*too late*'. We've got the Italian fleet but are being dangerously chivalrous about that. You can't trust any of these slippery foreigners. Why didn't we, at once, get Mussolini and clap him on an English ship?

26 September. This is what is called '*Battle of Britain*' Sunday; a day of Thanksgiving for our preservation from invasion and defeat in 1940. At St Michael's we only had read to us a letter from the Pope . . . Meanwhile, outside the church such a row of bands playing, people marching that the Rector had more than once to stop reading, an expression of petulant anguish on his face!

17 October. Met Tam after church. He, now a full-fledged priest – Revd Charles Hamilton Dicker – walked home with me and clearly wished to be asked in. But I thought of our minute joint of pork which has got to last for a week (and won't) and asked him to ring me up any morning and suggest a visit. But he is full of affairs and goes back to Leicester on Friday.

20 October. Horrible day. Bad Air Raid in the night which frightens me to death. And Winnie saying she doesn't like me to be alone, which means she's afraid of being alone herself. Like a Fool, she gets up, dressed and puts her head out of the window and talks to the men at the Malt House opposite. Pinyoun from 10 Castle Banks comes up too. And Winnie quite enjoys herself and is as tired as possible and as Black as Thunder next day.

20 November. Marjorie said that the scandal about Rowena Bingham and the Rector had suddenly and completely stopped – proceeding as it did mainly from the office of the local paper, where Lionel Cooke works. I think Rawlings has threatened an action for libel.

8 December. I get so dead sick of the Teheran Conference between Churchill, Roosevelt and Stalin that I throw down *The Daily Telegraph*. The Turkish Premier is there now. I rather agree with Dittmar, the German military correspondent: "If the allies are in a position to invade, why don't they do it *instead of talking so much.*"

11 December. Met Mr Bates who amazed me by saying that Mrs Bates [with high blood pressure] was coming out of the hospital tomorrow morning, but going back on Monday morning! After all the fuss – chatter, sympathetic notes and Bates with tears in his eyes – we all feel that this is a provoking anti-climax.

25 December, Christmas Day. As the butchers have handed out pork to every one for their Xmas joint, we, Mrs Jervis, Mrs Phelps and I, were a little crest-fallen at being given *PORK* at the White Hart. But it was very nice and a really wonderful pre-war Christmas pudding to follow. And the White Hart very festive with decorations. Walton very much 'mine host' - perhaps rather too much so! He certainly lifts his elbow! . . . Had some supper and went to bed, thankful that this farcical celebration was over.

26 December. Feast of Stephen, so we had that stirring hymn 'The Son of God goes forth to war'. With the lines that always thrill me: 'They braved the tyrants' brandished sword, the *lion's gory mane.*' You shiver! You see the lion!

28 December. Dear Mabel in tears of gratitude at the present – £20 – we had clubbed together to give her. I felt such a beast for not giving more than £2. I could have run to £5.

31 December. Went to see Mrs Adams and took her at her request 2 pears, my last biggest ones. A Miss Hoare from Barcombe there. After she went Mrs Adams said: "A nice woman but not a nice name." I said it reminded me of the old story. The City Magnate's wife at a Guildhall Banquet. A Mrs Hoare also there. The City Magnate's wife, much embarrassed, addressed her throughout the feast as Mrs W: "Between you and I, Mrs W."!

1944

20 January. Yesterday darling Margery's parcel came, so beautifully packed with Xmas ribbons and paper. Made me want to cry, but nowadays I am always on the point of tears if I were weak enough to let them come. Tea, sugar, biscuits, potted meat, liquid milk, Horlick's Milk. For Winnie a little silk handkerchief and a tiny bottle of scent. Winnie enchanted . . . Winnie also got from Margery a tin of cocoa already sweetened. To Winnie I gave no tea, and shall not in future . . . since I found she had been taking tea to the men at the Malt House. I hope she accepts this omission as a delicate reproof.

21 January. About 10 the most awful raid. A regular dog fight going on just over the roof, so it seemed. I was so childishly terrified that when the clock struck I was afraid they might hear and drop a bomb. At 10 o'clock another alert and at 4 o'clock the most awful row; bombs, gunfire, the hum and drone of planes [1].

26 January. Met Miss Davey who said had I seen the *Invasion Barges* [2] in the river beneath the Bridge?

12 February. At the White Hart Mrs Walton had kindly put me at a little table with Mr Bates. More trouble at St Anne's House. Johnson the cook still in the Midlands . . . Gardener laid up again. Furnace gone wrong again! Mrs Bates not at all well.

18 February. I told Jean I had tied up £5000 in trust for Margery's children, she only to have the interest during her lifetime. Jean thought in view of the war and also the fact of Margery being in America, this a great mistake. The children are grown up, the investments are paying badly, some not at all. Also if I live, and if the Government goes on with its mad cat 'social' schemes I may have to draw on the capital myself. Shall write to Harold [Blaker].

1 Four people killed at East Hoathly, East Sussex.
2 A puzzling reference as invasion barges were moored no nearer than Piddinghoe, seven miles down river.

22 February. Intense cold. Whirling cold. On Saturday I ordered a treacle tart of Pinyoun for today. Winnie and I are wondering how on earth she is to get down Keere Street [3] (sure to be like an ice slide) and also whether a sensitive treacle tart, just, so to say, *weaned* from a warm oven will stand up to the climate. Harold Blaker took away rough draft of my new Will. It leaves Margery everything absolutely, instead of £5,000 (Ernest's money) being in Trust for her children. For the rest £200 to Winnie; £25 to Joan; the studio and garden - 7 Castle Banks - to Emily. My diaries as already arranged to the SAS. Harold told me that when the bomb fell in Ferrers Road quite near 'The Lodge' [4] he went round to see how his mother was. Ida and Flora warned him to say nothing about bombs: "We told her it was only gun fire". So they took him upstairs and all talked about gun fire. But directly her daughters went out of the room, old Mrs Montague Blaker, with a cautious look round, asked: "*Harold, where did the bomb fall?*" He also said that in the old days loafers – like Pilfold – always assembled on the bridge and were called *Bridge Ornaments*.

27 February. The Rector raved and ranted about the evil of bombing Germany. A nice Lenten sermon!

29 February. I mended my Shetland Wool dressing gown. I don't want to start wearing the new one, it is for my last illness! Mrs Milne said, and not long before she died, although she nor I suspected it: "I have *one* pair of silk stockings left, and am keeping them for my burial."

3 March. Winnie . . . has had a chat with 'Smiler' (one of the four Georges at the Malt House) . . . 'Bert' (surname Skinner) was seen by a policeman selling bacon in a local shop (the *Fool!*) Gander, the greengrocer from Fisher Street, mixed up in it. The whole town a buzz.

7 March. Went to St Anne's House. Mrs Bates more wraith-like than ever and far worse than when she went to the hospital. Johnson, the cook, their only

3 Steep cobbled street outside the town wall down which the Prince Regent was reputed to have driven his horses for a wager.
4 Mrs Montague Blaker's home in King Henry's Road.

servant left, who has been with them for 20 years is leaving for good on Thursday . . . The position seems desperate, yet they don't want to sell the house and all the lovely things in it.

8 March. After tea Mrs Adams came, full of what the town calls the 'bacon ramp'. Essex at The Bull [5], whose son's portrait she has been painting, says that about 100 people are involved for receiving stolen property: three town councillors, one called Pate, a little grocer in Lansdowne Place . . . one Bank Manager and an official *"in a very high position"*.

9 March. Lewes, usually so sedate, is now stirred by yet another excitement. Members of the Town Council object to going to St Michael's for the Assize service because of the Rector's Pacifist views. They say it is not the *"Church of the Judicature"* but that the first Assize service was held there in 1908, whereupon Dr Belcher put up the notice (just like him!) . . . Anyhow it's been held at St Michael's for nearly 40 years . . . Meanwhile the Rector goes over the road to Roy Lawrence, the Under Sheriff and demands and insists that the service is not held at St Michael's. Playing into the Council's hands to save his own face (rather mixed, but let it pass!). So it is to be at St Anne's, for this time anyhow. [6] This will give that little absurdity Fowler-Tutt a longer route along which to peacock in her Councillor's robes.[7]

10 March. I went to Communion. And in his priest's office Rawlings is just the same as any other priest. *But I've done with him.* His Pacifism is a point of view. I neither agree nor sympathise, but I understand, and he is no worse than the Bishop of Chichester. His domestic scandal – it is not for me to judge. But he cares nothing for St Michael's, nor for the views of his congregation. He has emptied the church, he never visits, he cares for nothing but play acting[8] and (but we mustn't be malicious!) *I've no use for him* – except in the Sacraments of the Church when he becomes impersonal.

5 After the Godfreys moved, Bull House became a restaurant. Now owned by the SAS.
6 The Assize Service is still held at St Anne's Church.
7 Miss Fowler-Tutt during WWI objected to Rodin's *The Kiss* and was instrumental in its return to Edward Warren.
8 Rev Rawlings, a keen amateur actor, founded the still thriving Lewes Little Theatre.

15 March. Been all over the town trying to get a *Sussex Daily News* with a report of our 'Bacon' trial. Not one to be had. But 'Bert' (Skinner, by name) the thief has only been put on probation for a year, and Gander, the Receiver, fined £50. He, Gander, the liar, said he had no idea the bacon was stolen property or he wouldn't have touched it! Meanwhile those who bought it, including the *'official in a high position'*, are not even mentioned and get off scot free. The whole thing a crying scandal and the townspeople indignant.

16 March. Met the Manager, Mr Mills, of the Bacon Shop (Malt House) . . . he said he was *amazed* at the leniency of the sentences and scandalised at no mention being made of the people who bought the bacon, hundreds of poundsworth going on for months. Said it should have been tried by the Judge (the Assizes now on) and not by local magistrates. He, Mills, doesn't know, as I do, the 'graft' that goes on in this town, riddled as it is by Freemasonry.

20 March. Winnie said she had some sad news. Dear Mrs Bates died in the hospital on Saturday night. . . . I shall miss her terribly. The last time I saw her was on March 7th, more wraith-like than ever. I hugged her when we parted and she put her sticks of arms tight round me and said: "The truest friend a woman ever had." That was our parting. I wrote a note a few days afterwards saying I didn't want to make myself a nuisance of coming too often, but would take my chance in a few days. Wrote Mr Bates.

30 March. Met Mr Bates looking very downcast, poor man. So I asked him to walk with me . . . We looked at the hills and we spoke of those days when we often met there with our dear dogs, Zeb and Emma and Spangles.

1 April. I find I can no longer go up the Mount by the path to pick the primroses . . . turns me giddy to stoop. So I go up the steps and if the time comes when I can't do even that I will go up on all fours. For go I must and will.

3 April. Letter from Ida. Poor Ida very much in the wars. Suddenly taken ill at the end of February, bronchial pneumonia. No joke at 82 . . . Odd. How we hated each other and fought and struggled for so many years! And now left

alone in the world and old - I shall be 80 in October - she turns to me, her letter concluding: *'My love – dear Alice – always'*.

28 April. Emily, Brighton . . . The sea was so blue and the sun so warm that we sat on a seat staring at the barbed wire on the sea side of the road, where you are not allowed to go. Emily says she heard that by next autumn the piers, now cut in halves, will be joined together again. I said I wouldn't go on too soon! Let a few people get drowned first. . . . Hannington's is practically empty, which depresses me. So mixed up with my school days at Gothic House, Hurstpierpoint. All of us out for our morning walk, crocodile fashion. Miss Rowland behind with her inevitable umbrella, which she used as a shepherd uses his crook. Samuel Hannington driving by in a Victoria on his way to the little station at Hassocks.

2 May. When I picked up *The Daily Telegraph* and saw a photograph of 5 bald-headed gentlemen sitting in conference (Colonial Premiers with Churchill, looking as if they were yawning) I flung it from me in disgust. Muddle-headed politicians for the last 25 years have let us in for this. Baldwin, with his pipe and his pigs[9], the worst of the lot.

20 May. Mrs Byng-Stamper and Caroline Byng-Lucas there [White Hart] squired by a very attentive young man, clearly an artist[10]. Wonder if he, or they, paid for the lunch?!

2 June. Caroline Byng-Lucas came looking very decorative as usual. And not made up at all except for lipstick. This made her more real and easy to talk to. They are having a meeting at Miller's on the 28th with the view of forming some sort of society for preserving old houses in Lewes, should they be threatened. She told me – and I hadn't seen it – that after Lewes was bombed last January twelve month there was a notice put up in the window of the Southdown bus office. 'Do not fret. You will have a larger and a lovelier Lewes, after the war'. God help us! She also told me that Mr Godfrey had

9 Three times PM, a Worcestershire man, his pipe and pigs became a favourite theme of caricaturists.
10 Duncan Grant, who helped the Ladies of Mller's hang their exhibitions.

said that he, they – the Byng-Stampers and Mrs Dudeney – were the only people cared a hoot about preserving old Lewes. Mrs Byng-Stamper has bought the bow-fronted Regency house [11] (where Miss Akehurst had her wool shop) next to Westgate Chapel. She says it is lovely, quite unspoilt. A bombed-out family from North Street have been put in there and the house stinks. When they can be got out I am to be taken over it.

6 June. *The Invasion starts*[12]. . . . Jean arrived at 11 with the exciting news. Bulletins on the wireless every 2 hours. She will come again at 4.30 to give me the latest news. Told Winnie, who was dressed for departure and was wrapping up her shoes to take to the cobbler. "*Terribly exciting, Winnie – the Invasion.*" "Yes", said Winnie: "and as fast as you have your shoes re-soled they wear through again"!!

16 June. Communion at 12. I do think that a priest, before he vests and goes to the Altar, should clean his shoes! . . . The Rector now announces in a letter to the Town Clerk that if the Council again send Elphick to prison for refusal to firewatch, he – Rawlings – will, as a protest against what he calls an act of 'tyrrany' refuse, also, to firewatch unless Carvill's will give him Elphick's job as a carpenter! I wonder how he stands ecclesiastically over that? Hasn't he and isn't he paid for a wholetime job as Rector of St Michael's?

17 June. Met the Rector and said, with a pleasant, yet dangerous smile: "I'm very sorry – after all these years! – but I can no longer approve of you." He just gave *his* smile, charming and careless, and made off.

18 June. 8.30 There has just been an open air service on Castle Banks; then came an Air Raid warning, so the congregation 'scat'. As I sit here and write, these awful, pilotless planes [13] (the German's 'secret' weapon) are thundering,

11 Westgate House, 93 High St. Here from 1947–9 the Ladies installed the Scottish painters Colquhoun and MacBryde.
12 D-Day. The biggest combined land, sea and air operation of all time.
13 Jet-propelled aircraft capable of 400mph. Known in Germany as VI, in Britain as buzz bombs or doodlebugs. A 'Bomb Alley' ran across Sussex, Surrey and Kent to London.

or so it seems, just above the roof. Jean feels exactly as I do, terrified by these mechanical things, doing their devilish work so uncannily – so alone.

20 June. Dusart, who washed my hair, comforted me over the pilotless planes. He says that so long as they roar overhead (a most terrifying noise) you are safe. But if the noise instead of gradually dying away suddenly stops – then! I said: "Then is the time to jump out of bed." Dusart laughed: "There wouldn't be any time." But, with an attempt at soothing: "It would be all over in a moment". He says they carry only one bomb weighing about a ton. Before this I met Lionel Cooke who said they, the planes, could not get to Lewes the hills making some obstacle. I've heard this before, pray God it's true. These things are killing people wholesale . . . And no one – not even Mrs Blaker at 95 – remembers such a cold spring and summer. The north-east wind which never drops hinders our Invasion. On the other hand the Germans can't easily launch their pilotless planes.

21 June. Colder than ever. But in spite of this and the drought, my roses were never so lovely. . . . I stand half way up the Mount and thank God, with all my heart for bringing me here and showing me how to make a garden.

23 June. The Flying Bombs are now upsetting the cows – even a newly calved heifer staggered up on its long legs and ran round the field. Cows giving less milk, even ducks laying fewer eggs.

24 June. Met Margaret and went into her house for a bit. Her parrot, who lives in the dining room and hates intruders, said: "*Go to Hell*".

3 July. At one o'clock an Alert and then the most terrific noise as the Flying Bomb was overhead. After that, gunfire. I was in my bedroom taking my hat off. Terrified, as always now, fell on my knees. This Collect – for the 4th Sunday Trinity – very steadying. At 3 and again at 3.30 the infernal things came over again. Mrs Jervis to tea and she certainly made a big hole in Cruttenden's cake . . . I got out of bed this morning and there, if you please, were 4 fat pigs being driven to market. So rustic and non warlike! For me! Not for them! I thought of Mrs Sander's pet pig, *Belinda*, who was scrubbed

once a week and one day swallowed a cake of Lifebuoy. "And what happened to Belinda in the end?" "Oh. She went to market," says Mrs S casually.

4 July. Mr Matthews, the Rector of Southover, told Mrs Jervis that the Old Brewery House [14] there, occupied in the war by a German called Schwartz (who ran a Button Factory at Barcombe Mills) has lately been altered in some way and behind one of the walls they found a transmitter. So the Button Factory was only a blind. He was a spy.

5 July. All day long I wasn't a bit well and lay curled up on the sofa, staring at the hills and remembering the wonderful times, for many years, I had on them. (Wish I could learn a little philosophy, realise that in October I shall be 80 and so sink into the greasy, moribund state of extreme age). *I will not.*

11 July. Mrs Jervis said that in the *Daily Mail* she read that a Flying Bomb exploded quite near a large country house near London where German Officers are imprisoned (may be Trent?) No damage done to the house, except a good shaking. In the Park, trees uprooted and a crater. German officers, viewing this from the windows went in a deputation to the Governor and demanded that they should be removed to a safer place!

15 July. Met Georgie Beard . . . he said that he had talked with Mr Elwell who told him that the danger in London from glass, owing to the flying Bombs, was now not very great "*as there is very little glass left.*"! I was very glad to see Billy Massey after tea. He looked very white and tired. We talked about the danger to Europe even after Germany is beaten, of the young Nazis, utterly barbarous! Billy said, as many say, sterilise the lot. Which is un-Christian and, also, impossible. Too many of 'em. Then he said: plenty of waste spaces on the earth, dump them down in Siberia or the North West provinces of Canada.

24 July. Margery sent me the boys' addresses, Julian is in the Army and now being trained for the Army in Alabama. Jamie is somewhere roundabout

14 Once part of Verrall's Brewery.

Chicago, and training for the Navy. He wrote his mother: 'We have to scrub the decks *at least once a day.*' I thought this irresistible. They get no leave, Julian for 6 months, Jamie – as a radio technician – for 10. But thank God it is sure to be over before then.

25 July. For the first time I felt that I really understood Mrs Jervis and was fond of her. She is so lonely: all that glittering, wearying manner is simply a smoke-screen. Her life until Jervis died so happy, so uneventful. The adored only daughter of the Holmans, the perfectly adoring wife of the Revd Eustace Jervis. She is longing for the war to be over, when she will sell St Michael's House and get a small house at Eastbourne, where she has 10 cousins! How different from my up and down life. Always standing outside and apart. As Sir Louis Mallet once said: "I understand you – at last. Always with us, yet never *of* us." Anyhow I'd rather have my life than Florence Jervis's, and may I be defended from 10 cousins. One sister is enough for me to handle.

27 July. Mrs Lomas told me of 4 men at Isfield with a horse and cart. A Flying Bomb came over. 3 men lay in the ditch, the 4th man stood by the horse. The 3 emerged, asked him why he didn't take shelter. "I couldn't leave the horse. It might be frightened". (How lovely that is).

5 August. Jean says that Hester at Chelsea is on the edge of a nervous breakown owing to the Flying Bombs. But the police, to whom Jean has been, say she can't come here even to her own sister *unless she has been bombed.* The whole 'banned area' [15] affair seems to be a farce, Brighton crowded and more crowds pouring in. Hester says there is great feeling in London about Parliament dissolving for 7 weeks at such a time, £600 a year, free first class railway travel and off they go. Also, at the Admiralty, where Billy is, men are saying that we ought to warn Germany that if she sends over one more Flying Bomb we will select some German town – when and where we don't say – and bomb it until not one living thing is left. They argue that we should never be

15 From 1940–1944 a strip of 10 miles in depth of the Sussex coast was prohibited to all except residents or those with a bona fide purpose for entry.

forced to do it, the German bully being what he is. Anyhow, Londoners seem to have reached their limit of endurance.

6 August. Wretched night. Four Alerts, these Flying Bomb devils thundering over head. Four big bangs at intervals. I think that slogan of 1940–41 *'We can take it'* is wearing rather thin!

15 August. Jean arrived with great news – *we have invaded the South of France!*

23 August. Alert at 5.30 this morning, then the thunder overhead of the Flying Bomb, then a flash of light, then a terrific bang. It was shot down at Paygate, Ringmer. In a cornfield, and the corn had been cut!

24 August. The Germans have virtually arrested poor old Petain and taken him to Germany. *We have taken Paris!* Things begin to look up.

31 August. Letter from Vere. Vere says as the ban is off can she come for a week . . .?

1 September. George Beard said at lunch [at White Hart] that Sir Stephen Demetriardi [Mr Bates'son-in-law] found an excellent temporary cook for Mr Bates, but he sent her packing almost at once: *"I caught the woman coming down my Front Staircase"*!

14 September. Every day from 7 in the morning till late night planes going over, taking food to France and bringing home our wounded. Meanwhile we are 9 miles inside Germany and have taken Le Havre. I was feeling so happy to realise that no longer is there the danger of this house being bombed, when Mrs Jervis brought the rumour that Hitler's second secret weapon V2[16] had been over London and the Midlands – only a rumour. Will not be mentioned in the press nor on the wireless.

16 Long-range rockets, 15 tons in weight, carrying 1 ton warheads. Gave no warnng as they landed vertically.

1944

15 September. Am now told that the Black-Out does not end here on Sunday, we are too near the coast. We seem down here to have had our full share of misery . . .

30 September. Dr Irvine said . . . that I would never realise how old I was – did I expect to go scot-free of all ailments? I said yes: that I had always imagined I should go on, more or less until the end. And, when it came, die of pneumonia or heart, within a week. It appears that things don't happen that way, or won't with me.

21 October. My birthday. I came down to find the table very gay . . . Today I think so much of Mrs Bates who always came with a trug full of late roses and rosemary, even last year when she was too weak to come upstairs. Some of the rosemary cuttings I struck each year and it is in fragrant bushes on the Mount.

1 November. Winnie Hardy came on Monday to "enquire" after me as I had not been "seen about". Sounds as if I were already a ghost! I now take only an academic interest in the war, as Mr Churchill says that it won't be over till the summer at the earliest and that there may be "years of guerilla warfare after that."

10 November. I was glad to see Billy. He's looking white and thin – complains of not getting proper food. We talked of Germany. He is inflexible. Thinks that dividing Germany into small states as before 1870 not enough. There should be *no* Germany. Up to the Rhine given to France, the Ruhr to Holland, other bits to Czechs, Poles, Russians and so on. That the German people in a generation would become absorbed into these different nationalities. Sounds too good to be true and he admits that vested interests would never allow it. We are up against financiers all the time, mostly Jews. Hitler in a sense was right in his aversion to them, though nothing can ever excuse his persecution.

291

22 November. Frightful bang at 5.30 am. Doors and windows shook. Winnie has been told by the bacon men at the Malthouse that it was a V2 bomb. Hit Newhaven Harbour [17], has done great damage there. Here windows in the High Street broken, especially down Cliffe. Met Mr Beckley. He said seven people killed at the Newhaven Paris Hotel and railway impossible between Newhaven and Seaford.

25 November. I sat half undressed by the fire till 12 when he [Dr Irvine] came. Pummelled my unhappy stomach but didn't hurt it. Says that although Dr Vallance was quite wrong 14 years ago when he said this tumour should have been removed [by the minor op], impossible to do it now as I should never come through the operation. Even if I did my general health would be no better than it is now, which is pretty good considering I'm 80. Meanwhile the wretched thing is merely causing me inconvenience, fatigue and some spoiling of my figure. But it takes all the kick out of life, and I no longer put on my joyous 'celestial' earrings – all blue enamel and golden stars! I stick to silver ones. Funny!

29 November. Had a day in bed. Was warm and happy, waited on by Winnie who is an angel. My life depends on her.

4 December. Got from Baxter's 4 exercise books for next year's diary.

10 December. Billy arrived . . . he says that Zog, that brigand – once King of Albania – is in England, a basement flat, very luxurious and with bomb proof shelter in the Piccadilly Hotel. That puppet King Peter of Jugoslavia also living here in luxury. "Both of them lunching, now and then, with the Queen of England" says Billy. He knows a man who helped to decorate Zog's flat! We shall never get rid of these royalties – Zog, Peter, the Kings of Norway and Greece, Queen Wilhelmina and the rest. Every one of whom took to his (or her) heels directly the Germans invaded. Sick of the lot!

17 An ammunition barge broke loose from its tug and hit a landmine on the rocks. One person killed.

11 December. Am too seedy with this, that and t'other to go out. My life is really a burden. I am as David said the last time we met: *"Alice, I am so tired: And yet I don't want to go."*

16 December. Met Pilfold who actually taking his pipe out of his mouth, warmly wished me a Merry Christmas. Cadging for a tip.

21 December. Beastly cold misly day. Didn't go out. Dr Irvine came . . . he will do everything possible to avoid an operation. Once I dreaded it beyond measure but now I am so ill, my body a torment, that I don't mind. Especially as he thinks I might not come through and I have made up my mind that I will not (what grisly stuff to write in a Diary!)

22 December. Margery writes that Julian, so she has heard, may go to Australia. She bravely says that the only thing is to 'sit tight and be cheerful'. But I know what is in her mind, as in mine. He may have to fight the Japanese. My darling! I wish I could live long enough and have the power to save you from every grief.

23 December. Met Mrs Jervis. . . . She gave me – secretly – one of her 8 toilet rolls. I am to tell no one.

25 December, Christmas day. White Hart 1 o'clock. The lunch quite the worst I've ever eaten anywhere. Coarse beef, not carved, just chinked off – Mrs Jervis had a piece of gristle as long as a finger. Mashed potatoes, evidently cold ones warmed up and not really hot, coarse Brussels sprouts and some tolerably good Christmas pudding.

26 December. Mrs Brough said that the shortage of Toilet Rolls is because the Air Force had collared the lot, 2 rolls to each pilot. Something to do with scattering leaflets.

31 December. Jean came at tea time. Billy has been demobilised: she has been prepared for this and dreading it. Doesn't know how they can live on her tiny income. Billy has nothing. It does seem odd that the Admiralty has no further use for a man so capable and travelled and such a linguist. He is scrapped simply because of his age.

And so ends 1944 – bad luck to it. And so begins 1945. Wonder if I shall see 1946? Doubtful.

* * *

[The next diary breaks off abruptly on 5th January 1945. Mrs Dudeney had a stroke and was cared for to the end by her devoted Winnie. The war in Europe ended in May and Japan surrendered on 14th August. Alice Dudeney died on 21st November and her ashes were placed in the grave of her husband Ernest in Lewes Cemetery.]

INDEX

Adams, Mr & Mrs WD, 248, 253-4, 261-2, 280, 283

All Saints Church, 33, 189

American Saturday Review, 120

Amos, Mr and Mrs TW, 213

Ancaster, Lady, 124

Anglesey, Marquis of, 159

Anne of Cleves House, 10, 138n, 168

Arkwells, 149, 170, 175, 186, 196, 256

Ashdown House, 231, 240

Baker, Vere (Sullivan), 7, 39, 49, 67, 78-9, 92, 109, 117-18, 121, 123, 137, 159, 173, 177, 221, 264, 290

Baldwin, Stanley, 189, 285

Baring, Maurice, 44, 107, 246

Bates, Mr RG, 69n, 98, 120n, 157, 161, 168-9, 173, 178, 189, 207, 217, 224, 230, 257, 279, 281, 284

Bates, Mrs RG, 69, 88, 112, 147, 153, 178, 200, 207, 218, 220-22, 224, 230, 245, 257, 263, 266, 279, 281, 284, 291

Batup, James, 60, 99, 126, 244

Beard, George, 105, 253, 277, 288, 290

Belcher, Rev Dr H, 14, 19, 277

Bell, Vanessa, 258n, 270n

Belloc Lowndes, Mrs, 44, 96-7, 183

Berners, Lord, 159

Beveridge Report, 267-8, 273

Bingham, Rowena, 276-7, 279

Blaker, Harold, 102, 104-5, 135, 165-6, 249, 281

Blakers, 10, 21, 244, 282, 287

Blighty, 36

Bodle, Miss, 8

Bodle, Brig. Gen. William, 8

Bookman, The, 73

Boyce, Miss, 7, 91, 103, 135, 172, 205, 219

Boyle, Lady (Louise), 101, 180, 218, 238, 258

Brack Mount, 80, 95, 105n, 197-9, 202, 229, 244

Brough, Mrs AS, 186, 205, 213, 227, 244, 257-8, 267, 270-1, 293

Bryne, Lady Alice (Clemminson), 39-40, 104-5, 166

Bryne, Sir William, 166, 205

Bull House, 283

Burbidge, Mrs, 30-3, 38, 43, 47-50, 102, 116

Burdett, Osbert, 241n, 260

Byng-Stamper, Frances, 242, 248-51, 269, 285-6

Byron, Mrs GA, 73, 80

Calvert, Rev TC, 50

Carr, Mary, 82n, 227

Castle Banks (No 10), 226, 279

Castle Banks (No 7, Lean-to), 126n, 129, 176, 206-7, 221, 237, 251, 253, 282

Castle Banks (No 9), 163, 165-6, 226

Castle Lodge, 60n

Castle Place, 104n, 252

Castle Precincts House, 30-1, 33, 37, 48, 142-3

Cecil, Lord Hugh, 71, 83, 93-4, 145, 246

Chamberlain, Neville, 96n, 209

Chamberlain, Sir Austen, 96

Charteris, Evan, 106n, 124, 158

Charteris, Lady Dorothy, 158

Chichester, Bell, Bishop of, 231, 283

Cholmondeley, Marquis & Marchioness of, (see Alice Dudeney) 15n, 53, 93, 103, 105, 113, 124, 175, 221, 246, 250, 273

Christie, Agatha, 99n

Church Times, 91

Churchill, Lord Ivor, 106

Clark, WE, 248

Clarke, Mr & Mrs, 233

Clarke, Rev ADC Mackay, 14, 33

Clydesdale, Marquess of, 106

Coats, Mrs Dudley, 107

Collins, 50, 57, 72, 92n, 93, 102, 119-20, 138, 148, 154, 158, 162, 173, 181, 183, 279, 287

Cooke, Marjorie & Lionel, 274, 276

Corner House, The, 39n

Coward, Noël, 115

Croft, The, 266, 272

Crumbles Murder, 69-70

Cust, Hon Lady, 145, 152

Park Lane, No 25: (see Alice Dudeney), 146n, 156, 173, 182, 184, 219, 238

Parker, Miss, 124, 128, 139

Pearson, C Arthur, 185n

Phelphs, Mrs G, 250, 266, 279

Phoenix Ironworks, 138n, 147, 274

Pigeon House, Angmering, 1, 6, 192, 205-6

Pilfold, Mr & Mrs James, 164, 166, 188, 196, 273

Pinker, Ralph, 10, 22-3, 28, 30, 57, 75, 79, 82, 97, 119-20, 137, 156, 159, 170, 178, 183, 209, 245-6,

Pinyouns, 97, 226, 235, 279, 282

Playfair, Nigel, 44-5

Pocock, Kate (Dudeney), 45-6, 51, 67, 133, 136n,

Port Lympne: (see Alice Dudeney), 15, 40, 47, 49, 53, 83, 96-7, 106, 115, 220, 238

Prince Edward's Road, No 8,

Priory Crescent, 272

Prince of Wales, 113

Pryce, Richard, 32, 36, 44

Pryor, Frederick, 11, 13-14, 43

Ranson, Mrs, 247, 276

Rawlings, Mrs K, 80, 274

Rawlings, Rev K, 80, 108, 131-2, 161, 178, 209-10, 213, 225-6, 233, 246, 257, 260, 271, 274, 277-9, 282, 286

Red House, The, 190, 262, 266

Reeves, 234

Renton, Dr, 6, 35

Review of Reviews, 53

Rogers, Mrs A, 231, 240

Roth, Cecil, 228, 233, 238, 242, 258

St Anne's Church, 104, 108, 164, 283

St Anne's Crescent, No 56, 150

St Anne's House, 69n, 258

St Martin's Lane, 13, 17, 21, 269

St Michael's Church, 1n, 25, 58, 68, 161n, 193, 228, 262, 283

St Michael's House, 169n, 289

St Pancras RC Church, 68n

Sargent, John Singer, 91, 106, 135, 246n

Sassoon, David, 100, 115-16, 126, 129

Sassoon, Mrs Arthur, 158-9, 172

Sassoon, Sir Philip: AD falls out with, 59; air force party at Trent Park, 113; Brighton visits, 100, 192; first invitation to AD to Port Lympne, 40; first letter to AD, 15; first meeting with AD, 15; flying, 96, 103, 220; Georgian exhibition, 146; Hampton Court Garden Party, 207; host to AD before America trip, 135-6; House of Commons, 82, 103, 135; illness and death, 219-20; *The Sassoon Dynasty*, 242, 246, 249; polo, 96; letter to AD re book dedication, 25; portrait, 135; reconciliation with AD, 63; Sargent exhibition, 91; scattering of ashes, 220; Silver exhibition, 121; *Third Route, The*, 122n; Trent Garden Party, 166; will, 220-1

Sassoon, Siegfried, 160n

Shelley, John, 37, 95

Shelley's, 147, 218, 258, 266, 267n

Shiffner, Lady, 188

Shiffner, The Misses, 244-5

Simpson, Wallis, 193-4, 215-6

Sinnock, Winnie: AD's dependance on, 150, 292; engaged by AD, 72; fear of raids, 239, 269, 274, 299; kindness to AD, 132, 267; legacy from AD, 272, 282; meets Polish airman, 278; reaction to D-Day, 286; relationship with 'bacon' men, 243, 282; sees Spitfire dogfight, 237

Sitwell, Osbert, 158

Skues, 49, 75, 139, 147, 151

Smith, Miss Gabell, 100, 177

Smith, The Misses E & N Harvey, 8, 19, 22, 51, 180, 211-12, 218, 236

Smythe, Miss Bertie, 39n, 204-5

Smythe, Miss Mabel, 39, 58, 95, 149, 179-80, 189-90, 204, 210, 280

Sotheran, Mr & Mrs H Cecil, 73, 80-1, 86, 111, 114, 212, 230, 244

Southease Church, 209

Spokes, Mr (Junior), 216

Spokes, Sidney, 104, 152, 154, 186, 209, 212-3, 252

Stacpoole, Henry de Vere, 82

Stanley, Lord & Lady, 106

Stenhouse, Mrs JR, 70, 78, 87

Stevens, Mr F Bentham, 198, 201